Ellicott City, Maryland Mill Town, U.S.A

A historic tour of Maryland's unique 18th
century mill town, and a partial account of
the lives of some of its outstanding residents
– both past and present.

By
Celia M. Holland

2003 Update by
Janet P. Kusterer
Charlotte T. Holland

Janet Kusterer
Charlotte Holland

View of Ellicott's Mills, Md., 1854. By John Schofield
– Maryland Historical Society

TO MY HUSBAND
AMOS THORNTON HOLLAND

Without whose patience and understanding this
book could not have been

INTRODUCTION TO THE 2003 EDITION

Ever since her student days at the Institute of Notre Dame in Baltimore, Mother demonstrated a passion for writing and the printed word. There followed, prior to an early marriage, a brief but adventurous tenure as a cub reporter for THE BALTIMORE SUN where the assignments included covering the 5th Regiment Armory fire, a promotional visit to the city by Clark Gable, and an Annapolis to Baltimore interview with Governor Ritchie, in the governor's limousine.

From early childhood I can remember Mother's tireless submissions to the Ellery Queen Mystery Writer Contest and others, where she tested her skills and endurance, and grew all too familiar with the rejection slip, though often with words of encouragement. Then, in the mid to late forties, her short stories and verse became a regular feature in THE TRISAGION, a Catholic enterprise of the Trinitarian Fathers of St. John DeMatha, a journal of which she soon became editor.

Mother's interest in history and historical writing slowly matured following her marriage to my father, Amos Thornton Holland, who was reared by his grandparents at Warfield's Forest, more commonly known as Oakley Farm, near Lisbon. There she became immersed in the tales of fortune and misfortune of the family cousinhood with names such as Burgess, Dorsey, Gaither, Henderson, Howard, Warfield, and others; it was an education deeply enriched by our residence there of more than six years.

A decade later, from University Park, Mother took up what would prove to be a quarter century effort to record the stories of old homes and families of Howard County in two series of newspaper articles in the County's principal papers. The present book is the product of some of those articles, often rewritten and enhanced. ELLICOTT CITY, MARYLAND. MILL TOWN USA was published in 1970, went through three printings and has long been out of print. In 1987 she published her most ambitious work, OLD HOMES AND FAMILIES OF HOWARD COUNTY, MARYLAND, of which P.W. Philby, erstwhile Director of the Maryland Historical Society, wrote: "What a great and comprehensive work this: historical, demographical, and genealogical."

It is with much pleasure that I give Historic Ellicott City, Inc. permission to republish this special printing of ELLICOTT CITY, MARYLAND. MILL TOWN USA. All proceeds from the sale of this printing are to go to that splendid society in furtherance of its good works, which were close to Mother's heart. She would be immensely pleased and honored.

James C. Holland

Manatawny
Shepherdstown
February 2, 2003

ACKNOWLEDGMENTS

It is with a deep sense of gratitude that I acknowledge the help of all those who contributed to the contents of this book. To the residents of Ellicott City who welcomed me into their homes, permitted the taking of innumerable photographs, and placed at my disposal all available records, deeds, family papers, and personal knowledge of the area, I am most appreciative.

To the pastors of the three churches included, as well as the members who shared their knowledge with me, I am also indebted. And to those business men and women who gave of their valuable time, I again say thank you.

Particular mention is due a number of persons who contributed so much of their time and effort to assure the accuracy of this work. They are: Miss Laura Hanna and Mr. Edwin Hanna, Jr. of nearby Temora; Mrs. Alda Clark of Keewaydin, founder and first president of the Howard County Historical Society; Senator James Clark, Jr. and Judge John L. Clark; the late Mr. and Mrs. Richard Talbott of Patapsco Heights; Mrs. Jean Hannon, president of Historic Ellicott's Mills, Inc,.; Mrs. Doris Thompson, editor of THE HOWARD COUNTY TIMES; Mr. Louis Dorsey Clark, past president of the Historical Society; Miss Mary Dorsey Clark, secretary of the Historical Society; Dr. Benjamin Mellor, treasurer of the Historical Society; Miss Jeanne Simons, director of the Linwood Child Center; the late Dr. M.J. Fitzsimmons of the Patapsco Pharmacy; Mr. Samuel Caplan, business man and owner of a number of local landmarks; Mrs. Mildred Werner of Ellicott's Country Store; Mr. Lewis Simpson, distinguished architect, formerly of Maidstone, England; Mr. Henry L. Sandlass, architectural consultant to the Friends of the Patapsco Institute, Inc.; and Mrs. Louise Hawkins, former editor of THE CENTRAL MARYLAND NEWS. Also, Mrs. Norman Betts, formerly of Main Street, Mrs. Louise Kraft Boone of Quaker Hill, and Mrs. John B. Loughran, all lifetime residents of Ellicott City.

To my son and daughter, James and Charlotte, who spent countless hours proof-reading the manuscript and offering constructive criticisms, I can say only - thank you.

To Dr. Verne E. Chatelain, professor emeritus of American history at the University of Maryland, I wish to express special thanks for his critical reading of the manuscript and his contribution toward the structure of the book. His continued interest has been a source of constant encouragement.

To one and all I am deeply grateful and hereby acknowledge that without their generous assistance and cooperation, this work could not have been completed.

Notwithstanding the contributions of all those mentioned above, the errors are the author's alone.

Celia M. Holland

TABLE OF CONTENTS

Page

Introduction to 2003 Edition v
Acknowledgments vii
Preface to the 2003 Edition xi
Preface xiii

History of Ellicott City 1
First Terminal of the B.& O. Railroad 13
The Jonathan Ellicott House 22
The George Ellicott House 26
The Old~Emporium 33
The Patapsco Hotel 37
St. Paul's Church and School 46
Lilburn 66
19th Century Log Cabin, New Cut Road 78
The Howard County Times and Its Editors 81
Ellicott's Country Store 100
      (The Walker-Chandler House)
The Howard House 108
The Howard County Fire Department 115
Emory Methodist Episcopal Church 121
34 Church Road 130
Castle Angelo 133
Linwood 139
The Patapsco Female Institute 149
Mount Ida 183
The Old Manse 190
Ellicott's Second School 199
(Home of The Central Maryland News)
The First Presbyterian Church 204
      (Howard County Historical Society Building)
Ellicott City's Jail, Constables, Sheriffs and Police Force 209
The Hayden House 218
      (Former Home of the Board of Education)
The Howard County Courthouse 223
Lawyer's Row 228

                                                              Page
18th Century Log Cabin--Merryman Street 231
E.A. Talbott Lumber Company 234
Disney's Tavern 241
16 Columbia Road 246
Tongue Row 250
Keewaydin 254
Search Enclosed 260
274 Columbia Road 263
Talbott's Last Shift 268
Quaker Hill 274

Bibliography 286
Index 290

Note: Except where otherwise noted all photographs are by the
author. Copies of prints, sketches or paintings by Royal Hart
Studios, Lanham, Maryland.

PREFACE TO THE 2003 EDITION

We are grateful to Professor James C. Holland for granting permission for this one-time printing of his mother's ELLICOTT CITY, MARYLAND. MILL TOWN USA and for donating all royalties from that printing to Historic Ellicott City, Incorporated. This publication is also made possible in part by a gift from the Stephen Smith family of Annapolis and Howard County.

Historic Ellicott City, Inc. is a nonprofit volunteer organization founded in 1974 with the mission of preservation, education and restoration in Ellicott City. Through its efforts the Ellicott City B & O Railroad Station, the Thomas Isaac Log Cabin, the George Ellicott House, and the Heritage Orientation Center have been restored and preserved. It is our hope that this book and others will promote interest in a community and region so rich in history.

When Celia Holland first published her book, Ellicott City was the hub of a farming community, where people did their basic grocery and clothing shopping on a Saturday morning. For better or worse, this agricultural land is now for the most part home to thousands of suburbanites who look to the Historic District for its unique mix of restaurants, shops, sightseeing and entertainment.

It is the goal of Historic Ellicott City, Inc. to preserve the integrity of the original book while including a new supplement to each chapter relating the principal changes that have occurred to the town and its properties in the intervening 30 years. This is by no means a comprehensive accounting of the history of each site in this time period––a daunting task to say the least––but rather an overview of the current state of each property.

Janet Kusterer, executive director and past president of Historic Ellicott City, Inc. and a locally employed professional writer, and Charlotte Thornton Holland, vice president of

Historic Ellicott City, Inc. and Celia Holland's daughter, wrote the supplemental text. Special thanks are due Roland and Enalee Bounds for their historical perspective and to all the property owners who shared their buildings and their stories so generously. Any errors are the responsibility of the writers.

Janet Kusterer
Charlotte Holland
Ellicott City
July, 2003

PREFACE

It has been said that in writing a preface to a book the author is, in effect, doing one of two things. He is either making an attempt to explain his reason for having written the book, or he is offering an apology for having written it in the first place. This being the case, the writer will not debate the issue but shall, instead, offer an explanation of how this book came to be.

In 1960 there appeared in the pages of one of Baltimore's daily newspapers an article on Ellicott City—the mill town "untouched by progress." Although there were those who still had faith in the future of "the improbable seat of Howard County," based on its past, there were also those who believed just as firmly in the physical impossibility of ever restoring the little mill town. It was the latter conclusion that this writer could not readily accept despite the seeming apathy on the part of the general public.

Having been a resident of Howard County for a number of years, and having raised my family on the farm my husband called home—Oakley Farm, the last of Warfield Forest—it was inevitable that I should become more than a little interested in our environment. This naturally included the quaint but sadly neglected little town that serves as county seat.

Upon rereading the aforementioned article a few years ago, I found myself still debating the issue, albeit a bit hesitantly, but finally concluded that with a little publicity and a good "shot in the arm," Ellicott City could indeed survive and reclaim its former position of historic significance and prestige. Needless to say, I was fully aware of the fact that this goal could not be achieved unless public interest could be sufficiently aroused.

In 1964, after much consideration, I decided to approach the subject through personal contact with those county residents whose roots were also buried deep in its soil. These families, mostly descendants of Howard's first families, received me in open accord and enthusiastically offered complete cooperation in this uncertain project. This cooperation has never since been witheld or with-drawn.

The initial step taken was through the pages of THE CEN-TRAL MARYLAND NEWS, Ellicott City's new and dynamic news-paper. A series of more than fifty articles on historic homes and buildings to be found within the confines of Howard County was pub-lished and warmly received. This series included a number of landmarks in the little mill town itself.

There followed still more encouragement from the people of Howard County and many requests to publish the articles in book form. I agreed.

At first it was my intention to include Ellicott City as a part of the whole—a book on the entire county. But upon closer scrutiny it became more and more apparent that the mill town warranted special and individual attention, so great is its potential. It was then that I decided to change my course of action. By this time I was convinced that the little town must not die, and that perhaps I might personally be instrumental in administering that much-need-ed "shot in the arm"—active and constant publicity. A book on the subject seemed the logical answer.

After consulting with a number of people who were just as anxious as I to see the town restored, including members of His-toric Ellicott's Mills, Inc. and the Howard County Historical Soci-ety, I started compiling all the material that had been gathered during my travels and interviews. Much that was revealed by a number of Ellicott City's senior citizens and lifetime residents, and which had never before appeared in print, was set in order. Legend and lore, as well as personal interest stories, were also included. For it was unanimously agreed that all available infor-mation should be permanently recorded before it faded from mem-ory and was lost for all time.

Thus it is that after more than four years of constant re-search, the author has finally been able to piece together a history of Ellicott City, featuring many of its venerable and historic build-ings, as well as the stories attached to them.

It is to be understood that the writer in no way wishes to im-ply that she considers herself infallible. But she does ask that her history be accepted in good faith for what it is—the result of an honest, unhurried, and sincere effort to record the facts exactly as they were revealed to her, including incidents pertaining to persons, places, and things which left indelible marks on the im-mediate area.

This, then, is the author's conception of Ellicott City, Maryland's 18th century mill town, scene of many historic events. If when the tour is completed even a handful of people come to know and to love the little town as does the writer, this work will not have been in vain.

C. M. H.

University Park, Md.
January, 1969.

BIRD'S-EYE VIEW OF ELLICOTT CITY, MD.

-From an old postcard

ELLICOTT CITY, MARYLAND
MILL TOWN – U.S.A.

Ellicott City, center of frustration and fulfillment, of disappointment and surprise, of failure and success, is the heart of Howard County. It is to some a dismal town, lacking in both color and charm. But to others it is a completely fascinating place, offering as it does a clear and precise picture of another era.

Its boundaries, as described to the writer, are as follows: "...on the east, the Patapsco River; on the west, Matthew's Store; on the north, the grounds back of the Patapsco Institute including Linwood; and on the south, the Hazelhurst property (Lilburn)." Although the little mill town may take in a few extra acres, for all practical purposes this outlined area does indeed constitute the town proper.

To the casual observer passing slowly through the snarl of its downtown Main Street traffic, or creeping up the narrow and winding roads, or meeting head-on its completely uninhibited Saturday rush hour, Ellicott City has little to offer but headache, irritation, and complete disillusionment.

But to the man of vision, the man of foresight, the pattern changes. As he cautiously approaches the little "Alpine Village" to observe its charm, he finds immeasurable satisfaction in the architectural stability such as is seldom found in American vil-

1

lages of this period. In actuality, such a man recognizes the little town for what it is—a historic gem.

The muddy and polluted waters of the Tiber recall the days of yesteryear when beauty instead of waste covered the bed of the old river. The Patapsco becomes once again the majestic waters at the base of the Tarpeian rock and the beautiful Female Institute, and Main Street is late 18th-century Main Street, U.S.A.

Muddy roads appear once more and wagon wheels sink to their hubs in mire only to be routed from ruts sometimes two feet deep, to plunge ever onward over the first section of the original western pike ingeniously built by the immortal Ellicotts and Charles Carroll of Carrollton. Once again Ellicott's Mills takes in all that land east of the Patapsco River where, in the beginning, the business section of the picturesque little town thrived.

Slave labor is accepted as a way of living despite the fact that Joseph Ellicott, father of Andrew the surveyor, shared with his brothers and Mr. Carroll a deep sense of the injustice of slavery as a way of life. We find him upstream at the Upper Mills at Fountainvale as he opens his heart and his mind—as well as his home—to a man not of his race. Benjamin Banneker, Negro and object of his deep respect and admiration, is seen perusing the books of the Ellicott family library.

It is this same Mr. Banneker who is credited with having built a clock in 1754 which "not only told the time of day, but struck the hour." Historians agree that this was one of the first clocks of its kind to be made in this country.

We see him again on that memorable day when President George Washington, at the persuasion of Thomas Jefferson—then Secretary of State—summons him along with his renowned friend, Andrew Ellicott, to take over the planning and surveying of the nation's capital. Although both men still suffer from a lack of public recognition, it was indeed their work that bore fruit and ultimately brought to a conclusion the planning of the city of Washington, initially presented by the noted but temperamental Pierre L'Enfant.

But long before this dream was to become a reality, three brothers—John, Joseph and Andrew Ellicott—brought to Ellicott's Mills from Pennsylvania their knowledge and skill and founded here their first Maryland settlement, paying the total sum of three dollars per acre for land and water rights. The year was 1772. After a series of setbacks and much public ridicule and scorn, they eventually proved themselves and their theories and have since gone down in the annals of history as true American pioneers.

Aside from their knowledge of milling they introduced many "firsts" including the wagon wheel brake, the use of lime (plaster) to restore the productivity of the soil, a form of architectural construction that has outlasted most other forms in the country both in strength and appeal—with or without constant upkeep—a new faith in a new community (Quaker), and many other accomplishments too numerous to tabulate.

The first four-sided clock known to have been made in this country was invented by Joseph Ellicott who, upon recognizing the genius of his son Andrew, welcomed his assistance despite his extreme youth. Then in 1789, the first steamboat saw the light of day when John Ellicott, son of the first John, demonstrated this new process of motion as he ran his small boat down one of the larger mill-races, using this theory of propulsion. Had he not suffered the loss of one arm during the initial experiment, it is conceivable that he might well have preceded Robert Fulton in the invention of a larger and truly profitable vessel propelled by steam. The Ellicotts are also credited with having built the first grain elevator in Maryland which was equipped with machinery for the manufacture of the finest flour.

Ellicott's Mills was many things to many people. It was one of Maryland's first mill towns, indeed, if not the first. It was the heart of the Howard District of Anne Arundel County, later to become Howard County. It was the home of the immortal Ellicott brothers, carved from a wilderness beside a river, and gradually, the home of many millhands and merchants alike. It grew and grew, becoming the mainstay of nearby farmers who soon adopted the Ellicott theory that wheat, and not tobacco, was the most profitable commodity to be raised in the area since it did not wear out the soil. Neither did it reduce the profit to the farmer. Instead, it increased his earnings, even as it sustained the good earth.

Thus it was that the Ellicott brothers were directly responsible for such families as the Dorseys, the Clarks, the Hammonds, the Ridgelys, the Warfields, and others remaining in the area rather than moving on to Kentucky or Tennessee as had been planned. Several years of tobacco cropping had taken its toll. But with the advent of the Ellicotts and a new way to restore the soil to its original fertility, the landholder once again saw his margin of profit rise and life resumed its former pace. The feeling of insecurity which had engulfed the entire district no longer plagued the landed gentlemen, and once again the pleasures of social activity were restored.

All this—and more—was the direct outcome of the adoption of the theories set forth by three mild and humble men—John, Joseph, and Andrew.

*   *   *

From the beginning the Ellicotts enjoyed the confidence of Charles Carroll of nearby Doughoregan Manor who not only accepted their views but who, as has been seen, inevitably assisted in building that section of the National Pike, then a private road, between Ellicott's Mills and the Manor.

Always progressive, even in his declining years, Mr. Carroll was one of the staunchest supporters of the Baltimore & Ohio Railroad. On July 4th, 1828, at the age of ninety-one, he made his final public appearance when he laid the cornerstone of the B. & O. terminal in Baltimore. He considered this act second only in importance to his signing of the Declaration of Independence. The old Baltimore depot is known as Mt. Clare and still stands in the shadow of a great roundhouse on Poppleton Street.

Meanwhile the original Ellicott mill and all its dependent buildings, as well as the homes of the Ellicotts and their employees, became the nucleus of a spreading community. Disney's Tavern became the center of activity, while the Chandler House and the Quaker Meeting House were fast becoming local landmarks. Finally, in 1830 Ellicott's Mills received national recognition as the historic site of the first railroad terminus in the country.

There followed a trip by the first horse-drawn car, then a race between another and the famous Tom Thumb, invention of Peter Cooper. The outcome of this race which pointed up the inability of an animal to maintain indefinitely a steady pace or speed, led to further and improved development of the steam engine and eventually, to the present-day network of criss-crossed train service now serving the nation. But despite the part the little town had played in the development of the railroad system, on December 31st, 1949 Ellicott City—where it all began—lost its passenger service from Baltimore. Today a daily freight car or two is all that remains for the busy town wherein railroad service, as such, was initiated so many years ago. The tiny village and its contribution were soon forgotten.

However, the Baltimore and Ohio Railroad Station remains with the outline of the old turntable intact. Well-preserved and typical of its day of glory, the original terminal is still maintained by the B. & O. Railroad Company. Although some minor repairs are needed, it stands much as it stood more than a hundred years ago.

Following the construction of the railroad, more homes were erected, some of stone, others of frame. Among the more prominent were the Hayden house atop Court House Hill, Lilburn on the crest of College Avenue, the Fort house (later the Heine house) on Fels Lane, and the John Heavey house on Main Street.

The Fels Lane area had become the town's principal residential section. Here court was held in one of the homes during the building of the present courthouse. However, when another building in the same neighborhood was equipped to serve as the first jail, it did not contribute to the atmosphere of the remaining residences. This development was primarily responsible for the withdrawal of many of Ellicott City's first families and the ultimate deterioration of the entire vicinity.

By 1850 Ellicott's Mills had seen many changes. Beautiful churches and schools including the Patapsco Female Institute, Rock Hill College, St. Paul's Catholic Church, and Emory Methodist Episcopal Church had come into being. There was at least one hotel, the Patapsco, and a bank. Angelo Cottage was attracting visitors from nearby Baltimore. College Avenue and Columbia Road, with its inimitable Tongue Row, had come into their own. It was a time of peace and progress.

In 1851 Howard District of Anne Arundel County became Howard County and the new courthouse atop the hill took on the importance of the seat of local government. In 1867 a city charter was secured for Ellicott's Mills and the name was changed to Ellicott City.

But before this came about new rumblings were heard. Father and son argued among themselves, and the day was soon to come when brother would kill brother, and families would be torn apart. With the outbreak of war in 1861 the sympathies of the people of Ellicott's Mills were divided, as they were throughout the state. But contrary to general belief, the majority of the small town's citizens favored the Union. Nevertheless there were those who slipped across the Potomac to serve in the Confederate ranks. Thus the small town's heartbreak was as deep as the rest of Maryland's, the borderline state.

A list of Confederate soldiers who died in this tragic conflict —the War Between the States—is to be found on a monument standing on the lawn of the courthouse. The writer questions whether any names were understandably overlooked or lost, since the list of casualties seems unbelievably low in number when we consider the fact that with but few exceptions the surrounding agricultural area was almost solidly in favor of secession and against the abolition of slavery.

When viewing this monument it would be well to keep in mind that this list represents only the known members of known families who made the supreme sacrifice. Should some mother's son lie abandoned in an unmarked grave, the town and county hereby accord him full recognition. Unfortunately, a list of equally brave Union soldiers who perished defending their beliefs remains tragically missing, since the small town's 20th century sympathies are unmistakably pro-southern.

It is also a matter of record that today the people of the entire state consider themselves of strict southern origin and stubbornly refuse to be called Northerners. Geographically, they are correct. However, at the time of the Civil War the Mason-Dixon Line was not in fact the dividing line between the North and the South. After a vain attempt to remain neutral, Maryland virtually became a melting pot of conflicting emotions and was ultimately christened—by both armies—"the borderline state." The waters of the Potomac literally divided the North from the South, although many people on both sides of the river shared varied degrees of conflicting loyalties.

Howard County as a whole—and Ellicott's Mills in particular —played a small but significant part in this mighty struggle. Here men of the 1st Maryland Cavalry, C.S.A., better known as the Howard Dragoons, took their stand and tried, albeit in vain, to keep the Union troops from reaching their objective. A skirmish is believed to have taken place at the bridge spanning the Patapsco. This bridge, once one of Maryland's best-known covered bridges, remained standing until the early 1920s when it was destroyed by fire.

During the skirmish, the use of a secret weapon known as the Winan Steam Gun, invented and introduced by Charles S. Dickinson, a dedicated southern sympathizer, was planned as a final means of repelling the enemy. However, both gun and its inventor were taken captive, but not before Mr. Dickinson had succeeded in removing some vital parts, leaving the weapon a useless burden to the Union troops.

After four long years hostilities ceased. A new and united country was born, and all persons were declared free and equal.

*   *   *

But even as the memory of the war remained fresh and bitter in the minds of the people, Ellicott's Mills, now known as Ellicott City, was plagued by still another and even more devastating personal tragedy. On a disastrous day in 1868 the rain fell on the new city in such torrents that the Patapsco rose five feet in ten minutes. Starting in the western reaches of the river where eighteen inches of rain had fallen within half an hour, houses, stores, sawmills, and bridges were swept away. Gathering momentum as it approached the defenseless little mill town and widening its path of destruction, the Patapsco roared through the valley claiming thirty-six lives and causing a loss of no less than a million dollars in damages. A vivid and tragic account of the catastrophe follows:

> The mighty stream had gathered in its onward march, trees, timbers, houses and bridges. It entered the town with a thunderous roar, and began its terrible work of death and devastation. Now it began to tear the place to pieces.
>
> On an island formed by the river and the mill race, a row of 13 houses stood and the occupants realized their danger much too late. When the water demolished the first house, the people fled into the next one, and so on until they were all crowded into the last one which was built of stone. Here they hoped they would be saved, but in the end it was hurled from its foundation. Thirty-six men, women and children were sent down into the boiling cauldron, before the horrified eyes of their relatives, assembled and helpless to aid them as they stood on the shore.
>
> For many months the gruesome search for the dead was conducted on either side of the valley, among the matted driftwood and along mud-packed shores. Some of the plants of industry were rebuilt and activities resumed, but some never recovered from the flood. The old Patapsco has overflowed many times since then, but never has it written such a dark page in its history as that of 1868.
>
> Visitors today who pass through the quaint town of Ellicott City, often wonder why most of the homes are perched on the high hills, but it could be that the original builders held vivid memories of how terrible that quiet, peaceful stream lying below could become when the rains come.

*   *   *

With the passing of time the memory of the horrifying aftermath of the flood subsided and little by little the small town resumed normal activities and pursued a new course of living. Along with the rest of the nation the community witnessed the gay nineties, initiating a period of frivolity unprecedented in the history of this country.

Ellicott City, as an incorporated town, reserved the right of licensing the sale of hard liquors to within the city's limits. It became the only "wet spot" in the county and taverns mushroomed and flourished. Patrons from all over the county, as well as the adjoining areas, made Ellicott City their headquarters when in search of liquor and other alcoholic beverages.

On the south side of West Main Street a tavern keeper erected a sign reading "First Chance Saloon." The incoming visitor in search of a drink hardly needed further persuasion to make this his first stop. At the other end of town—just west of the border—another equally enterprising innkeeper erected a similar sign, this one reading "Last Chance."

Ellicott City remained the center of boisterous gatherings and prolonged drinking parties until October, 1919 when the passage of the Volstead Act put an end to such scenes and the "wet spot" became as sedately "dry" as the rest of the country.

Meanwhile, in 1914 the commission form of government was adopted. Three commissioners were elected for four year terms. At the same time the Patapsco River was made the eastern boundary of the city, dividing Howard from Baltimore County, and the flour mills and Ellicott homes—other than Mt. Ida—were no longer within the county limits.

On July 1, 1935 the town's charter was revoked by the state legislature, ending the city government. This bill was introduced by the late Senator Joseph L. Donovan. To date there are no incorporated towns in Howard County.

Shortly before the turn of the century Ellicott City again felt growing pains. Emory Methodist Episcopal Church was almost fifty years old when the First Presbyterian Church (now the home of the Howard County Historical Society) was erected. The old Howard County Fire Department Building followed, and a picturesque row of small buildings opposite the courthouse—the first of which was standing in 1878—became known as Lawyer's Row. Here no less than twenty-three men practiced law.

Convenient to the courthouse itself, Lawyer's Row saw no

carriages or other conveyances brought to the hill by the men who thus earned their livelihood. All available space, which must indeed have been limited, was reserved for ox-carts, wagons, and all types of carriages and surreys used by men and women seeking legal aid. The client's parking needs were considered of primary importance.

The courthouse, sitting atop one of Ellicott City's seven hills, was reached by roads winding around and through the sides of the rocky terrain. It was a steep-pitched hill, but since so many of the town's attorneys lived within walking distance of the noted building, it was reached by climbing "the Mount" on foot or by ascending a series of steps running from Main Street "down the block" and backtracking to the hill itself. It could also be approached by entering either the Howard House or Disney's Tavern, climbing several flights of stairs, passing through the back yards, and climbing still another flight of steps.

Once they arrived at their offices not many men were inclined to take to the streets of the town for bread or sustenance at lunch time. More frequently than not snacks were carried—a sandwich or two, plus a piece of fruit or cake—and a pitcher of well water was obtained from the nearest source when wine or ale were not available. Pot-bellied stoves supplied the necessary heat during the winter months and kerosene lamps burned well in to the evening hours. The eight-hour day and five-day week were unheard of. Only on the Sabbath did man earn a respite from his daily routine.

But hardship bred only professional stamina. Cases were carefully prepared and eventually, with the clearing of additional ground, the men of Capitoline Hill brought their carriages and vehicles and life became more tolerable. Luncheon meetings came to be the custom of the day, and life was good as friends and fellow attorneys met to swap yarns or discuss cases.

The courthouse and Lawyer's Row still stand and together constitute one of the most fascinating areas in Ellicott City. It is to be hoped that some use will always be found for these unique buildings, minute as they are. For Capitoline Hill without Lawyer's Row would be like Capitol Hill (at Annapolis) without its ancient and treasured Treasury Building.

⁂   *   *

As can be seen, with the passing years Ellicott's Mills has grown and become the nerve center of an ever-growing county. As

Ellicott City, it remains the county seat, although the retention of this honor was challenged briefly in 1965 and 1966 when some thought was given to replacing the old courthouse with a new and larger structure to be erected "somewhere outside the confines of the small town." Public reaction to the suggested move was spontaneous resulting in a decision to retain Ellicott City as the seat of government. Subsequently, additional ground was purchased, a large addition to the original courthouse was made, and county government from within the little mill town continued uninterrupted as it had for the past century or more.

In November, 1968 a charter form of government was adopted. In January, 1969 Omar J. Jones, former principal of Howard High School, was elected the county's first chief executive, defeating Jack L. Larrimore, Howard County's chief of police. The three Democratic county council candidates—William S. Hanna, Edward Cochran and Hugh Nichols won over James M. Holway, Robert H. Marks and James H. Dietz, all Republicans.

Along with the three councilmen just elected, Alva S. Baker, a Democrat, and Republican Charles E. Miller also assumed positions on the council, filling the additional two seats of the five established by local charter. Both men chose to accept the positions on the basis of their membership on the outgoing Board of County Commissioners, rather than resign their board seats and run in the election. A third commissioner, Harry T. Murphy, Chairman of the Board, decided to resign his post and seek the county executive office. However, he was defeated in the Democratic primary elections in November.

Thus it is that Ellicott City today is the scene of much activity whether it involves the passage of an important zoning law or simply farmer's day in town. Curious tourists and residents of the new city of Columbia are being seen more frequently on the streets, some to peer into the windows of restored shops, others to seek out the old and historic landmarks. Camera enthusiasts also find much to their liking. There is an atmosphere about the place that is hard to define. It must be seen to be appreciated.

With this in mind, the writer offers a pictorial tour and study of this remarkable little community. Its past, upon which its future rests, is presented as accurately as human effort and research will permit. Barring unintentional oversights and possible misinterpretations, the author hereby presents historic Ellicott City as she sees and loves it. For Ellicott City is authentic Marylandia. But more than that, it is truly Mill Town, U.S.A.

*   *   *

2003 UPDATE

Ellicott City celebrated its Bicentennial in 1972, a celebration that was greatly anticipated but almost didn't happen.
While planners ironed out party details, something happened that
diverted everyone from more frivolous pursuits, and had the
potential to make or break the town.

Possibly the most significant event to occur in Ellicott
City in the last thirty-plus years is the natural disaster named
Tropical Storm Agnes, which occurred in June, 1972. The
destruction caused by the raging waters was a turning point for
the town, as building owners had to decide whether to rebuild or
leave. As the waters receded they left a trail of mud, ruined merchandise and broken building materials.

The town folk banded together, cleaned up, and began the
long metamorphosis that would transform the town from a nondescript strip of businesses to the attractive historic but contemporary mill town jewel it is today. Obstacles were raised every
step of the way, but miraculously the town did come together to
celebrate its Bicentennial and the beginning of a new era for
Ellicott City. As preservationists gathered with politicians on the
parade reviewing stand, their conversations looked not only
backward to a celebrated history, but also forward with optimism.

Historic Ellicott City, Incorporated was established in
January 1974, initially to assist in the preservation and restoration of the Ellicott City Baltimore & Ohio Railroad station building. On January 23, 1974, Articles of Merger were signed
between Historic Ellicott Mills, Incorporated and the Ellicott
City Bicentennial Association, Incorporated, creating the new
organization. Around this time, changes in ownership on Ellicott
City's Main Street brought about several façade changes to major
properties, which caused those interested in preservation to look
for methods of control.

The Howard County governmental structure had recently
changed to that of County Executive and County Council, but the
County had not adopted Historic District Zoning Regulations.
Historic Ellicott City, Inc., with the assistance of those who had
worked to establish the Annapolis Historic District, drafted legislation to establish Historic District Zoning.

Following its adoption, legislation was filed to establish
the area which had formerly been the confines of the corporate

limits of Ellicott City as Howard County's first Historic District, and Howard County's first Historic District Commission was appointed. Through the work of preservationists such as Jean Hannon, the Ellicott City Historic District was placed on the National Register of Historic Sites in 1980.

In 1977, Howard County established the Ellicott City Restoration Foundation, charged with the oversight of the Ellicott City community development, and state funds became available to retain a historic preservation consultant. This finally led to the first Ellicott City Master Plan, the 1980 Murphy Williams Study, " A New Life for an Old Town," and Howard County committed to preservation efforts, which had been underway within the newly formed Historic District of Ellicott City.

But troubles continued. Even as the town began to rebuild, another storm, Eloise, hit in 1976, causing further destruction. The unique topography of the area made it particularly suscepti- ble to fires as well, which are reviewed in the chapter on the fire department.

In 1997 Ellicott City marked the 225th anniversary of its founding with a year-long program of planting celebration gar- dens and general neighborhood sprucing up. One of the most sig- nificant garden additions is the Mill Stone Park, located at the corner of Main Street and Ellicott Mills Drive, across the street from the Thomas Isaac Log Cabin. The Longfellow Garden Club maintains this garden, which features mill stones retrieved from the Patapsco River.

In 2001 Howard County marked its 150th birthday with another year-long celebration. This 'Sesquicentennial' milestone was observed with special events by many of the town's organiza- tions. Since being named a Historic District in 1974, the town has benefited from the oversight of a variety of groups, which emerged to address the various needs of the community.

Among those located in Ellicott City are the Howard County Historical Society; Historic Ellicott City, Inc.; The Ellicott City Restoration Foundation; The Friends of the Patapsco Female Institute Historic Park; The Historic District Commission; The Ellicott City Business Association; The Howard County Arts Council; and the Ellicott City Colored School, Restored.

In 2003, a new Ellicott City Master Plan was submitted to the County Executive to be used as a planning tool in the 21st century.

*   *   *

B. & O. Station, as depicted by Ted Koppel

FIRST TERMINAL OF THE BALTIMORE AND OHIO RAILROAD

In 1827, when first the idea of a railroad system was conceived by men like George and Alexander Brown, Philip E. Thomas, Charles Carroll of Carrollton, Samuel F. B. Morse, Peter Cooper, Thomas Ellicott, Benjamin H. Latrobe, Johns Hopkins, William Patterson, and others, available transportation was far from adequate. Existing facilities were both crude and unpredictable.

In 1868 Professor Henry Onderdonk, historian and former president of the Maryland Agricultural College (now the University of Maryland), put on record a brief but precise picture of the situation in his book, HISTORY OF MARYLAND. According to the Professor, in 1824 the first steps toward economic stability were taken, via interstate commerce. A corporation was formed—known as the Chesapeake and Ohio Canal Company—and plans for the building of the canal were disclosed. With its terminus located at Georgetown, a new fear gripped the city of Baltimore. For upon completion of this project, trade with the west would undoubtedly become

13

extremely limited, there being no visible means of competing with
the newly formed company either by land or by water routes.

A complete and accurate description of prevailing conditions
may also be found in George W. Howard's book, MONUMENTAL
CITY, published in 1873. It reads in part:

> ...The western trade, which, before the Revolution,
> had been conveyed on the backs of packhorses, walking
> in single file through the narrow paths which led across
> the mountains, now required for its transportation the
> huge canvas-covered "conestoga" wagons, which, with
> their teams of six or eight horses and jingling bells,
> used to traverse the old Braddock's road and the turn-
> pikes that had been constructed as far as the navigable
> waters of the West. The relics of this method of trans-
> portation may yet be discerned in the immense yards,
> made for the accommodation of these wagons and teams,
> attached to a few of the old inns in Baltimore that have
> yet escaped the march of improvement.

Professor Onderdonk's account continues:

> At this time (1824), rail roads were an untried novel-
> ty. In England, the engineers and capitalists were agi-
> tating the subject of this means of transportation be-
> tween Liverpool and Manchester—the first passenger
> rail road ever constructed—and simultaneous with this
> movement the leading citizens of Baltimore were con-
> templating the organization of the Baltimore and Ohio
> Rail Road—the first in this country.

From 1827 through 1830 Alexander Brown and Sons were a-
mong the chief supporters of the development of such a system.
The first steps were soon to be taken. At a meeting held on February 12, 1827 twenty-five of Baltimore's leading citizens gathered
to consider the possibility of establishing such a service, thus openly competing with navigation up the C. & O., the Erie, and other
canals west. New ideas were already fermenting in the minds of
these progressive Americans.

The meeting was held at the home of George Brown in Baltimore and a memorial was at once presented to the legislature. A
charter was granted in less than ten days after formal presentation.

A lawsuit with the Chesapeake and Ohio Canal Company with respect to a right of way for the railroad soon followed, but a compromise was effected.

The following excerpts from a series of letters written by Alexander Brown to his brother William in London are self-explanatory:

> ... The people in this country have lately been turning much of their attention to the formation of Rail ways.

Then in mid-February, 1827:

> The Community seems to take a deep interest in it and a charter has been applied for.

By June 12, 1829 Mr. Brown reported that "much time is devoted to details about wheels, flanges, and other phases of construction."

THE STORY OF ALEXANDER BROWN & SONS, authored by Frank R. Kent (1925) reveals the following entry: "...subscription books were opened on March 20, and forty-one thousand seven hundred and eighty-one shares of stock almost immediately subscribed." A total sum of $4,178,000 was contributed or pledged by 20,000 people.

By April, 1827 a company had been organized with the following men elected to the Board of Directors: Alexander Brown, Charles Carroll of Carrollton, Thomas Ellicott, George Hoffman, Talbot Jones, William Lorman, Isaac McKim, John B. Morris, Robert Oliver, William Patterson, William Steuart, and Philip E. Thomas. Mr. Thomas was chosen president and George Brown, treasurer.

On July 4, 1828 Charles Carroll of Carrollton laid the cornerstone of the Mount Clare Station in Baltimore and the event was signalized by the most imposing procession ever seen by the people of Maryland. Work was begun shortly thereafter with Baltimore as the eastern terminal. By June 14, 1830 thirteen miles of road reaching from Baltimore to Ellicott's Mills were completed, and the railroad was put in operation.

The small passenger cars, resembling in many particulars the old-style stagecoaches, were placed on the track and drawn by horses over strap-iron rails. (Sail power had also been tried on windy days but proved of little value.) The freight cars resembled large square boxes on wheels and were covered with white cotton material similar to that used for wagon sheets.

The horse-drawn cars stopped at Relay Station which then stood not far from the Thomas Viaduct over the Patapsco River. Here a fresh change of horses took up the burden. The Viaduct itself was completed in 1835. Designed by Thomas Latrobe, it was the first curved and arched railroad viaduct to be built in the United States.

On August 30, 1830 the initial journey in this country by steam was made from Baltimore to Ellicott's Mills. Peter Cooper was the inventor and builder of the "miraculous locomotive" and in the cars were many of Baltimore's and Maryland's leading citizens. People from widely scattered areas and from many states also came to see a railroad in operation, and to enjoy a ride on the cars for the gratification of their curiosity. Since Congress had been requested to take a million dollars worth of stock, a great number of members of that august body also examined the railroad and rode in one of Winan's carriages.

The B. & O. Railroad as such was probably the third or fourth railroad to be erected in the world. There were short runs from Stockton to Darlington (England, 1825); from Manchester to Liverpool (1830); and a still shorter line in Delaware County, Pennsylvania, privately owned by one Thomas Leeper, quarriman. A few other minor runs existed but none to equal that which was conceived by the men heretofore mentioned. Public recognition as the builders of America's first railroad was given them, and in time financial assistance was forthcoming from the United States Government, although the exact amount contributed has never been definitely determined.

With the advent of the railroad and the building of the first terminal within the town's limits, Ellicott's Mills achieved national fame. The little village became the center of attention and enjoyed much publicity.

* * *

According to legend, this newly-acquired fame originated on that eventful day (August 30, 1830) when the historical race between the Tom Thumb and a horse-drawn carriage took place. According to one source, "the Tom Thumb was making its way back to Baltimore with officials and friends of the railroad, when it encountered at Relay Station another vehicle on the second track. This vehicle was driven by Stocken and Stokes, great stage proprietors of the day, and the cart was being pulled by a gallant gray of great beauty

and power. From this point on, all parties were determined to
have a race home. At first, the gray had the best of it, but when
the whistle blew and the steam flew out of the engine, the train
gained on the horse. The pace increased, the passengers shouted,
the horse snorted, and the engine puffed. The tiny train passed the
horse, but just then a small band blew off the engine and before it
could be replaced, the horse passed the little open car. When
steam was again resumed, the horse was too far ahead to be overtaken and came in winner of the race. But the real triumph was
Peter Cooper's, for the success of the first steam engine in America. "

*   *   *

Although at one time the horse-drawn car seemed more steady
and reliable and actually won the initial race, subsequent and daily
rides to and from Ellicott's Mills (from Baltimore) broke down the
stamina of the beast and made him bow his head to the inevitability
of locomotion. With the advent of the railroad, Ellicott's Mills
grew in stature and importance and the town's economic stability
seemed assured.

A station of granite, with turntable, was erected in 1831 and
still stands in an excellent state of preservation. It was, however,
a warehouse-looking building at first, with as many doors as windows. In the early days of the 20th century a telegraph office with
a bay window to observe moving trains was added, as were colored
glass windows. An egg stove warmed the offices and waiting rooms,
later to be replaced by a more modern heating system.

Today the building consists of a freight landing, a waiting
room, ticket office, and other "modern facilities." The second
floor, which once served as baggage room, remains bare. The
outline of the turntable where the Iron Horse revolved for its return trip to Baltimore remains visible at the south end of the station. Handy luggage carriers, picturesque but crude by today's
standards, still stand beside the building. Although there is no
longer any use for them, they are in perfect operational condition
and add still another touch of nostalgic authenticity to the old structure.

When the depot was first erected there were signs of fierce
Indian battles having taken place on the site, as evidenced by the
great number of stone tomahawks, axes, and arrow points found in
the area.

Although the line was greatly extended within a few years,

gradually reaching Cumberland, Ellicott's Mills maintained its position as one of the most important towns along the entire route since the receipts for freight—due to the enormous output of flour and other grain products—far exceeded that of any other point between the two extremities.

The first railroad advertisement ever published was issued by the B. & O. Railroad, advertising "4 brigades" of cars to run between Baltimore and Ellicott's Mills. The fare was twenty-five cents.

While in office (1833-1836) Governor James Thomas announced the completion of the B. & O. as far as Harper's Ferry. There was much rejoicing. The legislature was again called upon for assistance, this time to advance a loan of $2,000,000. The loan was granted. The B. & O. was now a national project.

In 1838 the area surrounding Ellicott's Mills, then known as the Piedmont area of Upper Arundel, was declared a district. The railroad was greatly responsible for this development. In 1851 the district became a full-fledged county with the railroad having pushed on farther west. In 1880 the central office of the B. & O. stood on the northwest corner of Baltimore and Calvert Streets, in Baltimore, where it remained for many years. It was a six and one-half story building and at the time, one of Baltimore's finest.

Passenger service was good for many years. Then on December 31, 1949—with the decline in "travel by train"—the last passenger train ride between Ellicott City and Mt. Airy was given a number of notable persons. Among those who enjoyed this honor was the late Miss Pearl Mercier, a former teacher from Lisbon School who lived to celebrate her 40th anniversary as a teacher in the Howard County Schools. She was accompanied by a group of her former students.

Miss Pearl, as she was known, was the granddaughter of Mr. Charles Woods of New York, one of the three original contractors (Matthew, Woods & Hall) who laid the first B. & O. tracks from Baltimore to Ellicott City. Miss Mercier was believed to have been the last survivor of the immediate families.

Today only freight cars travel over the beds of this historic route. But the people of Howard County—and of Ellicott City in particular—take great pride in their Railroad Station. For, as the first building of its kind in the country, it is a monument to the initial system of public transportation from east to west.

The old fieldstone building is considered one of Howard County's most historic sites. It enjoys national as well as local fame. At one time, in addition to the daily schedule, weekly runs or excursions were made to view some of the native landmarks including Tarpeian Rock, Castle Angelo, and the beautiful Patapsco Female Institute. The town became a summer resort, attracting such notables as H. L. Mencken who got his first taste of printer's ink in this small town in the office of THE ELLICOTT CITY TIMES, now THE HOWARD COUNTY TIMES.

For more than a decade the late Charles L. Gerwig, then editor of THE TIMES, spent countless hours in an attempt to have the station declared a National Historic Site. His many sacrifices and years of dedicated work seemed to go unrewarded. Then shortly after his death, because of the continued efforts on the part of his family and the support of THE TIMES, interest in the significance and historic value of the old building was revived.

A letter to the Honorable Stewart L. Udall, Secretary of the Interior, from Senator Joseph D. Tydings of Maryland followed. In it Mr. Tydings urged the Secretary to "...consider the historical worth of this station, in a nation with its heritage so closely tied to the development of its rail systems."

The people of Ellicott City waited anxiously. The possibility of a railroad museum in part of the building was discussed openly by historians and residents alike, while erstwhile dreams of celebrations, with appropriate costumes of the first arrival, were once again renewed, B. & O. officials willing. Then on Thursday, November 21, 1968, THE TIMES announced the good news to its readers:

ELLICOTT CITY STATION IS NATIONAL MONUMENT

Bold headlines followed by a modest but happy article, after years of hard work and perseverance!

The man responsible for this quiet victory is no longer with us. But because of him, and because of those who took up his cause after he was gone, the quaint granite building at the foot of Main Street will not disappear. It will, instead, be recognized once again as the place where it all began so very many years ago and—at long last—take its rightful place in the annals of American Railroad history.

* * *

2003 UPDATE

Research done since the publication of Celia Holland's book uncovered a few errors that need to be corrected. Among the most significant are the following: (1) Messrs. Morse, Cooper, Hopkins and Latrobe were not involved with the incorporation of the railroad system; (2) on July 4, 1828 Charles Carroll of Carrollton dedicated the first mile marker, not the cornerstone of the Mount Clare Station in Baltimore; (3) the Thomas Viaduct was designed by Benjamin Henry Latrobe, Jr.; (4) most accounts give August 28, not August 30, 1830 as the date of the initial steam journey in this country; (5) the carriages which were a part of the initial steam train were the property of Ross Winans; (6) the stage coach proprietors in the legendary Tom Thumb Race were Stockton and Stokes; and (7) the first known turntable at the Ellicott City Terminus was constructed in 1863, and the telegraph office was erected in 1856 or 1857.

At the height of the destruction caused by Tropical Storm Agnes in 1972, floodwaters rose to 10 feet around the railroad station, with the potential of destroying the facility. Historic Ellicott City, Inc. evolved to respond to the community's desire to save the Ellicott City B & O Railroad Station, the oldest railroad terminus in America, and the first stop on the line west from Baltimore.

Although interested citizens had worked to have the station declared a National Historic Site in 1968, its future after the storm was in question. As private entrepreneurs investigated the structure with thoughts of purchase, the local preservationists interceded between the Baltimore and Ohio Railroad Company and Howard County government officials. When the B & O agreed to lease the building to the county for a fee of one dollar a year, the preservationists agreed to research the structure with hopes of opening it as a museum.

With funding from the Maryland Historic Trust, a Historic Structures Report was written by Andrew Cascio. In January, 1974, Historic Ellicott City, Incorporated was formed to lead the way in preserving the station. A restoration project was undertaken, which resulted in the opening of the station as a museum, on August 1, 1976.

The first major restoration of the Railroad Station Museum was completed in 1983. A ceremony commemorating the restoration was held May 14, 1983 and the Sagle Memorial Library, housed in the Museum, was dedicated the following day. In 1997 a return to the station of a replica of the Tom Thumb, the train that was pitted against a horse in the legendary race of 1830, celebrated the sale of the Railroad Museum building to Howard County by CSX Transportation, which had purchased it from the

B & O. The sale paved the way for the second, and most ambitious, restoration of the Railroad Museum, completed in 1999.

A unique public-private partnership including Historic Ellicott City, Inc., Howard County government, CSX Transportation, The Maryland Historic Trust, the State Highway Administration, and the Federal Highway Administration has ensured the future of the Museum by completing the extensive restoration that allows for the optimum use of the facility for education and historic interpretation.

The restoration accomplished the following: it restored the east wall and engine house to their original status; it recreated the 1863 turntable as a static exhibit; and it restored the original section of 1831 track into the building. In addition, it recreated the outside passenger staircase, developed a new visitor traffic flow for better historic interpretation, and added the amenities of outside lights and fencing.

In March of 2000, a three hundred foot length of railroad siding was restored at the Museum, permitting the running of a small passenger car next to the Old Main Line and paving the way for future use for excursion and exhibition trains. In August, 2001, the Station celebrated its 25th anniversary as a Museum and in June and July, 2003, commemorated the 175th anniversary of the founding of the Baltimore & Ohio Railroad.

* * *

2003 photo by Charles Kyler.

THE JONATHAN ELLICOTT HOUSE

Across the Patapsco River bridge at the foot of Main Street and opposite the Ellicott City branch of Wilkins & Rogers, Inc. — which stands on the approximate site of the original Ellicott's Lower Mills—there are two houses of granite. The first was erected by Jonathan Ellicott and the second by George, both sons of Andrew and Elizabeth Brown Ellicott of Bucks County, Pennsylvania.

Although they are today located in Baltimore County, it must be remembered that prior to the year 1914—when the Patapsco River was designated the new eastern boundary of Howard County— they were in fact within the town and county limits. Also, being the last of the original Ellicott homes still standing, to exclude them from this history would be sheer folly, since they clearly represent the early days of the small town's existence.

The house farther west and closer to the Patapsco River bridge was the first to be built and was erected in 1782 by Jonathan, oldest son of Andrew and Elizabeth, when he was but twenty-six years of age.

Very little has appeared in print concerning this particular member of the Ellicott family, although his talents and accomplishments certainly matched those of the rest of his illustrious kin.

Born November 9, 1756 in Bucks County, Pennsylvania, he married Sarah Harvey, the niece of the wife of his uncle Nathaniel

Ellicott. Following a brief residency in their home state the young couple moved to Ellicott's Mills where he became the proprietor of part of the mill property.

When hardly more than a boy, Jonathan Ellicott served as a captain in the Revolutionary War in 1777 but saw no action, although he did manufacture swords which were used in the battles of Monmouth and Cowpens. According to Charles W. Evans, historian and genealogist, Jonathan may have been dismissed by the Society of Friends for these actions, but if so was reinstated, "for he was an exemplary member of the Society" after the war until his death.

He was the originator of the Baltimore-Frederick Turnpike in 1797, and it was his plan that was used in the building of the bridge over the Monocacy River in Frederick County in 1807. This bridge, better known as the old Jug Bridge, has an inimitable legend attached to it. It is said that the trowel master carefully sealed a demijohn of whiskey in the huge stone jug that marked the eastern end of the bridge, after which it was named. Although the bridge itself has since collapsed, the old stone jug remains intact, having been moved to the new highway where it can be seen by all.

Jonathan Ellicott was by nature a progressive and active businessman. Yet despite his many responsibilities, he still found time to serve his fellowmen through both civic and religious projects. But true to his Quaker beliefs, he remained an humble and retiring person who preferred working quietly, thus avoiding the limelight as well as the price that must be paid for constant publicity. He valued his privacy above all else and shared his triumphs only with the members of his immediate family.

When the firm of Ellicott and Company was dissolved in 1812, he received as his share that portion of the property known as the Patapsco Flour Mills. As in all past ventures he was again highly successful.

Mr. Ellicott lived in the stone house heretofore identified until his death in 1826. His widow Sarah outlived him by fourteen years and remained in the home he had built for her, where they had raised their family of twelve.

During the Ellicotts' lifetime the house was a simple but sturdy structure. But it was known far and near for its gracious hospitality. A warm welcome was extended to all who stopped there, whether early or late. It is said that its rooms were constantly filled with guests.

Described by Mr. Evans as having been "of a plain and substantial character, built in accordance with the simplicity of Friends," the Jonathan Ellicott House has since undergone a number of changes and is today one of the more handsome structures in the area. Unfortunately it is not in the most desirable setting, but rather, as part of the Wilkins-Rogers property, faces the imposing but unpicturesque main building. The same house in a wooded area would be strikingly beautiful.

*　　　*　　　*

When first erected the old home had a single-story porch running across the entire front. A path from the pike led to the house, while a mill-race separated it from that of his brother. Flowering shrubs and colorful bushes grew in abundance. However, the present stone wall and side picket fence were added at a much later date, as were the shutters. A more ornate entrance was also substituted for the severely plain doorway at the time of restoration. For unknown reasons the first-floor windows have twenty-four panes, the second floor, eighteen, and the third, twelve.

The house has been compared by many to homes dotting the countryside of Mr. Ellicott's native state. Although this comparison is partially true, it is to be remembered that most of the older Pennsylvania farmhouses were constructed of red brick made of Pennsylvania clay. The use of stone, more plentiful in Maryland than in our neightboring state, is scattered there, while most of Ellicott City is built of the same rock upon which the town itself stands.

In Pennsylvania the construction of a stone house in the 18th century usually indicated wealth on the part of the builder, while in the area of Ellicott's Mills native granite was chosen primarily for economic reasons due to its abundance. Few areas outside this vicinity yield so great a quantity of this mighty rock. Keeping in mind its almost indestructible qualities, the Ellicotts showed great wisdom and foresight in their determination to use this local product. For many of the original buildings still stand, despite fires and floods and the ravages of time and the elements.

Jonathan Ellicott died the wealthiest of the Ellicott family, leaving a large estate. The other members of the firm, although they lived handsomely, died "possessed of very moderate fortunes."

Building as he did "in accordance with the simplicity of Friends," and despite the few ornamental embellishments, Mr. Ellicott's house still reveals the clean and beautiful lines that only simplicity can achieve. Short of an Act of God, such as carried away the old mills, the Jonathan Ellicott house seems destined to stand for many years. For a program of preservation, as outlined by the new owners of both houses, is now in the drafting stage. The possibility of maintaining them as offices or testing kitchens is under consideration. Upon inquiry, the writer was assured that as of this writing, future plans do not include the demolition of the old landmarks.

*   *   *

Although there has been considerable progress made in Ellicott City due to the restoration program now underway—sponsored by Historic Ellicott Mills, Inc. and the Howard County Historical Society—there are still many more buildings of comparable beauty dotting the hillsides of this remarkable town. They cry out for recognition and need only the touch of interested and knowledgeable owners. With the obvious renewal of public interest in this project, it is conceivable that the remaining homes and buildings of ancient vintage may yet be rescued from total annihilation.

If enough people can be convinced to study with care the dignified and uncluttered lines of the Jonathan Ellicott home, as well as the minor alterations which accent its structural excellence, and in turn apply this knowledge to the reclamation of the remaining landmarks, a complete restoration of the historic little town can be achieved.

Needless to say, such an ambitious program would, of necessity, be both costly and require time and patience. But upon its realization, the original 18th-century mill town would enjoy once again its former prestige as the historic and picturesque center of Howard County, and indeed, of all central Maryland.

Such an achievement is the hope and dream of all who really care.

*   *   *

2003 UPDATE

We read with sadness the words Celia Holland wrote about this beautiful house. She wrote, "Short of an Act of God, such as carried away the old mills, the Jonathan Ellicott House seems destined to stand for many years." The ink was barely dry on the manuscript when the fury of Tropical Storm Agnes struck in June, 1972, and destroyed this shelter of the Ellicott family that had withstood two centuries of natural challenges. Only recently restored at the time, the granite structure was ripped apart by the raging waters, and completely dismantled by the fire department soon after the floodwaters receded.

THE GEORGE ELLICOTT HOUSE

East of the Jonathan Ellicott house stands the H-shaped or double house built in 1789 by George Ellicott, brother of Jonathan and fourth son of Andrew and Elizabeth Ellicott. Although more than twice the size of his brother's, George Ellicott's house is of far more severe lines and has undergone less change. One might say it has merely been conscientiously maintained.

George Ellicott, who was born March 28, 1760 married Elizabeth Brooke of Montgomery County, whose ancestors came to Maryland in 1650. The ceremony took place in December, 1790. There were seven children of this marriage.

Together with his brothers and sharing the expense, George Ellicott opened the original road from Ellicott's Mills to Baltimore. An earlier project, a road from the mills to Carroll's Manor, was also conceived by the Ellicotts, although in this instance Charles Carroll of Carrollton assumed at least half the expense. The actual work was done by slave labor. It is further recorded that although his brother Jonathan was the originator of the road to Frederick Town, it was constructed after a survey by George Ellicott, then a youth of seventeen years. He also excelled in mathematics and was one of the finest amateur astronomers of his time.

He was very active in Indian affairs, taking part in the Great Indian Council of 1799 held in Upper Sandusky, Ohio, as well as a conference held in Baltimore in 1802 at the old Fountain Inn then

26

on Light Street. A conference with Little Turtle, a famous Indian
Chief, was followed by another meeting in Washington. A letter to
his wife dated "4th of 1st Mo: 1801" reads:

> ...We reached Washington last evening, dining pleas-
> antly at John Chew Thomas' at noon; it rained slowly
> to the end of our ride, but we did not get wet. This
> morning we called on the Indians, the Little Turtle with
> his brother Chiefs, and their interpreter, William
> Wells. They seemed well pleased to see us. We then
> waited on the Secretary of War, and, afterwards, on
> the President of the United States (John Adams) who re-
> ceived us in a very friendly manner, and says he shall
> do all he can to put a stop to the introduction of liquor
> amongst the Indians. We then called on Gen'l Smith (a
> Senator in Congress from Baltimore). He thinks it will
> not be advisable to hand our memorial, until the house
> has got through the business of the census, with which
> it is now engaged, and the next day after tomorrow we
> expect to hand it in. We are at Rhodes' Tavern, rooms
> to ourselves, and a good fire.

As can be seen, a concentrated effort was made by those present to stress the dangers and "evil effects of spiritous liquors then
being sold to the tribes." This culminated in the assignment of
George Ellicott to write a memorial to Congress, bringing about
the passage of a law making it illegal to sell intoxicating liquors
to the Indians. The memorial reads as follows:

To the Congress of the United States:
    The memorial of the Committee appointed for Indian
Affairs, by the Yearly Meeting of Baltimore, respect-
fully represents:
    That a concern to introduce amongst some of the In-
dian Tribes, northwest of the river Ohio, the most simple and useful arts of civil life, having been for several years laid before our Yearly Meeting, a committee
was appointed by that body, to visit them, to examine
their situation, and endeavor to ascertain in what manner so desirable a purpose might be effected. A part
of that committee, after having obtained the approba-
tion of the United States, proceeded to perform the service assigned them, and the result of their inquiries

and observations, as reported to the Yearly Meeting, was, that the quantity of spiritous liquors, with which the Indians are supplied by the traders and frontier settlers, must counteract every measure, however wise and salutary, which may be derived for the improvement of their situation.

The truth of this assertion is abundantly confirmed, by a speech made before us, by the Little Turtle, a Miami Chief, (of which we herewith transmit a copy for your consideration,) and we also acknowledge our belief, that the evil is of such magnitude, that unless it be altogether removed, or greatly restrained, no rational hope of success in the proposed undertaking can be entertained. We are, therefore, induced to solicit the attention of the National Legislature, to this interesting and important subject, which we consider involves, not only their future welfare, but even their very existence as a people.

Signed on behalf of the Committee by
Evan Thomas,   John McKim,
Elias Ellicott,   Joel Wright, and
John Brown,   George Ellicott.

On still another occasion—this one involving a journey among the Indian tribes from February 23rd to May 27th, 1804—George Ellicott, Gerard T. Hopkins, and others including a practical farmer, a carpenter, and a blacksmith, travelled about two thousand miles, their mission being to instruct the Indians in farming methods and procedures. Indications are that the trip was highly successful and understanding between the white man and the Indian was undoubtedly furthered.

An interesting account of a visit to Ellicott's Mills by Little Turtle and other Indian Chiefs during Christmas week of 1807 was recorded by Martha Ellicott, the most observant of George's children. Says Charles W. Evans in his account of the Ellicott family: "Having heard so much of Little Turtle, Martha was determined to be present when he and the other chiefs were introduced at her father's house."

The group invited included Little Turtle and Rushville, Chiefs of the Miami nation; the Beaver and Crow, of the Delawares; two Shawanese Chiefs; and Marpau and the Raven, Chiefs of the Potowatamies. Only Marpau, who was of a "very warlike disposition,

and the brother of Tecumseh and the Prophet, who, in 1811, openly revolted from their allegiance to the United States," declined.

Martha, then twelve years of age, recorded her memories of
the event later in life. The following is her account of the incident
in her own words:

> The Little Turtle and Rusheville, the Beaver and
> Crow, and the two Shawanese, were dressed in a cos-
> tume usually worn by our own citizens of the time: coats
> of blue cloth, gilt buttons, pantaloons of the same col-
> or, and buff waistcoats; but they all wore leggings,
> moccasins, and large gold rings in their ears. The
> Little Turtle exceeded all his brother chiefs in dignity
> of appearance—a dignity which resulted from the char-
> acter of his mind. He was of medium stature, with a
> complexion of the palest copper shade, and did not wear
> paint. His hair was without any admixture of grey, al-
> though at this time he was fifty-seven years old. His
> dress was completed by a long, red, military sash a-
> round the waist, and his hat, a chapeau bras, was or-
> namented by a red feather. Immediately upon entering
> the house he took off his hat, and carried it under his
> arm during the rest of the visit. His appearance and
> manners, which were graceful and agreeable in an un-
> common degree, were admired by all who made his ac-
> quaintance. When seated at the table, they seemed to
> enjoy the repast which was set before them. A large
> dish of hominy—a national dish with the Indians—had,
> with a variety of other dishes, been served up especial-
> ly with reference to their tastes, and was very accept-
> able to them. The Raven, on taking his seat, immedi-
> ately pointed it out to his wife, who sat at his side, and
> spoke for the first time since his entrance, to request
> to be helped bountifully to the hominy, having seen noth-
> ing he liked so well since he had left the woods.

The visit ended very agreeably; the deputation shook
hands with the Friends who had entertained them, and
returned to their hotel. They found Marpau and his
wife quietly seated by the fireside, but soon understood
that they had just returned from a walk, having passed
the day on the hills and in the fields on the banks of the
Patapsco.

Both Marpau and the Raven, whilst on their journey,
were careful to present themselves on all occasions

where there was a chance of their being seen, painted
and adorned in their most approved style. Thus, while
in Washington and Baltimore, although in comparative
retirement, as he did not go out, Marpau was said to
spend two or three hours daily in the duties of the toilet, painting his face, dressing his hair, and arranging
his appearance, by a small mirror held up before him
by his wife, who stood near him for the purpose of pro-
nouncing occasionally on the effect produced, and giving instructions. Similar attentions were conferred by
the wife of the Raven on her husband, but as he was of
lower rank and rather older than Marpau, his toilet was
less elaborate and occupied less time.

Martha Ellicott concluded her account with these words:

The day after the dinner party, all the Indians went together to visit the places where Marpau and his wife
had walked the day before, and the day following they
all departed for their homes in the west.

Emma Willard, famous educator and scholar, gave the following information in her AMERICAN REPUBLIC. The author offers it in conclusion:

After the inauguration of James Monroe, in 1817,
the Indians of Ohio ceded all their lands within its limits to the United States; they were allowed by the conditions of cession, to remain on the lands subject to
the laws of the United States; but very few of them embraced this alternative; the rest chose to emigrate beyond the Mississippi. The history of the red people
from this period is full of sad interest.

*   *   *

After the partnership of the Ellicott brothers was dissolved
in 1812 George Ellicott "worked the mill for rolling iron, on the
Patapsco, at Ellicott's Mills, which was built by the brothers in
1807, and to which was afterwards added the rolling mill for
sheathing copper." He died November 29, 1853 in his 73rd year.
But his home still stands almost as he built it. Today a roadway
separates the house from that of his brother's where once a mill-

canal had run.

The unbroken lines of the old stone house are unbelievably austere, although at one time the southern exposure was softened by a full front porch. It is further noted that both houses which face the Patapsco once overlooked a broad span of green, with "nothing to impede the view but here and there an ornamental tree."

A small frame entrance between the two sections does not appear in a photograph made in 1854, nor does the lovely main entrance with its pediment crowning a doorway flanked by side columns.

It is interesting to note that the windows of the front section differ from the rest of the house in that they have four panes of glass, while those in the rear, bordering on the pike, are similar to those in the Jonathan Ellicott house, with twenty-four panes on the first two floors, and twelve panes in the dormers.

The west wall of this same wing was built with no windows at all, a practice followed by many of our early pioneers who thereby hoped to shut out the worst of the wintry blasts. It is possible the west windows of the front section were cut in at a later date.

As in the case of his brother's home, it is also conceivable that the George Ellicott house will stand for another century or more.

Since the house served as an Ellicott home for more than sixty years, it is appropriate that this narrative be closed with a quote from the obituary notice of Elizabeth Brooke Ellicott who outlived her husband by twenty-one years. Upon her death, November 29th, 1853, at the age of ninety-one, the notice ran:

> ...She was the last Ellicott of Ellicott's Mills, where she had lived uninterruptedly for sixty-three years. The events and Chiefs of our Revolution were familiar to her; she had exulted in the peace of 1783; she had talked with Washington, Franklin, Jefferson, Adams, Madison and Rush; her vigorous mind, improved by careful and continual reading, made her fit company even for them. She was a sincere and ardent lover of her country and its institutions, and had travelled over a great portion of its territory; she loved to speak of its beautiful scenery, its happy liberty, and its future prosperity.

She was, after all, the wife of George Ellicott and the mother of his children. It is only right and just that when observing the house in which they lived, they both be remembered for their many contributions to the history of this great nation. Their charity, sense of duty, and unflinching courage in the face of adversity, have left an indelible mark upon the minds and hearts of all who cherish the warm and fascinating history of the immortal Ellicott family.

*   *   *

2003 UPDATE

In light of the unfortunate destruction of the Jonathan Ellicott House, which had been located next door, local preservationists set out to ensure the same fate of devastation by floodwaters did not overtake the George Ellicott House. An incredibly ambitious project was launched to move the house across the street to higher ground, a project that was completed in 1989 by a partnership of Historic Ellicott City, Inc. and Charles Wagandt's Oella Company.

The renovation of the property is striking, combining respect for the building's history with modern functionality. This combination is quite rare and should be greatly admired. However, unable to find tenants of its own, the partnership sold the property to OccuHealth, Incorporated, which today maintains the beautifully restored building. The company offers occupational, healthcare, and environmental resources. Although it has been moved out of the low flood plain, the building is still in an area subject to flooding, so it is hoped that such a fate does not loom in its future.

THE OLD EMPORIUM

Returning to Main Street from the Ellicott homes, one re-crosses the bridge spanning the Patapsco River. To the right and standing between the river bed and the underpass of the B. & O. Railroad, there is a single stone building now the property of E. T. Clark & Sons, a firm that has served the community for well over one hundred years.

Constructed of native granite and possessing the same archi-tectural features as the Ellicott residences and other 18th-century landmarks, the little shop is believed to have been built originally as a millhand's home. Spared the fate of its neighboring houses, all of which were swept away in the great flood of 1868, it is con-sidered one of the oldest structures in town.

With the destruction of most of the business district which was located on the east bank of the Patapsco prior to the flood, the town's merchants relocated west of the river and a new business area came into being. The old home in question soon became "Rad-cliffe's Emporium."

The stock carried included staples and fancy groceries, no-tions, underwear, dress fabrics, footware, hats and caps, paints, varnish, oils, glass, and "only lines carried by a first-class house." S. J. Radcliffe & Son also sold coal and wood, kerosene, coal oil, and other household necessities, in addition to which they owned and operated a kiln in which they burned oyster shells, thereby creating a form of lime for use in the fields. It is said they were prepared "to ship orders of any magnitude."

The Emporium was a well-stocked store and followed closely the pattern of operation set forth by the Ellicotts. However, there is no record of the Radcliffes having carried such luxury items as silks and brocades or fine china from overseas, as did Ellicott & Company. Nevertheless, the old Emporium and the Radcliffe kiln are still remembered by some who recall the store as it was in the late 1880s.

Although there was but one major industry in Ellicott City, the Gambrill Flour Mill, smaller businesses gradually appeared. A variety of shops opened their doors and before long Main Street became Main Street, U.S.A.

To quote one source, a former resident and member of a prominent family:

> Main Street was lined by a continuous row of shops, etc. Mrs. Annie Easton and Sons were the undertakers. Mrs. Dorothy Kraft and Sons were the butchers. Spirituous wants were supplied by Mr. O'Brien, Mr. Truehart, Mr. Curran, and Chris Eckert's Howard House Bar.
>
> Groceries were run by Mr. Hunt, Howard Dunkel and brother Jeff, and the patriarch of them all, Mr. Joe Leishear. He was of the old school, had such things as paper collars, etc., which he'd kept on his shelves for years. He would not tolerate paper bags and wrapped everything from pepper, salt, sugar and flour in manilla paper. His son Joe who assisted could not do a thing with him! His old colored man, Jake Henson, delivered heavy groceries on an old-fashioned drag!

Other businesses included Mrs. Fisher's Grocery Store, "right at the town pump, made by the Oldfields;" Laumann's Barbershop, where cupping and leeching were also done; Bierly's Shoe Shop, where boots and shoes were made by hand—ready-made ones being available only at Kirkwood & Getz; Buetefisch's Tailoring Shop, where the customer could make a selection from bolts of good, better, or best material; and Dr. Isaac Martin's Drug Store, operated by Dr. Martin and his two sons, Ike and Ross.

*   *   *

With the dawn of the 20th century Ellicott City remained little changed. But certain observations as recorded by Louis Dorsey Clark, past president of the Howard County Historical Society, offer a vivid and colorful picture of the average sights to be seen in the small town from the turn of the century through the early days of World War I.

There were the horse-drawn wheeled vehicles including Mrs. Garnett Clark's pony and cart; the donkey and special horizontal cart for the crippled Miss Mary Merrick of Linwood; the two-horse carriage of Louis T. Clark, overflowing with children; the rented daytons and buggies from the Gaither Livery Stable; the delivery wagons from Kraft's Meat Shop; the E.A. Talbott coal wagons drawn by two horses; the fine six-horse or six-mule teams, the animals often decorated with bells and tassels, pulling huge farm wagons of hay to Baltimore or wheat to the mill in Ellicott City; the long bus, also pulled by mules, carrying the religious students to St. Charles College which then stood across the Frederick Pike from Doughoregan Manor; and the striking two-horse American Express delivery van.

Numerous horses, most with vehicles, were to be found before hitching posts at the courthouse, churches, and up and down Main Street. On a fine day one could expect to see the Misses Ligon, descendants of Governor T. Watkins Ligon, riding proudly behind their coachman, or Johnny Pue on his fine horse.

Soon the buggies of Dr. William B. Gambrill and Dr. Gassaway disappeared from the streets, for they were among the first local physicians to switch to the new and temperamental automobiles. Mrs. Alda Clark, the Maccubbin sisters, and Mrs. John Rogers were among the earliest "suburban drivers."

During the winter months Main Street often became the scene of horse sleighs and even a few cargo wagons with runners substituted for wheels. But when the snow lay heavy, traffic was such that Main Street became a literal toboggan slide for the young and the young in heart.

*   *   *

In the 1920s Radcliffe's Emporium became the property of Louis T. Clark who operated a grocery store on the premises. Today it serves as part of an old and highly respected business firm —E.T. Clark & Sons, founded in 1845—and although minute in size, is of far greater historic value than the larger property facing on Depot Yard.

One entry in the daily sales logs of 1847 speaks eloquently of one form of service rendered by the company during that period, and is reminiscent of prevailing practices. It reads: "Placing irons on 4 prisoners—50¢ each. . . $2.00."

Although Edward T. Clark & Sons is no longer called upon to fill such orders, the people of Ellicott City do look to the owners to preserve the small building which reminds everyone, both resident and tourist alike, of another era when Ellicott City was Ellicott's Mills, and the little business house was the home of one of the earliest settlers—an honest and hardworking millhand.

* * *

2003 UPDATE

The Old Emporium, located next to the river under the railroad bridge, is the oldest riverside structure remaining in the area, having survived the terrible storm of 1868 and the pounding of Tropical Storm Agnes in 1972. Severely damaged by Tropical Storm Agnes, the building stood vacant for approximately ten years, but fortunately was purchased in 1982 from E.T. Clark of Clarks Hardware, by local attorney Robert C. Brown and his wife, Paula, who gave the old building new life with a major restoration.

At the time Mr. and Mrs. Brown purchased the building, it had no windows. The Browns valued such remaining special features as original hard pine on the second floor and obtained the services of a consultant nationally known for his work at Harper's Ferry National Park, who dated the building from the 1780's or '90's. A structural engineer did a site plan, and steel reinforcement was erected inside.

A hands-on restoration effort then ensued during which materials from the 1920's, 1930's, and 1940's were removed, new windows and first floor flooring installed, fireplaces reactivated and new electric and heating systems installed. A handsome, historically accurate landmark emerged from a vacant, deteriorating structure.

Over the years it has been home to a variety of businesses, from Appalachian Outfitters to a group of real estate development businesses today. These include Land Design and Development, Waverly Real Estate Group, Old Town Construction, The R/E Group, and Hamilton Reed Builders. The current owner of the building, Donald Reuwer, has had the office areas decorated using strong colors, handsome furniture, and art by local artists. Under his stewardship the building continues to thrive and delight into its third century.

Lottery poster showing the Patapsco Hotel with its second-story porch and boardwalk to the next building, 1834. – From the original at the Baltimore Museum of Art.

THE PATAPSCO HOTEL

On Main Street, west of the Patapsco River, there is a long three-story building still referred to as the old Patapsco Hotel. The present structure was built in the early 1920s from materials taken from an older hotel located on the same site. The original building, believed to date from 1830, was owned and operated by the McLaughlin family, the head of which was a son-in-law of Mr. Barnum who kept Barnum's City Hotel, the historic hostelry in nearby Baltimore.

Although the Patapsco Hotel was the scene of many historic events, no photographs of the old building have been uncovered by the writer. However, a lottery poster showing the first structure —as part of a group of buildings to be offered for sale—was circulated within a few years of its opening. Drawn by R. C. Long and lithographed by Thomas Cambell, it is captioned: "A Sketch from Rock Hill, advertising a Valuable real and personal property sold by Andrew McLaughlin by Lottery in accordance with Act of Maryland Legislature passed Feb. 19, 1834." Each piece of "Valuable real and personal property" was sold separately, the hotel having been purchased by a Mr. T. G. Brown.

The poster also sheds considerable light on the physical appearance of the first building. It is depicted as being three and one-half stories high with one oversized and two single chimneys piercing the roof. The top floor appears to have been a half-story and undoubtedly served as servants' quarters and storage space. A porch encircled three sides and a wooden walk connected the second-floor level with the next building which was used at the time as the Town Hall. According to the sketch, a vacant lot separated the two buildings.

Although the name Patapsco Hotel was never officially changed, it soon became known as the T. G. Brown Hotel, or simply, Brown's Hotel.

38

Little is known of the years during which Mr. Brown was proprietor. Only a single item has been called to the attention of the writer. This was a newspaper article which appeared in the Century Edition of THE TIMES, covering the history of old St. Peter's Episcopal Church. Although dealing primarily with this topic, it read in part:

> On April 7, 1842, when the hotel was the property of T. G. Brown and operated as the "T. G. Brown Hotel," a group of Ellicott City Episcopalians who had been attending services at Christ Church near Guilford, met to discuss the organization of a new congregation at Ellicott's Mills.
>
> Col. J. T. Williams served as chairman and J.K. Swain as secretary. Others included E. S. Williams, John Phelps, William Denny, William L. McLaughlin, George Ellicott, James Wingate, Charles Tucker, John Bosley and M. Lewin.
>
> A committee selected a vestry for the new parish, the first meeting being held on April 20, 1842. Rev. Alfred Holmead, Chaplain of the Patapsco Female Institute, was chosen as first rector...

Subsequent meetings were held at Brown's Hotel and resulted in the ultimate building of the first St. Peter's Church in 1854. (This building was destroyed by fire in October, 1939. A new church, located at Rogers Avenue and Old Frederick Road was completed in 1940.)

Thus it was that T. G. Brown's Hotel played a small part in the history and organization of St. Peter's.

*　　*　　*

In the early 1800s Ellicott's Mills had much to offer by way of natural beauty and climate. Uncluttered hills and valleys greeted the visitor. With the exception of the east side, where stood the mills and commercial district of the day, all the hotel windows overlooked extensive lawns and picturesque buildings.

From the rear one looked down on a number of small summerhouses. The vacationer could also enjoy an excellent and unobstructed view of Angelo Cottage. In the distance and farther west Mt. Ida—then one of the town's showplaces—stood out in bold relief, while to the north the Patapsco Female Institute, the largest and most magnificent of all the buildings, towered majestically over the entire town.

Although it is conceded that Mr. Long's poster undoubtedly depicts the buildings as seen through the imaginative eyes of an artist and tends to romanticize the small mill town, the buildings did exist and stood approximately as shown.

It is a matter of record that for a number of years following the construction of the railroad, tourists by the hundreds spent considerable time in the fascinating little town. With the fare to Ellicott's Mills from Baltimore a mere twenty-five cents, and the promise of a leisurely day or two spent in an inviting atmosphere beckoning, it can easily be understood why so many flocked to the area.

A unique service was extended to all who chose Ellicott's Mills as a summer retreat. Through an agreement made by the owners of the hotel and the B. & O. Railroad Company, visitors were taken directly to the hotel, by train, rather than deposited at the depot across the road. Upon their arrival the guests stepped from the platform of the train to the second-floor side porch of the hotel itself.

As early as May, 1830 three round trips from Baltimore to Ellicott's Mills were scheduled each day. With this schedule in effect the crowds swelled until an additional hotel was needed, and the Howard House was constructed in the late '50s.

A view of Ellicott's Mills published and sold by John Schofield in 1854 through the Patapsco Enterprise Office, New Town Hall, Ellicott's Mills, shows little or no change in the outward appearance of the Patapsco.

*   *   *

Many people from all walks of life found great pleasure in being a guest at the old hotel. Possibly the most famous of all was Henry Clay, the Great Compromiser and Senator from Kentucky. Having served as Secretary of State under John Quincy Adams (1825-1829), he ran for the Presidency as the Whig candidate in 1831 and again in 1844, losing in both contests. However his courage was such that, true to his beliefs, he made no attempt to conceal his personal feelings of alarm at the growth of abolitionism in the north, the most fiery and sensitive subject of the day.

His decision to attack the movement openly was looked upon with great concern by many of his supporters. His friend William C. Preston of South Carolina advised him against such action, warning him of the strong possibility of political suicide. Clay's reply —"I had rather be right than be President"—remains to this day one of the most courageous statements ever voiced by a man in public life.

A number of Henry Clay's staunchest supporters were to be found in the old line state where sympathies were with the South in many areas. In Howard County, the home of numerous slaveholders, he won the admiration and respect of many citizens. But in Ellicott's Mills, a manufacturing and mill town, contrary to general belief, most of the people did not share his political views.

Nevertheless, there is an oft-repeated story that while engaged in one of his presidential campaigns, Clay stopped at Ellicott's Mills and was seen standing on the balcony of the Patapsco Hotel looking out over the small town. Word spread rapidly and despite personal affiliations a crowd soon gathered and cried out for a speech. It being Sunday, a church bell rang out. The sound of it checked him before he had uttered a word. Raising his hands in an appeal for silence, he said gently, "My friends and fellow citizens, the notes of yonder church bell remind me that this is a day for prayer and not for public speaking." Then once again raising his hands, this time in silent benediction, he returned to his room as quietly as he had appeared.

*　　*　　*

The Patapsco Hotel today

The Patapsco Hotel was not always the scene of pleasant events. There were times when circumstances and conditions found it a dismal and frightening place. Such was the case during the War Between the States, since both Union and Confederate troops passed through the small mill town and, in fact, are said to have indulged in a mild skirmish within sight of the hotel. During this trying period many buildings lying in the path of moving troops were seized for one reason or another. It is a matter of record that both Lilburn and the Quaker Meeting House were besieged and pressed into use as hospitals. The Patapsco Hotel shared a similar fate. Since public sympathies in the little town were primarily pro-Union, and since Major McGowan—into whose hands the property had passed —was a loyal Unionist, the hotel became the unofficial quarters of the Union Army while in the area.

Edward Paul Duffy, a noted correspondent for THE BALTIMORE SUN at the turn of the 20th century and a writer of history on occasion, recorded this phase of Maryland history as follows:

> War history clings around the McGowan Hotel. It was the social centre for the Union officers whose commands were stationed in the vicinity, and, in fact, for sympathizers with the Federal cause. The McGowans were a military family, the father having been in former wars and two sons officers in the Union Army. One daughter was married to a Federal officer but a few months when he fell on the field, the victim of a Confederate bullet. His funeral took place from the old hotel, often afterward the scene of brilliant military social gatherings.
>
> East of the McGowan Hotel a tenpin alley which paralleled the railroad track was also used as additional quarters. The foundation which was still visible at the turn of this century has since disappeared.

*   *   *

The Patapsco Hotel faced still another kind of peril when, following the war, it withstood the horrifying flood of 1868. Although the Frederick Road and the bridge over the Patapsco River were carried away by the turbulent waters, and despite the fact that many homes and the Ellicott mill itself disappeared with the receding tide, the old hotel stood firm.

As late as 1879 the Patapsco was still operating as a hotel with Mr. T. Wilson as owner. He, in turn, sold it to the Hunt family who were still in possession of the property in 1905 although it was no longer being operated as a fashionable hotel, but was instead "rented in lodgings."

A few years later the Patapsco met an undignified and tragic end when a new owner took possession, tore out the interior, leaving only the side walls standing, and converted the historic old building into an ice plant. For ten years an effort was made to make the business profitable, but to no avail. The gutted building was abandoned temporarily, during which time the streetcars were not permitted to pass its doors for fear of collapse. The walls bulged and the once-lovely landmark became a hazard to life and limb.

In the early twenties a Mr. Pennington purchased the property, determined to salvage the site. After dismantling the old building stone by stone he rebuilt the Patapsco in its present form. All of the outer walls, as well as the windows and doors used in the reconstruction, were from the original hotel. Mr. Pennington made no attempt to replace the picturesque porches. Instead, he changed the plan of the ground level to include a number of stores. The rest of the building was converted into apartments.

Although the original hotel was gone for good, Mr. Pennington's contribution to the town did indeed restore dignity to the site of the former landmark. Once again "the old Patapsco" functioned as a place of shelter for residents of the small town and as a prospective center of activity. The starkly gutted building was given a new face and a new lease on life.

In 1923 another flood plagued Ellicott City. Water rose to a depth of six feet on Main Street, but again the Patapsco Hotel—the only building in Ellicott City to be rebuilt stone by stone—stood firm, although considerable damage was inflicted at street level and on the first floor.

The next owner was a Mr. Thompson who made his home there and operated a shoemaker shop in one of the stores. He rented out the remaining shops and apartments.

In 1952 during one of the worst floods to hit the little mill town, many buildings near the river were washed away as a wall of water eight feet high backed up and swept through no less than thirty buildings on Main Street. Again, like the rocky hillsides that surround this unique town, the Patapsco survived although its tenants were, of necessity, evacuated. Few structures of comparable size, including those of modern-day construction, could have sustained the repeated lashings of so many floods. Yet "old Patapsco" stood firm.

But with the porches gone and the wooden walk a thing of the past, until recently the landmark remained stark and lacking in character, despite Mr. Pennington's good intentions. All resemblance to the once-lovely hotel had disappeared.

Today a new and imaginative owner has purchased the well-known property. He is Mr. John M. Burbank, Jr., proprietor of Ye Olde Towne Gun Shop, one of the most attractive shops in town. Slowly the old hotel is coming to life again. There has been a general "face-lifting" of the store fronts, and appreciative and creative tenants have opened interesting and fascinating businesses. Included are: the Gun Shop, an art gallery, an antique coin and stamp dealer, and an antique and decor shop. There is also a two-store shoe repair which has occupied the same location for many years.

Through the combined efforts and talents of Mr. Burbank and Mr. Heselbach (of the Gallery CH), appropriate designs for new store fronts have been realized. Working as a team, the two men are credited with having remodelled all six stores, including the actual physical labor. With a little additional imagination and effort, and a great deal of patience, the entire building may yet regain an overall architectural charm. For the remodelled shops and granite walls, glistening from age and weather, already offer much by way of enchantment.

More than a hundred years ago the Patapsco Hotel attracted visitors from far and near. Once again tourists are returning to browse in the little stores and to recall the history attached to the building itself. Perhaps in the not-too-distant future the entire building will be restored, and the old hotel will once again become the pivotal point around which much of the town's life will revolve. Surely this is what Mr. Pennington had in mind when he dismantled the building stone by stone, determined to salvage the site.

With Ellicott City becoming once more a town appreciated for its historic interest, Mr. Burbank may well bless the day he came to the rescue of the mill town's once-famous hotel!

*   *   *

2003 UPDATE

The Patapsco Hotel is enjoying a renaissance. Owned by Land Design and Development and the Waverly Real Estate Group, the building has undergone a reconstruction, which retains the historic façade, while the interior has been modernized to accommodate 21st century taste. An antique shop, Retropolitan, occupies the first floor, and the upper floors were remodeled in early 2001 into six upscale luxury rental apartments. The owner added a patio and garden area behind the building for the enjoyment of the residents. Reserved parking for the apartment dwellers is located next door, behind The Old Emporium.

*   *   *

2003 photo by Charles Kyler.

St. Paul's Church as it appeared in 1910. In the background, Rock Hill College before the great fire of 1923.

-From the author's collection.

ST. PAUL'S CHURCH AND SCHOOL

Overlooking the banks of the Wild Cat Branch, a stream which parallels New Cut Road for several miles, there stands one of Ellicott City's finest landmarks—St. Paul's Catholic Church. Once described as "a jewel in an exquisite setting," St. Paul's tall steeple can still be seen from any of the small town's seven hills.

When Ellicott's Mills was first settled by the Ellicott brothers, the needs of the early Catholic settlers were provided by the chaplain of Doughoregan Manor, as well as the Sulpician Fathers from St. Mary's College, Baltimore.

A leaflet discovered among the effects of the Rev. H. B. Coskery, first resident-pastor of St. Paul's, reads:

> John Fahey arrived at Ellicott's Mills in 1822. There were only three Catholics about the mills. Mr. Mooney, Mr. Airlocker (or Erlougher) and Mr. Jones, and a colored man named John Joyce. There was no church here of any sect, except the Quaker Meetinghouse on Quaker Hill. The Catholics worshiped at the Manor, six miles distant. The first pastor was Reverend Timothy O'Brien, then Mr. Richmond, then Mr. Todrig, an Englishman, who was succeeded by Mr. Coskery in 1836 or thereabouts...

(John Joyce, the Negro mentioned in this account, was a freedman of Charles Carroll. His descendants still survived in the vicinity of the Manor until well past the turn of the 20th century. There may possibly be some in the area even today.)

Immediately after the development of the National Pike and the B. & O. Railroad, there was an influx of Catholics into the area in and around Ellicott's Mills. The new residents were of Irish, German, and English origin. Some settled outside the village wherever acreage was available, while others who sought jobs as millhands made their homes near the mills. Thus the original Catholic parish comprised most of Howard County and also portions of Anne

Arundel and Baltimore Counties.

Although the first baptismal registration is dated 1838, it is generally believed St. Paul's Church was begun in 1836, the year in which the deed was drawn. Archbishop Eccleston and Henry B. Coskery received the land from John Ellicott, son of Elias, and Andrew Ellicott and his wife Emily. The two lots were presented to the Catholic Church by the Ellicott family "for the nominal fee of five dollars."

Taking approximately two years to build, according to the parish registry "St. Paul's was blessed December 13, 1838," a claim verified by a stone in the old belfry tower. The original Patapsco Bank Building was standing at the time and was to be acquired by the church at a later date.

During the building of the now-famous landmark and before the parsonage became a reality (1844), Father Coskery and conceivably his successor, Father Piot, made Castle Angelo their home. During this period Mass was said in the quaint little structure, endearing it to many members of the Catholic faith who later settled in the area. Some thought was given to buying "the Castle" and preserving it as the site of the first Catholic service in the little town, but the plan never materialized, possibly due to the lack of funds.

In 1859 the church was renovated to include the erection of an apse at the east end, a sacristy to the right of the sanctuary, and a chapel for the students of Rock Hill College to the left.

In 1861 additional ground was bought from Victor J. Diffey and George Ellicott. It was this George Ellicott, son of the first George, who became the progenitor of the Catholic branch of Ellicotts. Although he never embraced the religion himself, his wife, the former Barbara Agnes Peterson of Calvert County, was a Catholic. The children of this marriage all followed in the mother's faith.

George Ellicott, being a man of broad mind and deep insight, apparently accepted without question his family's decision, although he himself was an active member of the Quaker Brethren until his reputation as a "swearing member" brought about his expulsion from the Meetings. Commented Mr. Ellicott following his humiliation: "They may expel me from the Meeting, but I'll be damned if they can knock the Quaker out of me!"

St. Paul's Church was built of grey granite from a nearby quarry and was originally sixty feet long, forty feet wide, and thirty feet high. The late Brother Fabrician, Professor of English literature at Rock Hill College, offered a vivid and candid description of the church as he first saw it in 1871:

The lower story is a large open room thirty feet by
forty, lighted by four large windows. It was first used
for a Sunday School, then for a small parish school, but
is now occupied as a lodge room by the Catholic Bene-
volent Legion. The main auditorium or church proper
is on the second floor and consisted in the beginning of
a large open hall sixty by thirty, with a plain flat ceiling twenty feet above and eight rectangular windows,
ten by four feet, four on each side.

These were of the old style cottage-windows with
diamond shaped panes of glass painted white. They
were divided into four equal compartments, the upper
portions turning outwards on pivots at the side, the under portions swinging inward on hinges. They have
since been replaced by stained glass windows of the
most modern type. The altar was at the eastern end
of the church and consisted of a neat wooden closed-in
table surmounted by a tabernacle flanked on each side
by three small wooden steps. All was painted in white,
tipped with gold.

Above hung a large oil painting in gilded frame, depicting the public confession of the apostle Thomas'
faith in his newly-risen Savior. On each side of the
main altar were shrines for the Blessed Virgin and St.
Paul the Apostle, statues of whom were supported by
strong wooden brackets springing from the walls ten
feet above the floor.

These statues were of wood painted white, and were
of almost heroic mould, entirely out of proportion to
the size of the church. That of St. Paul, with its stern
countenance, flowing beard, and massive sword, was
somewhat impressive; but that of the Blessed Mother
was anything but devotional. It was the image of an
Amazon, bold, masculine, defiant, with hair dressed
in the fashion of a hundred years ago. The wags of the
parish irreverently styled it "Old Queen Bess," and in
truth the name was quite appropriate. It was more of a
hindrance than a help to piety, yet its presence domin-
ated the entire room.

The walls of the church were unpainted, but down
each side were large framed colored prints of the Sta-

tions of the Cross. The pews were of the old-fashioned box-type with high backs and swinging doors. They were painted a dark brown. Straight across the back of the auditorium stretched a gallery ten feet wide and about eight or ten feet above the floor. Leading up to this was a wooden staircase on the right of the entrance, while on the left was an old confessional. The gallery was for the exclusive use of the colored members of the congregation, and for the village choir, at whose service was a large reed organ.

The entrance to both stories of the building was through a stone belfry ten feet square, with a door in the center of the basement floor, while two stone stairways led up to doors on each side of the tower for admission to the church proper.

A square room, six by six, lighted by a large window, served as a vestiblue. On each side of the swinging doors opening into the church, were two quaint holy water fonts or marble bowls resting on low wooden pillars painted brown. The belfry rose above the slanting roof of the church not more than ten or twelve feet. It had openings on three sides as outlets for the sounds of the bell, and was surmounted by a plain gilt cross.

During the winter months, the church was heated by two high sheet-iron stoves placed midway on each side of the room. Suspended from the ceiling at equal distances from each other, were two large bronze chandeliers supporting coal-oil lamps, to be used at the evening services, which seldom took place at night except during the Lenten season. In the beginning, there was no regular sacristy. The priest vested most probably at a table on the right side, and the vestments and altar ornaments were stored on shelves behind the altar.

During the pastorate of Father Starr (1870-73) tasteful and appropriate changes were made. The walls were frescoed, pews repainted, and Stations of the Cross erected. Large storage cases and closets for vestments and ornaments were installed in the sacristy. The painting of Thomas the Apostle which once hung over the main altar was removed to the rectory. A marble altar with proper liturgical equipment and a sanctuary light were installed. Two carved wooden statues of adoring angels were raised to flank the high altar. A crucifix of silver with a polished brass figure of the

Savior, as well as elaborate German silver chandeliers, highly
polished, added a note of luxury and radiance to the beautiful interior. Although not a wealthy parish, the parishioners were generous and strove only for the best in appointments, as they could afford them.

Then under Father Tarro (1883-1907), a brilliant and talented man, St. Paul's drew closer to its present appearance. The
main altar was rebuilt using panels of Scotch marble and the brilliant brass monogram "I. H. S." was mounted beneath the surface
of the altar. A new and beautiful brass tabernacle door replaced
the old, and "over the sacred receptacle, a neat boldachino in white
marble, surmounted by a cross, completed the happy transformation." The chancel floor was tiled, the altar steps improved, and
two massive candelabra replaced the adoring angels. Windows of
cathedral-rolled glass delicately tinted were installed, while new
pews, confessional, baptistry, and steel ceiling of chaste design
replaced the old. Two marble side altars were added. Outdoors a
graceful spire topped by a gilded Celtic cross reached skyward one
hundred feet above the earth.

Father Tarro set a precedent for beauty and religious significance in his small gem of a church. It has been claimed that at
the time, Ellicott City's St. Paul's was considered "one of the best
equipped churches outside the larger cities of the Archdiocese."
Father Tarro's successors have succeeded in maintaining the picturesque beauty that became St. Paul's heritage so many years
ago.

*   *   *

It has been said that no early history of this church could be
considered complete without mention of Mrs. Mary Richmond. A
devoted but humble person, she quietly took upon herself the full
responsibility of the sacristy, including the care of the vestments
and altar linens as well as the care of the altar and sanctuary itself. This self-imposed obligation represented much physical labor as well as liturgical knowledge. Today, these chores are shoul-
dered by a group of women known as the Altar Society. It was written of Mrs. Richmond:

> One venerable figure emerges from the shadowy past
> with a special claim upon the gratitude of St. Paul's
> congregation. Others did, good work, noble work for
> the honor of God and the beauty of his house; but there

was one so regular, so assiduous, so devoted to the
humble role she had taken upon herself, that no account of St. Paul's sanctuary would be adequate or complete with the name of Mrs. Mary Richmond omitted.
Through winter's cold and summer's heat, rain or
shine, early and late, her portly figure could be seen
trudging the road between her home and the church,
carrying on her arm a heavy basket containing the altar linens and the priest's vestments all beautifully
laundered and ordered by her own hands. Down one
hill and up another, year in and year out, with ever a
cheerful smile and kind word of neighborly greeting,
her presence shedding a benediction as she passed by,
she could be seen wending her way to her self-imposed
task of loving labor in the sanctuary of her Lord. How
she loved it! Peace to her soul, and green be her memory in the annals of St. Paul's!

Another honored parishioner closely identified with the early
history of St. Paul's was Mr. Joseph A. Ells, Sr. It is said of him
that he spared neither time, money, nor self in contributing to the
betterment of his beloved church and parish. Traces of his skill
and handiwork can still be found in the old building.

Through his labor a cellar was dug back of the basement of
the church so a stage could be erected for church entertainments.
He was responsible for the niche over the high altar where the sta-
tue of the Sacred Heart now stands, as well as the design of the
memorial windows. He personally paid for the tiling of the sanctuary, as well as a marble cruet stand. He "designed and executed the confessional and baptistry," and with the help of Mr. John
O'Brien, Jr. improved the choir gallery.

Other names indelibly engraved on the records of St. Paul's
include: the Onthanks, the Merricks, the McMullens, the Heaveys,
the Reynolds, the Kirbys, the Mulligans, the Wallenhorsts, the
Martins, the Hendricks, the Truehearts, the Van Lills, the O'Bri-
ens, the Loughrans, the Durkes, the McKenzies, the Tomminks,
the Powers, the Potts, the Siglers, the Bachs, the Burkes, the
Kavanaughs, the Mahons, Mrs. Joseph Ells, the Malones, the Hold-
ens, the Foleys, the Oldfields, and Miss Victorine Murphy.

Were the author to attempt to bring this list up to date, down
through the years, scores of pages would be filled, for the historic
landmark—old St. Paul's—has always enjoyed a generous and active congregation. So rather than omit a single name, unintention-

ally, the writer has focussed only on the early years of its existence.

*   *   *

Possibly the most famous of all St. Paul's social activities
was the annual church picnic, usually held on the 4th of July before
the harvest, or on Lady Day in August after the crops had been
gathered in. Brother Fabrician's description of this very special
event would be hard to surpass. It was a "must" on every parishioner's calendar and members came from far and near—from
Sykesville and Elkridge, from Paradise and Union, and from areas
not yet bearing official names. Said Brother Fabrician:

> The lassies wore long white muslin dresses, stiffly
> laundried, with high-necked waists and long sleeves—
> no 'peek-a-boo' waists in those days nor 'rats in the
> hair'—red or blue silk sashes around the waist, stream-
> ers falling behind, lace collars held in place by a rib-
> bon bow of the same hue as the sash they wore, or by a
> large cameo breast pin—an heirloom in the family—and
> broad flapping Leghorn hats or calico sun-bonnets
> adorned with ribbons and artificial flowers. These hats,
> no doubt, were the ancestors of the modern 'Gainsbor-
> oughs' and 'Merry Widow' and 'Chanticleers.'
> The swains sported low cut shoes, loud stockings,
> white duck pantaloons as stiff as a board, brilliant
> waistcoats or colored shirts, turn down collars and
> flaming red neckties, linen dusters, and broad-brimmed
> soft hats, mostly white or light brown. Many discard-
> ed collars entirely, substituting therefore a brightly
> polished collar-button in lieu of a tie. The elders were
> satisfied with more sombre colors—mainly light gray
> or brown: the matrons with vari-colored ginghams,
> and white or calico aprons, black lace caps or Shaker
> bonnets.
> From Hollifields and Ilchester, from 'the Folly' and
> the Manor, from Waterloo and even Sandy Springs—
> from all quarters came the farm-wagons laden with
> human burdens and good things to eat—the old, the mid-
> dle-aged—sturdy sons, buxom lassies—and children
> galore!
> There were the Carrolls, the McTavishes and the

Cromwells; the Benzingers, the Wymans, the Sands, and the Footes; the Cissels, the Dorseys, the Hammonds, and the Clarks; the Thomases, the Peters, the Whites, and the Warfields; the Gaithers, the Owings and the Forsythes; the Davises, the Talbotts, and the Sykes; the Watkinses, the Garys and the Browns; the Ellicotts, the Tysons, the Haines, and the Hunts—all the gentry and plain bourgeois—Catholic and non-Catholic alike, the one as generous, if not more so, than the other.

Strictly, it was a family gathering...and how their souls were knit together in bonds of reverence and love!

St. Paul's grew with the little mill town, sharing its successes and failures, advancements and setbacks, sorrows and joys. Each pastor in turn contributed something of himself to the parish and its people, as well as to the Church itself.

*   *   *

Rev. Henry Benedict Coskery, D.D., pastor from 1835 to 1840, was called to the Cathedral and made Vicar General. He served twice as administrator of the Diocese of Baltimore and although appointed Bishop of Portland (Maine) in 1854, returned the bulls, requesting that this appointment be withdrawn. His wish was granted. Father Coskery was totally unselfish. He was interested only in helping his fellowman, to the extent that when he died (Feb. 21, 1872) "the sum total of his worldly wealth was but thirty-two cents...."

Reverend Bertrand S. Piot, S.S., known as the pioneer priest of Western Maryland, served from 1840 to 1851. The simple wording of the records of his long pastorate bears witness to his modesty and humility. With no mention made of the effort on his part to raise the necessary funds to maintain and improve his parish, his ledgers read simply: "The organ was bought in December, 1839, for the sum of 360 dollars—(I think)." Other purchases included the burial ground (1841), $225.00; bell (1843), $172.00; priest house commenced in 1844 (no figure); stone wall and two flights of steps (1846), $228.00; stone steps to the church (1847), $290.00, etc.

Father Piot's devotion to two other principles remained unchanged until the day of his death. He was strictly opposed to slavery, spending much time instructing the slaves of his parish and baptizing them. He became their undisputed champion, although his mild and charitable disposition won for him the respect of his opponents as well. He was also an ardent temperance advocate, organizing the highly successful St. Paul's Temperance Society. When Father Piot died in 1882 he was a beloved and revered old man. He was buried in the cemetery he had founded. His tombstone, which for years lay buried beneath wild and unruly overgrowth, was recently unearthed by the present pastor.

Father Piot's successor was Reverend Bernard J. McManus who served as pastor a scant two years (1851-53). Father McManus was a man of great intellect. He was an outstanding scholar. Yet he knew and loved the people entrusted to his care. He was never too busy to help when help was needed, but his greatest joy

St. Paul's first school, formerly the first Patapsco National Bank Building.

lay in an intelligent conversation with one of his contemporaries— or with a group of young people who shared his interests.

No man who enjoyed the privilege of a friendship with him remained untouched, for as with any person of true value, his humility and concern for his fellowman surpassed all his other remarkable characteristics. And he possessed many.

Upon his death it was written of him that he was a man of "clear, sound judgment...a wise counselor...[and] no one was more loved and esteemed by both clergy and laity than he." In speaking of his friend, His Eminence James Cardinal Gibbons once said: "My soul is knit to the soul of Father McManus, as the souls of David and Jonathan were knit together."

Father McManus was succeeded by Rt. Rev. Augustine Verot, S.S. (1853-58), who was destined to become the first Bishop of St. Augustine, Florida. As such, he became known as "the Rebel Bishop" during the War Between the States.

Father Verot was a saintly and religious man who brought many converts into the Church. He was also responsible for the return of numerous lapsed Catholics. It was during his pastorship that the cemetery was enlarged, the purchase price of two hundred dollars for the additional land being loaned him by Mr. Joseph Kuhn.

Known as an excellent speaker, Father Verot was also an exceedingly intelligent writer. He is credited with having written one of the finest Catechisms ever published in this country.

Right Reverend John S. Foley, D.D. (1858-64) was another of St. Paul's former pastors who was later elevated to the rank of Bishop. On November 4, 1888 Cardinal Gibbons, a life-long friend, consecrated him Bishop of Detroit in the Baltimore Cathedral.

John Foley and his Brother Thomas Foley shared a rare distinction in that they were both consecrated bishops of the Church. It is said that "with the exception of His Eminence Cardinal Gibbons, no episcopal consecration ever held in Baltimore Cathedral met with more genuine and widespread approval than those of the two Foley brothers."

Rev. Thomas O'Neill (1864-70) was one of St. Paul's most colorful and dynamic pastors. A curt and abrupt man, he possessed a "caustic wit and sledge-hammer logic." He was highly respected but feared by many. His theory of "brimstone and fire" was delivered in full force at each and every service. Although not a man of eloquence, his sincerity and honesty won for him the loyalty of the entire congregation, despite personal likes or dislikes.

His approach on matters of money and financial support was equally blunt and to the point. A story is told of his shrewd observations on the occasion of one such appeal. When the basket was about to be passed, he turned slowly but deliberately toward the students from Rock Hill College, and in a quiet but unmistakable manner addressed the petrified group: "...I want you scamps to put no more buttons in the collection box. I have more buttons upstairs than would last a man a lifetime." He paused momentarily and the silence in the small church was all but unbearable. Then in a voice resembling an approaching storm he bellowed: "I want sound, hard cash, not buttons! If you can't give cash, give nothing at all; but keep your buttons. God knows you need them!" Without another word he walked to the altar and resumed the service. A sense of guilt swept over the perspiring boys, and for that one day at least, the sound of coin upon coin jingled and echoed throughout the little church.

Father O'Neill died November 21, 1874 and lies buried in St. Mary's graveyard, Emmitsburg, Maryland. Although there are none left to remember him, he and his abrupt approach on all topics have become legend in the history of St. Paul's.

*   *   *

Legend further tells us that during the final days of the Civil War St. Paul's was the scene of a scandalous attack combining pathos with humor. The event, which presumably took place during Father O'Neill's pastorate, was recorded March 26, 1864 following the registration of the baptism of one David Martin, soldier. The account reads:

> This carries us back to the Civil War Period, and to many Howard Countians will bring back memories of that troublous time in Ellicott and Elkridge. Then occurred a very stirring incident, the centre of which was St. Paul's Church.
>
> A body of Yankee cavalry had been stationed on Quaker Hill for some days—to the great disgust of Ellicott's citizens who were open and ardent Southern sympathizers. The Yankee soldiers, all non-Catholics, undertook one day to amuse themselves by entering St. Paul's and acting there most rudely, even going so far, tradition says, as to make one of their number don the sacred vestments and mimic the 'Sacred Mystery.'
>
> The entire townsfolk, without distinction of creed, were furiously indignant, but powerless to prevent the gross outrage. However, whether by train or telegraph or speedy horseman, the Catholics soon informed a regiment of Irish Catholic troopers then stationed at Relay.
>
> Quick as a flash these sprang to horse, and at breakneck speed shortly reached Ellicott's; but our brave Yankee heroes got wind of their coming, struck camp, and hastily beat a retreat. Dame Rumor, as usual, added to the account of the affair; and therefrom evolved the following humorous sequel.

> She maintained that the Irish Catholic troopers did surprise the Yankees in their sacrilegous act, and that the foremost Irishman raised his musket and shot down the vested ruffian as he stood before the altar; but that some days after, struck with remorse, he came to confess to Father Foley most contritely, not that he had shot a man, oh no! that was heroic! but that he had burnt a hole in the vestment!

Although there are those who question the validity of this tale, the story has been repeated to such an extent that it has passed into the hazy realm of folklore. Be that as it may, there are many who are still convinced of the authenticity of the story, with but one exception, since the events of those fatal years (1861-65) left other indelible marks on the history of the little mill town.

There are those who insist, along with a majority of our local historians, that Ellicott City—being an industrial center—did not in fact consist primarily of "ardent Southern sympathizers," but rather, that sympathies were divided as they were throughout the state. They argue further that despite wartime loyalties, it was the outrageous behavior that was resented and not the color of the culprits' uniforms. However, as is often the case, the traditional version affords more color and is, therefore, more readily accepted.

*   *   *

Right Reverend William E. Starr's contributions to St. Paul's have already been noted in this article. He succeeded Father O'Neill and was pastor from 1870-73. In 1908 he was invested with the Roman purple, as Monsignor, by His Eminence, Cardinal Gibbons. This title is an open recognition bestowed upon those priests who have contributed to an extraordinary degree valuable service to the Church.

The Very Reverend John J. Dougherty (1873-83) came to St. Paul's following twelve months of a most unusual assignment. When Archbishop Spalding died in February, 1872, to be followed twenty-one days later by the Reverend Henry B. Coskery, who was then serving as his assistant, the widowed diocese was placed under the temporary control of two young priests, one of whom was Father Dougherty.

Following a meeting of the Diocesan Council and the confirmation by the Propaganda at Rome, young Father Dougherty was appointed first assistant at the Cathedral from which, for a period of a little over a year, he "governed the diocese with great prudence and success." But failing health brought about his release from such burdensome duties, and he was offered the pastorship of St. Paul's in Ellicott City, which he happily accepted.

Father Dougherty had attended St. Mary's College from 1845–1856. Later, during his days as Prefect there, he had as students the Hon. Lee Knott, Reverend Doctor Eccleston (Episcopal minister), Father Sumner, S.J., John Lee Carroll, Dr. William Hand Brown of Baltimore, John F. McMullen, Sr., of Ellicott City, and other prominent men.

He was deeply loved by parishioners and students alike. Then after ten years of untiring service, he was ordered to St. Joseph's Hospital in Baltimore where he died in 1885, a victim of cancer. A memorial window was erected in his honor by the parishioners of St. Paul's where he "had spent the happiest days of his life."

Reverend Peter Tarro, D.D. (1883–1907), whose contributions to St. Paul's have also been reviewed here, was a discerning and talented man. Ordained a priest before the canonical age, he came from Italy to America. Here he served in many capacities: as assistant at St. Augustine's Church, Washington, D.C., then St. Stephen's, and finally St. Paul's in Ellicott City. His pastorate has been described as "the longest and most brilliant in the history of St. Paul's." In addition to the improvements already described, he also added an additional floor to the rectory as well as the existing mansard roof. A parish hall which was used as a Sunday School and center for all social activities was also erected.

At a farewell banquet given him the night before his departure many of Father Tarro's accomplishments were cited. But most touching of all was the tribute paid him by Mr. Joseph Ells, spokesman on that memorable occasion. Said Mr. Ells:

> You have left an impression on the minds and hearts of those who know you that will remain as long as life endures; and for those who follow us for many years to come, you have left a reminder of yourself in our little church, its towering steeple, memorial windows and beautiful altars—all of which have been put there by your untiring and unceasing efforts.

Father Tarro was then presented with a purse, an exceptionally generous amount having been donated by the people of St. Paul's, who found it difficult to bid him farewell. Among the many assignments that followed his transfer from the parish, the most interesting and rewarding was his appointment as pastor of Sacred Heart Parish, Mt. Washington, and chaplain at Mt. St. Agnes College.

Reverend Michael A. Ryan (1907-12) was the last of St. Paul's pastors about whom much has been recorded to date. A product of St. Charles College, and afterwards St. Mary's Seminary, he too was ordained by Cardinal Gibbons. After approximately sixteen years of duty at various parishes in the Archdiocese, he was sent to St. Paul's. In addition to physical improvements to the church and grounds, he is also credited with having instilled a stronger Catholic tone throughout the parish, and with increasing notably the attendance at public services and the reception of the sacraments. His success in the field of conversions was outstanding.

Upon his return to Baltimore in 1912, Father Ryan organized Blessed Sacrament parish and built its church. Later, he served as pastor of St. Peter's for many years, remaining in the city until 1920. During this time St. Paul's welcomed and said farewell to three more pastors: Reverend Dennis Keenan (1912-14); Reverend Thomas S. Dolan (1914-18); and Reverend Edward Southgate (1918-20).

One incident which occurred in 1918, during the pastorship of Father Southgate, bears repeating. Although unimportant in itself, it is indicative of the caliber of the people of the parish as well as their rector.

Minor repairs on the church buildings were needed, including a repainting of the well-known spire. The necessary work was begun early in November. In the meantime, the end of World War I was rapidly approaching. With the signing of the Armistice on November 11th, bells rang out throughout the county. The little mill town took part in the national celebration. That is, all but St. Paul's. For although the bell was there, so were the workmen who clung to the scaffolding. Fearing the vibrations might shake the painters from their precarious perch, the order was issued to keep the bell silent. It was a sad day for St. Paul's. But a better way was found to celebrate the happy occasion. Members of the little congregation gathered indoors and instead of listening' to the peal of the mighty bell, in quiet voices they recited prayers of thanksgiving, together with an earnest plea for continued peace.

When Father Southgate was called to serve elsewhere and the announcement was made that Father Ryan would be returning to Ellicott City, there were mixed emotions on the part of the people. The rapid turnover of superiors from 1912 to 1920 had only added to their sense of confusion and frustration. Father Southgate's transfer was looked upon as still another great loss, while at the same time the return of Father Ryan was deemed a completely unexpected and delightful turn of events. Father Ryan's second assignment to St. Paul's lasted until 1947.

It was through his efforts that in 1922 the old Patapsco National Bank building was acquired and converted into the first parochial school in Ellicott City. At the same time he also provided a two-room school in the parish hall for the Negro children as well.

On September 11, 1922 St. Paul's School opened its door to accept seventy-five pupils. During the first year there were six grades. Another was added in 1923, and the eighth and final grade in 1924. On June 12, 1925 St. Paul's graduated twelve students. It was a big day in the history of the parish. Margaret Miller, one of the graduates, was the recipient of the Archbishop's Scholarship to a Catholic high school. The following year James Lilley brought more honor to St. Paul's when he was awarded a similar scholarship to Mt. St. Joseph's in Baltimore. Both achievements reflected the excellency of training accorded the children by the School Sisters of Notre Dame who staffed the new school.

In 1942 Father Ryan welcomed an assistant, the Reverend Linus E. Robinson—later pastor of St. Bernard's Church in Baltimore—who cared for the parish during Father Ryan's long illness and confinement at Jenkins Memorial Hospital. In 1944 while still under the doctor's care, this courageous man celebrated the golden jubilee of his ordination to the priesthood. In 1947 he resigned his position as pastor of St. Paul's and remained in the hospital until his death on March 12, 1953.

In 1948 Father Daniel F. Cummings became the new pastor. He was followed by the Reverend Casimir F. Keydash, former pastor of St. Joseph's Church at Sykesville and St. Michael's at Poplar Springs. In August, 1962 Father Keydash was transferred to St. Patrick's in Baltimore, at which time he was succeeded by the present pastor, Reverend Nicholas W. Dohony.

*   *   *

Father Dohony, a personable and energetic man, has contributed greatly to the advancement of the parish as a whole, as well as the restoration and preservation of the original landmark. Responding wholeheartedly to Cardinal Sheehan's plan to preserve the buildings both as local and religious landmarks, the present pastor has worked diligently with members of the parish to establish a practical and feasible maintenance program.

Born in Baltimore County, he became a resident of Baltimore City early in life. After attending Loyola High School, he studied at St. Charles College and St. Mary's Seminary. On June 10, 1937 he was ordained by Archbishop Michael J. Curley at the Basilica of the Assumption of the Blessed Virgin Mary, then the Baltimore Cathedral, first Roman Catholic Cathedral in the nation. Following his ordination he was assigned to St. Patrick's Church, Baltimore, where he remained until 1956.

He then became the first full-time chaplain at the Maryland State Reformatory for Males at Breathedsville, a small town near Hagerstown, Maryland. At the same time he was appointed first pastor of St. Joseph's Church at Half Way. The little village, hardly more than a dot on the map, was so named because at one time it served as a stagecoach stopover "half way between Hagerstown and Williamsport."

In 1958 Father Dohony became pastor of Our Lady of Sorrows, Owensville, and Holy Family Church at Davidsonville. In 1960, upon the death of Msgr. John Eckenrode, he returned to St. Patrick's as pastor and remained in this post until 1962 when he was transferred to St. Paul's.

When Father Dohony first came to Ellicott City he was given an assistant, the Reverend Robert S. Flagg. In 1965 Father Flagg was succeeded by the present assistant, Reverend J. Edward Yealdhall.

*   *   *

On September 8, 1966 another milestone in the history of St. Paul's was reached when the doors were opened for the first time to a new school with all modern facilities. Located on St. John's Lane north of Route 40, on a 20-acre tract of land once a part of the Ramsburg farm, it is now accommodating more than 350 pupils. Sister Mary Kevin, S.S.N.D. was appointed first principal. Members of the order of School Sisters of Notre Dame—as well as lay teachers—complete the teaching staff.

On May 7, 1967 Mass was said for the first time in the new auditorium-church also located on the property. Although Masses will continue to be celebrated each Sunday in the old church on St. Paul's Street, Ellicott City at 7, 9, and 11 a.m., additional services will be held in the new building at 8, 10 and 12:30. The hall accommodates up to one thousand persons and more than three acres of land have been paved for parking facilities. The total investment to date is approximately one million dollars, a far cry from St. Paul's humble beginning.

*   *   *

On July 6, 1967 Father Dohony celebrated the 30th anniversary of his ordination to the priesthood. Feted by more than 250 persons at a banquet planned by James Lilley, Reginald Malloy, Albert Memmel and Edward Bloom, he was accorded full recognition for his years of active and superb service.

In addition to his regular clerical duties, this remarkable and well-organized man has found time to work with the Big Brothers Association, the Archdiocesan Holy Name Society, and the Sodality Union of Baltimore. He was also Pro-Synodal Judge for several years with the Matrimonial Court of the Archdiocese of Baltimore. But of primary importance to the people of Ellicott City and Howard County, Father Dohony has also succeeded in stimulating the interest of many people in the history of the ancient landmark and this has resulted in its preservation. The church itself has not only been restored to its original beauty, it also retains many of its early features.

The two adoring angels once again grace the high altar; the handsome confessional, constructed with great care by a man of deep devotion to both his parish and his faith, is still in use; the Scotch marble altar with the brass letters IHS, installed by Father Tarro, also remains and is used daily. These and many other architectural features are still to be seen, including the original choir-loft which served the needs of the choir itself, as well as the Negro members of the parish—the latter practice having long since been abandoned. The side chapel, once occupied only by students from Rock Hill College, has now become part of the church proper. And on a clear day, the vivid colors of the beautiful memorial windows still shed a rainbow of light over the entire church. It must be seen to be fully appreciated.

Father Dohony is responsible for still another development in the history of St. Paul's. Due to his persistent research, a portion of the long-forgotten burial ground has been identified and is now in the process of being restored.

One mile west of the 11-mile stone on Route 144, at Rogers Avenue, one can see the remains of a few headstones. They are on a hill on the south side of the road and overlook a small stream. This inconspicuous spot was once St. Paul's cemetery. Over the years it has been reduced in size since portions of the land have been sold on various occasions. Nevertheless, after much work and unravelling of brush and other debris, Father Piot's tombstone has been unearthed and at long last, one can read the inscription thereon.

*   *   *

Thus it is that after having weathered the storms of several wars and a number of devastating floods, the old church remains a monument to peace and an integral chapter in the greater story of the famous old town.

*   *   *

2003 UPDATE

Many changes have occurred at St. Paul's in the past 35 years. In 1966 the parish built a new school in the Ellicott City suburbs off Chatham Road. In 1974 these new school facilities became Church of the Resurrection Parish and Resurrection School. The school is now called Resurrection-St. Paul School.

Under the direction of Father Nicholas W. Dohony, the parish completed a major renovation of St. Paul's Church in 1975. The new design added a side entrance and vestibule, with new stained glass windows duplicating the pattern of those already in place. At this time they dismantled and rebuilt the altar to create two new altars, one of which allows the Mass celebrant to face the congregation. They removed and replaced old pews, and added new carpeting, air conditioning, and lighting. In 1976 they added a wood carving of St. Paul created in Italy.

Further renovations took place in 1992, under the guidance of Father Thomas J. Donaghy. These included adding a ramp to give handicapped access. Vents and insulation were added to combat the poor ventilation, which had led to peeling paint. Also, the old school became a new parish center, named Dohony Hall. In April 1996 the Historic District Commission gave their Award for Outstanding Achievement—Non-Residential Resource to the church for this new parish center.

Recent work on the facility includes an expansion to double seating, two new wings, new entrances, improved office areas, elevators, and a redesigned parking area.

In May, 1998, St. Paul's commemorated the 160th anniversary of its cornerstone laying as the oldest Catholic church in the county. The church's continuing series of expansions and improvements attests to this parish's great vitality, and that of the community in general. Recently completed are a $1.2 million renovation, which includes a new sound system, new heating and air conditioning, as well as a ground-level entrance from the parking lot. Yet, the modern amenities do not alter the historic, traditional feel of the surroundings.

In 1999, Cardinal William Keeler visited St. Paul's to celebrate the 161st anniversary of the laying of the church's cornerstone in 1838. Renovations to the parish building that once housed the school now provide space for religion classes. A reminder that the building once served as a bank is the vault, which remains in place, as it would be too difficult to remove.

Rev. Donaghy remains pastor of the church as of this writing, a church revitalized by an influx of new families to the Ellicott City area. There is a very active youth ministry and a strong religious education program. In July, 2001, St. Paul's, along with nine other historic churches in Howard County, opened its doors to visitors as part of a tour celebrating the County's 150th anniversary.

There the visitor could view numerous church artifacts including the marriage certificate of baseball legend George Herman ("Babe") Ruth, who married Helen Woodford at St. Paul's on October 17, 1914. With such an appreciation of history, continual renovation of facilities, and a strong, active membership, the oldest Roman Catholic Church in Howard County continues to thrive.

*　　*　　*

Lilburn. Front view showing the altered tower where the spirit is said to dwell.

Dining room at Lilburn with its mysterious chandelier

LILBURN

Although most towns in Maryland the size of Ellicott City have a number of attractions to lure the seasoned traveler, few can offer so many in so limited a space. As a rule you will find a stately courthouse or public building, one or two churches of great charm or historic significance, several extraordinary houses, and possibly one or more fine antique shops.

But unlike most other towns of equal size, Ellicott City truly abounds in all these things. In addition to an impressive courthouse, several old and historic churches and public buildings, a number of antique shops, a minute castle, and many extraordinary houses, the town also boasts a particularly handsome old home, believed by a number of people to be haunted.

Lilburn, once known by the local residents as "Hazeldene," is located atop College Avenue beyond St. Paul's Catholic Church. It is a massive grey stone edifice of Gothic design. Built in the mid-1850s by Richard Henry Hazelhurst, it consists of more than twenty rooms, all of which are exceptionally beautiful and of fine proportions. During his ownership the estate was completely self-sufficient, there being approximately 2600 acres.

There was at one time a cook's house or separate kitchen which has since disappeared. However, an old barn believed to be the original still stands, as does a granite three-story smokehouse, two floors of which are beneath ground level. An old brick carriage house which is built into the side of a hill also remains. Like the smokehouse, it is three stories high, the lower level having been used for the "everyday carriage," the second floor for the carriage master's living quarters and the top floor for storage.

Mr. Hazelhurst, who was born March 2, 1815 at Abingdon, Berkshire, England, came to this county when still a compara-

67

tively young man following the death of his first wife. Some time prior to the building of Lilburn he took as his second wife Elizabeth Virginia McKim by whom he had six children, five girls and one boy.

Maria Eleanor, the first child, was born August 24, 1854. She was followed by George Blagden, November 25, 1855; then Catherine Lilburn, the first child to be born on the estate, in 1857; followed by Margaret McKim, June 9, 1859; then Julia, born in 1861; and finally Elizabeth, in 1863.

Mr. Hazelhurst is known to have prospered in this country. He owned a foundry in Baltimore. Being a man of strong convictions, he made considerable money during the War Between the States by selling an inferior grade of iron to the Union Army toward which he harbored little sympathy. His loyalty to the Confederate Cause knew no bounds. In turn, when the Union Army passed through Ellicott City, Lilburn was not overlooked. All of the owner's fine show horses were confiscated.

For several years the house is said to have been used as a hospital. Since Mr. Hazelhurst refused to leave his home under any circumstances, it is assumed he and his family maintained limited living quarters during this period of occupancy. It has also been stated by a former resident, John Maginnis, of Chicago, that General Robert E. Lee, a close personal friend of Mr. Hazelhurst, visited Lilburn and that he referred to it as "his retreat."

It is recorded that in 1870, because of declining health, General Lee did indeed seek aid from a prominent Baltimore physician. It is also a matter of record that between tests he stayed at nearby Linwood, then the home of Mrs. Major Peter, his wife's cousin, on a number of occasions, making the possibility of a stop at Lilburn feasible. However, there is apparently no positive proof verifying this claim.

Mr. Hazelhurst's love for Lilburn was of such depth that despite the anguish he was to endure there, he insisted on remaining, bearing in silence his deep and successive sorrows. On February 26, 1858, a scant three and one-half years after the birth of his first child, tragedy struck for the first time as he and his heartbroken wife stood by silently watching the life of the adored child slip away before it had even had chance to fully blossom.

For a number of years the Hazelhursts knew a quiet sort of peace, although it is said that despite the birth of her other children, Mrs. Hazelhurst never fully recovered from the loss of her firstborn. Then in 1887, after having also endured the shattering and humiliating experiences of the Civil War, Elizabeth McKim

Hazelhurst departed this life leaving the man she loved to face widowhood for the second time, and to accept alone the successive deaths of two more children. In 1891 Catherine Lilburn, thirty-four years of age, joined her mother for whom she had grieved deeply. Then in 1893 Julia, who had been married a brief two years, died at the home of her birth, apparently during childbirth.

Little by little parcels of land were mysteriously disposed of —perhaps to raise funds following the havoc wrought by the war— until the estate consisted of approximately 1200 acres, less than half the original holdings.

Then at long last on February 21, 1900, after almost a half-century of personal heartbreak and disillusionment, Richard Henry Hazelhurst breathed his last at his beloved Lilburn. He was survived by three children, one of whom was to follow him within five years (Elizabeth, in her 43rd year). George Blagden and Margaret McKim Hazelhurst alone survived.

Mr. Hazelhurst, who had served as vestryman at St. John's Episcopal Church, was mourned by all who knew him. He had been successful in many ways. Nevertheless, he had also suffered far more than most men. His endurance and quiet dignity under stress and strain aroused a deep and abiding sympathy in the hearts of his associates as well as the respect of all who came in contact with him.

Although he has become a legendary figure in Ellicott City history, he was, in fact, a very real person with very real problems. It is not likely he will be forgotten.

*   *   *

There followed a number of owners, one of whom stands out due to his colorful but eccentric personality. This was a Mr. Wells, "father of two gorgeous red-headed daughters," and the holder of the first pew in St. Paul's Catholic Church. Born in England, he was a recluse who shut himself and his handsome family off from the rest of the town. He planted a seven-foot hedge around Lilburn, defying anyone to invade his privacy. On Sundays when he ventured forth to attend Mass, he was politely addressed by his fellow-parishioners as "Mr. Wells," his first name never being used by anyone for fear of his reaction to such unsolicited familiarity! Even on these occasions he restricted his daughters' communication with others to a brief exchange of words with Father Ryan, the pastor.

A story is told of one brave man, a native of Ellicott City, who attempted a conversation while on the trolley car en route to

Baltimore. He received an abrupt and sharp reply in return for his efforts. Said Mr. Wells in his distinctive British accent: "Young man! Just because I did permit you to sit next to me in the trolley seat, do not think you have reason to attempt to speak to me!" He paused long enough to scowl at the intruder, then added briskly: "You are never to address me again, sir!" And turning toward the window he averted his eyes from those of his offender's for the balance of the trip.

Upon their return to the little mill town the story spread with fantastic speed. Eyebrows were lifted, questions were asked, brisk comments were made, and respect turned to cool tolerance. Needless to say, Mr. Wells was never again annoyed by superfluous conversation! Even upon the death of Mrs. Wells, when the townspeople relented temporarily in their feeling of antagonism and called at Lilburn to pay their respects, they were refused admittance to the house.

Mr. Wells was ultimately found dead in the library, apparently a victim of a heart attack. After a reasonable interlude his daughters went to Europe where one became the wife of an Austrian Count.

*   *   *

It has been claimed by a number of people that following Mr. Wells' death the old house became an Oddfellows Home. However, one highly respected citizen who has been deeply involved in the town's progress all his life claims that although plans were made to purchase the property for this purpose in 1910, nothing came of it due to a lack of funds. Others say it served for a brief period as a home for retarded children. But again, this statement has been denied and there is no record of such an institution having been established there.

*   *   *

It was during the residency of the Maginnis family that the strange and ghostly noises were first publicly noted, descending from the top floor of the tower. According to Mr. Maginnis (of Chicago) who was raised at Lilburn, the many tragedies that took place in the beautiful old home while the Hazelhursts were still in residency there were believed to have been responsible for the presence of the saddened spirit.

Having borne the death of his first child followed by the embarrassments and harassments of the war, plus the succession of deaths heretofore described, Mr. Hazelhurst was believed to have come to think of Lilburn as a place of tragic memories and unbearable frustration, rather than the happy and carefree home he had planned. Finally, his spirit broken, he who had dreamed of Lilburn as a place of beauty and complete happiness departed this life, as we have seen. But whether or not he ever really abandoned Lilburn is a matter of conjecture.

At first there was only the sound of footsteps overhead, originating in the top room of the tower. Weird noises followed. Then unexplainable and mysterious experiences were witnessed by various members of the Maginnis family. Nevertheless, the new master of this eerie house was as determined as had been his predecessor that his children would be raised here, ghost or no ghost. His decision was final.

It was Mr. Maginnis, Sr. who restored many of the original features of the house. He also installed the first heating system, using hot air ducts, and redecorated the entire house, making of it one of Ellicott City's showplaces.

But he is best remembered for a truly generous and nostalgic custom he established to initiate the holiday season. Each year on Christmas Eve he held open house for all the servants of Ellicott City. Such a gesture was heretofore unheard of and won for him the respect and admiration not only of the invited guests, but of their employers as well.

The custom came to an abrupt and tragic end in the early 1900s when the tree caught fire in the living room. The flames spread rapidly through the house due to the suction of the otherwise comforting hot air ducts. Although no one died in the fire the house was completely gutted, leaving only the beautiful spiraling stairway hanging grotesquely in mid-air. The tower was destroyed, possibly due to the necessary but destructive work of the firemen in their attempt to save as much as possible of the beautiful home.

Many whispered that one of the Hazelhursts had undoubtedly returned and had almost succeeded in destroying their old home, although they could not agree among themselves as to the identity of the spirit. Nevertheless, superstitions being what they were, the townspeople were convinced that surely now people would leave the place alone. Accepting this recent occurrence as indisputable evidence of the existence of a supernatural being, the town waited.

However, Mr. Maginnis was not convinced. Being a man of courage and fortitude—if not of inexhaustible patience—he completely rebuilt the interior exactly as it had been before with one exception. In his anxiety to complete the job and reoccupy the house, he failed to notice that the third-floor landing was not joined to the second floor by means of a stairway! Instead, it resembled a hanging balcony suspended over the hallway below. The effect was rather appealing. But to reach the third floor, one had to cross over to another part of the house and approach the top floor by way of the back stairway. Mr. Maginnis was irritated. But he was also restless. Intent on moving back, when the error was discovered he decided to "let it be," and so it is even to this day.

The only obvious change made by Mr. Maginnis was in the restoration of the tower. Instead of restoring the original Gothic peaks he replaced them with parapets, thereby giving it a more massive appearance. The townspeople said nothing but inwardly shook their heads. Believing now that they knew who it was that haunted the house, they again wondered and waited. Would this deliberate change aggravate the original builder? How would he who had taken such pride in the Gothic beauty of his home show his displeasure? Disillusionment does strange things to mere mortals. How, then, would it affect a spirit?

Soon the noises were resumed and the footsteps overhead seemed louder than ever. Again they originated in the new and altered tower. Would a man of Mr. Hazelhurst's character resort to this type of reciprocation just for the sake of a few Gothic spires? Or did the disastrous fire itself bring back anew the memory of his own sad times, making him pace all the harder back and forth, back and forth....

No matter what his reasons, Mr. Hazelhurst did nothing to harm any of his successors. He simply remained in what he still considered his own home—if, indeed, the ghostly resident was the genial but frustrated old man.

In the early 1930s the Maginnis family left Lilburn. Although they too loved the place, for reasons best known to themselves, they abandoned their estate and today return only occasionally for a brief glimpse of their former home.

*   *   *

Stories of strange happenings at Lilburn spread throughout the town until most of the local residents were afraid to approach the old granite "castle," let alone purchase it. But one lady who visualized Lilburn as it must have been, recognized all its potential beauty and persuaded her husband to let her try her hand at bringing it back to its original grandeur.

Again the land had dwindled away until there was but a fraction of the estate left. Mr. and Mrs. Weaver, the new owners of the house, had only moderate success with the interior. However, Mrs. Weaver, a dedicated gardener, was far more interested in restoring the grounds to their former elegance and charm. Whether or not there was any similarity between her exquisitely planned gardens and Mr. Hazelhurst's initial landscaping is not known. But the story persists that Mrs. Weaver was particularly talented in her chosen field and achieved great success in her attempt to restore picturesque beauty to the gardens of the castle on the hill. The patterns of her plantings still remain.

Judging from the outline of her work, a constant reminder of her obvious good taste, the present owner commented, "She must have been a very lovely lady." This tribute and the gardens themselves make it reasonable to assume that she will always be remembered for her contribution to Lilburn.

Upon her death the next owners were Dr. and Mrs. William F. Gassaway. Mrs. Gassaway was a daughter of the Weavers and she and her sister inherited Lilburn jointly. Upon the death of her sister Mrs. Gassaway became the sole owner.

The Gassaways, choosing not to live there, converted the house into apartments and held the property until early 1965 when they sold it to Mr. and Mrs. Sherwood H. Balderson, the present owners.

*   *   *

The Baldersons, who have five children ranging in age from fourteen to twenty-six, have completely restored the beautiful old home. By removing the temporary walls of the erstwhile apartments, they have revealed once again Lilburn's many splendid and original features. The house now sits on ten acres of ground, still enough to do justice to the grand old structure.

As you enter the handsome hallway you are immediately aware of the fact that there is no stairway in sight. To the right a truly magnificent gold and silver dining room, featuring a fine collection of antique furniture, greets the eye. The walls are panelled, sections of the upper panelling being covered with gold brocade. Coordinating floor-length window drapes help stress the grandeur and size of the room. Over the center of the long satin-like table hangs an exquisite crystal chandelier. The room is truly beautiful.

Returning to the entrance hall and bearing left, the visitor passes beneath a graceful archway and faces the lovely spiraling stairway. It is this same stairway that is complete only to the second floor, although there is an illusion that it runs to the top of the house.

The colorful living room with its deep reds and blues, features furniture from all parts of the world. The Baldersons, being connoisseurs of Oriental art and furniture, have hung a huge painting from the Far East over the living room mantel. The painting, an unusual but colorful composition, dates from 1776 and is understandably one of the family's most prized possessions.

At the far end of the room there stands an imposingly beautiful Steinway piano, believed to have been made the same year the house was built. It is of solid rosewood and perfect in every detail.

A large closed-in porch with exposed rafters colorfully painted opens off the living room and looks out over a long sweep of emerald green lawn. In the rear of the house an outdoor patio furnished with charming white wrought-iron furniture affords still another lovely view. From here one can see the small white tenant house as well as the top floors of the old meat and carriage houses. With the progressive loss of land which originally surrounded Lilburn, the horse stables are no longer located on the Balderson property but have now passed into the hands of a neighboring landowner. However, from any side of the house the view is arresting and most inviting.

The master bedroom, done in shades of deep blue and white with touches of gold, boasts a bed that could be mistaken for the Lincoln bed in the White House, with a small canopy added. Furniture of the same period is scattered around the room, as well as foreign pieces, which blend beautifully. The bed faces an unusual blue-grey marble fireplace with a conversational grouping of wingback chairs facing it.

All the fireplaces in the house have marble mantelpieces. Chintz-like wallpapers are used in the girls' rooms, while those occupied by the Balderson boys are typically masculine.

Young John Balderson, who graciously conducted the writer through his home, enjoys the privacy of a room in the tower itself just beneath the top floor where the spirit is believed to reside. His experiences with "the ghost" have been numerous and varied. Having heard the sound of footsteps on an almost nightly schedule for the past five years, he has chosen to ignore it. Although some people now blame the disturbances on the presence of squirrels or bats between the two floors, possible access to this space has not been found despite a very thorough examination.

Even though the Baldersons were familiar with the rumors attached to Lilburn long before they decided to make it their home, they have never known fear.   They feel instead a sense of compassion for the deceased whose beautiful home eventually became a house of sorrows. Says Mrs. Balderson, "We do not want to drive out or exorcise the presence at Lilburn. We feel that whatever it is is a tortured spirit—certainly not an evil one."

Although the family has witnessed some rather disturbing incidents, Mrs. Balderson adds, "I am not a mystic, yet I know and believe that the 'thing' at Lilburn has more of a right to be here than I."

It has been reported that at one time a succession of events led to a near-breakdown for this gracious lady, necessitating a trip away from Lilburn and "its constant happenings." Upon reading the report Mrs. Balderson commented, "I have never felt fear— only compassion. And my husband feels exactly as I do. Nor would I ever leave Lilburn under any circumstances. Mine is a love affair with the house."

Mr. and Mrs. Balderson are further convinced that the "presence" has been one of sorrow "which seems to have grown to one of more-or-less contentment." Although they are two of the least likely subjects for a seance or a haunting, they are at the same time sensitive enough to admit things have occurred that can neither be explained nor casually dismissed.

Since no one knows for certain who the spirit might be, the Baldersons admit that there are ample reasons to suspect that any one of the members of the Hazelhurst family could be guilty. It is conceded that Mrs. Hazelhurst might to this day be standing within the confines of her young daughter's room—Maria—still trying to reject the memory of the tragedy which deprived her of her first child's love.

One incident of unusual impact took place in the hallway outside the door of the room that once served as Maria's nursery. The family pet, a seventy pound Weimaraner, was found in the hall in a state of frenzied panic. He was on full point toward the rear of the hall, his hair up on end, his teeth bared in a vicious snarl. Leading him gently downstairs and out of doors the family watched as the animal shook in terror, becoming violently ill. The dog will no longer go near the hall where he suffered this experience. Keeping in mind that the incident took place outside Maria's nursery, for some time it was thought that Mrs. Hazelhurst was undoubtedly the tormented soul.

But with her husband having had to bear not only Maria's

death but the aftermath of the War as well, and the loss of his beloved wife, followed by that of two more daughters, it seems more logical to conclude that most people can overcome a single tragedy, but few can carry the burden of so many. Yet the true identity of the spirit, if indeed there is one, shall probably remain unknown.

While standing in the room on the top floor of the tower, presumably the home of the "thing," John Balderson pointed out the sepulchral windows which open out, casement fashion, locking with wrought iron locks. On more than one occasion these windows have been found open despite the fact that all members of the household disclaim having been near the room at the time. Finally, Mr. Balderson decided on a more positive approach. On a day when the servants were off duty, he and his family went to the tower while he tied each of the windows closed with stout rope. They returned to the patio and upon looking up a few minutes later, much to their dismay, noted that no less than three windows again stood ajar. Retracing their steps hurriedly, the confused family found the rope lying on the floor. With all members of the household accounted for during the entire procedure, none could venture an explanation.

For a time, other than the sound of the eternal footsteps overhead, the Baldersons enjoyed a respite. Then one evening, while entertaining friends for dinner, their conversation was suddenly interrupted by a muffled noise from above. Conversation ceased and gradually the exquisite crystal chandelier started swaying. Back and forth...back and forth.... It stopped as abruptly as it had started only to repeat the procedure a second and third time, leaving the host and hostess without a logical explanation. Their guests were bewildered and obviously alarmed. But when the incident did not repeat itself again they made a determined effort to overlook this strange experience. Nevertheless, the memory of that evening remains with them.

When the author questioned young John regarding his feelings today and those of his family, he informed her that they had reached one definite decision. So long as the "thing" did not interfere with their lives or cause any harm to descend upon them, they would live with the strange noises and unnatural incidents. But should there be any actual appearance or contact, or should anyone suffer physical harm, then all things would be taken into consideration and a decision reached at that time.

"But," repeated Mrs. Balderson, "we feel that whatever it is is a tortured spirit—certainly not an evil one. We also believe that peaceful co-existence with the occult is possible." Lilburn seems to be a vivid example of this possibility!

With a house of such great size, if indeed there is a spirit—and it is not too difficult to concede that there definitely seems to be one—there should be ample room for both the Hazelhurst mystery and the charming and openly-sympathetic Balderson family.

Perhaps it is truly possible that with persistence, this coexistence can continue, and he who suffered so much when master of the place shall eventually find satisfaction and contentment in merely observing the peace and tranquility that have at long last descended upon Lilburn.

Surely this is as Mr. Hazelhurst had planned it.

*   *   *

2003 UPDATE

Lilburn's current owners, Chris and Janet Cotter, were married in 1993 and moved to Lilburn soon after. The huge home was a decorating challenge, so they called in the experts, and Lilburn became Historic Ellicott City, Inc.'s 13th Decorator Show House. The beautifully decorated home received over 6,000 guests in a one month period in the fall of 1997, making it one of the organization's most successful efforts.

Now consisting of seven acres, the property retains only a few of the original outbuildings. Still standing are two structures—a three-story stone smoke house next to the pool, and a three-story brick carriage house behind the tower. Another house next door may be part of the original set of outbuildings as it is built on an old stone foundation.

Initially, Chris Cotter maintained his advertising business in Lilburn's tower, where, in keeping with Lilburn's tradition, one of his employees once felt the presence of the friendly ghost that occupies the tower. Kristine Poorman was at work one day in an office on the second floor of the tower when she heard "a big bang" that sounded as if it had come from one of the floors above her.

Thinking Janet Cotter's father—who was often working on repairs at Lilburn—might have fallen and hurt himself, Kristine went to investigate. On entering the hall she noticed that the chandelier was rocking back and forth. On further investigation Kristine found absolutely no one in the tower on the floors above her. She was alone in the tower part of the house. Due to the company's expansion, rather than ghostly visitations, Chris Cotter moved his business to Main Street in the summer of 2000.

The family, as well as the business, has expanded in the years of the Cotters' ownership. In the past few years the couple has adopted two daughters from China, Marielle and Julia.

LOG CABIN—NEW CUT ROAD

When returning to Main Street from Lilburn by way of College Avenue, it is well worth a few moments of the tourist's time to visit still another interesting landmark located on nearby New Cut Road. Hugging the edge of the pass on which it stands, it can be reached by taking a sharp left turn at the junction of College Avenue and New Cut Road, within sight of St. Paul's Church. A short distance down the narrow lane one comes upon an unusual sight, seldom seen in this part of the country, but strongly reminiscent of the Deep South—a "duplex" or "joined" log cabin.

Believed to have been built in the mid-1800s, its history is vague and all but non-existent. However, a study of the acreage held by the Talbott family in 1732 when Talbott's Last Shift was described as "being on the Patapsco and consisting of 1120 acres," leads one to suspect that the unique cabin stands on land once a part of this vast tract.

The John Talbott property was later divided and sold, part of it going to George Ellicott who, in turn, sold it to Benjamin Dorsey, and another part going to Edward and Richard Talbott. Edward Talbott increased his holdings to 1031 acres, but upon his death little remained of the estate. His heir, Edward A. Talbott, sold the remaining 11 1/4 acres, all that remained of the once-sizable property, to James W. Rowland in 1850.

Meanwhile, the Ellicott portion of the land changed hands a number of times over the next century, a part of it eventually becoming once again a possession of two members of the Ellicott family. It is a matter of record that all that land on which Lilburn and St. Paul's now stand was at one time the joint property of John (1805-1866) and Andrew (1801-1866) Ellicott, sons of Elias. It might well have been during their ownership that the little cabin was erected. But this theory remains a matter of conjecture.

Another school of thought tends toward the suspicion that the cabin might have, instead, been a part of the Lilburn estate which came into being in the mid-1800s when first Richard Henry Hazelhurst erected his handsome home atop the hill. Keeping in mind that at one time the Hazelhurst property consisted of well over 2600 acres, it is equally conceivable that the old quarters may well have been the erstwhile property of "the ghost of Lilburn." (See chapter on Lilburn.)

Upon close scrutiny, the primitive features of the structure and the pronounced joining of logs in the center of the double building strongly indicate that the elongated cabin sprang from a smaller and less unique one. For, as was the custom before slavery was abolished, as the enslaved family grew, so grew their quarters.

Although information pertaining to the picturesque cabin on New Cut Road remains vague and must necessarily be based only on knowledge of the customs of the period in which it is thought to have been built, the spectator will find it both interesting and fascinating. For it conjures up once again an almost-forgotten period in the history of Ellicott City when the little town was divided in loyalties, as was all of the Old Line State.

Thus it stands, a relic of pre-Civil War days, almost within stone's throw of the bridge where a skirmish is said to have taken place, and well within the shadow of old St. Paul's, scene of still another type of "skirmish." (See history of St. Paul's.)

Although the humble cabin is one of Ellicott City's lesser landmarks, and one that is seldom viewed as such, it is an interesting one, recalling as it does an obscure and all-but-forgotten phase in the history of the small mill town.

*   *   *

2003 UPDATE

Unfortunately, not all the properties covered in Celia Holland's book continue to be preserved. As she noted, "the humble cabin is one of Ellicott City's lesser landmarks, and one that is seldom viewed as such...." Over the years the cabin languished, and although Historic Ellicott City, Inc. approached one owner about purchasing the structure, this offer was not accepted. In the late 1990's the land's owner, Historic Ellicott Properties, looked for a new owner and a new home for the cabin, but to no avail.

According to a company spokesman, the cabin became a safety hazard, with one part collapsing toward the river and one part leaning toward New Cut Road. The company sought and was given permission by the Historic District Commission to remove the derelict building. Neighbors recall seeing a wrecking company swinging a steel ball against the building to completely knock it down.

It was reported that some pieces of the old logs were collected as souvenirs, but most are now lost. One hopes that renewed interest in our local history will prevent such losses from occurring in the future. It may have been a "humble cabin" but it was ours, and our history needs to be honored and not dismantled.

*   *   *

First permanent home of THE HOWARD COUNTY TIMES, erected in 1926 by Mr. Stromberg.

THE HOWARD COUNTY TIMES AND ITS EDITORS

In 1840 when upper Anne Arundel County was designated a separate and distinct district, to be known as the Howard District of Anne Arundel County, the need for public communication was resolved when Edward Waite and Matthew Fields founded the first newspaper in the area, calling it THE HOWARD FREE PRESS. Published at Ellicott's Mills, its circulation was in proportion to the new district's population. Initiated primarily to publish official notices and orders, the paper also covered general news—in capsule form—as well as short items of local interest. But all articles were brief, as was the paper itself.

In addition to publishing the FREE PRESS, the owners also did job work and furnished stationery for the commissioners of primary schools throughout the district.

Unable to make a financial success of the venture, Mr. Fields sold his share in the newspaper and plant to James Wingate of Ellicott's Mills in 1842 and returned to his native Rockville where he founded THE MONTGOMERY COUNTY SENTINEL in 1855. Ironically, this paper was destined to be sold by his descendants to a future owner of THE TIMES, Paul G. Stromberg, as shall be seen.

(It is of interest to note here that THE SENTINEL, which is still serving Montgomery County today, is the oldest weekly news-

81

paper in that county. Publication was interrupted only once since its founding—during the War Between the States—when Mr. Fields was imprisoned as a southern sympathizer. Following his death the paper remained a family enterprise until purchased by Mr. Stromberg.)

Meanwhile Mr. Wingate, successor to Mr. Fields as part owner of the HOWARD FREE PRESS, changed the name of the paper to THE HOWARD DISTRICT PRESS. Being a man of meager means he operated on an extremely limited budget. He was even less fortunate than his predecessor. After five years of fruitless effort he was forced to declare himself bankrupt, signing over his interest in the paper to Richard Chaney in March, 1847.

Due to a lack of funds on the part of successive owners, mismanagement and the failure of the paper to produce sufficient revenue, it changed hands as well as names repeatedly during the first twenty years of its existence.

Shortly before the country became enmeshed in the Civil War it became known as THE HOWARD GAZETTE. With John Schofield, originator of the best-known prints of the small mill town as publisher and editor, the paper finally achieved its first semblance of success.

Among the lithographs published and sold by Mr. Schofield was an early view of the town entitled "Panoramic View of the Scenery on the Patapsco River for 7 miles—above and below Ellicott's Mills, Maryland." This lithograph was in three colors—brown, black and white, and measured about 24 x 36 inches in size. A small train in the foreground is reminiscent of those pictured in Currier & Ives prints.

Possibly Mr. Schofield's best known print of Ellicott City was done in 1854 by E. Sachse & Company of Baltimore. It is a composite of twenty-two subjects with twenty-one historic buildings and sites forming a border around the principal subject, a view of the town itself. Bearing the title "View of Ellicotts Mills from the Heights above Elizabeth Ellicott's Residence," this chromo-lithograph is approximately 18 x 26 inches. Although photographic copies of both prints may still be found, the originals have become scarce and are today considered collector's items.

In addition to the two well-known prints, Mr. Schofield is also credited with having published the first known photograph of Ellicott City in the June 18, 1857 issue of THE INDEPENDENT, a paper with which he had been associated for a number of years before acquiring THE GAZETTE.

*   *   *

In 1869 when John R. Brown, Jr. son of John Riggs Brown (Browne) of Good Fellowship, Woodstock, purchased the paper, it was known as the HOWARD COUNTY RECORD. Mr. Brown christened it THE ELLICOTT CITY TIMES, and before long it was referred to simply as THE TIMES, the name by which it is known today.

Mr. Brown, who was born at Woodstock, was described by a contemporary writer as "the brilliant editor of the ELLICOTT CITY TIMES." As a newspaper man he was well liked despite his cryptic editorials. During his ownership the paper grew in size and prestige. It was published each Saturday and subscriptions cost two dollars per year, "in advance."

In addition to taking an active part in many civic programs, Mr. Brown also found time to become one of the original founders of the Howard County Agricultural Society. During the war he had served with the Confederate Army in Company A, First Maryland Cavalry. A bachelor, he died at an early age in 1877, leaving no one to succeed him.

For the next year (1877-78) Louis (Lewis) J. and J. Harwood Watkins, sons of Dr. William W. Watkins of Richland, and grandsons of Col. Gassaway Watkins, Revolutionary War hero, were the new owners. It was Dr. William Watkins who, as a delegate to the Legislature in 1838, "urged and secured a subdivision of the large county of Anne Arundel, and when Howard District, which he created, finally passed into a County in 1851, he was chosen its first State Senator."

Louis Watkins held the office of Clerk of the Court (1873-1888), as had his father before him. J. Harwood, an attorney of some repute and youngest son of Dr. William, died while still a young man.

In 1878 the paper was purchased by J. Thomas Clark, a member of another well-known Howard County family. Born and raised at Clarksville, he was the son of William and Albina Watkins Clark, and the brother of Dr. Thaddeus Clark. Kin of the former owners of THE TIMES, Thomas Clark also numbered among his illustrious ancestors the aforementioned Col. Gassaway Watkins as well as the Clagett family, one member of which became Maryland's first Episcopal Bishop.

Mr. Clark married the only daughter of John Hardy of Clarksville, and although he lived his entire life in Howard County, after giving up the proprietorship of THE TIMES, he became an official in the nation's capital, which position he held for many years.

Possibly the best known of all the editors and publishers of

THE TIMES was Edwin Warfield who succeeded Mr. Clark as owner from 1882 to 1886. His record as a public servant is as outstanding as it is varied. Having served as Register of Wills in 1874 (succeeding Benjamin H. Dorsey, deceased), he was re-elected to the office in 1875. He went on to become State Senator in 1881, President of the Senate in 1886, Surveyor of the Port of Baltimore under President Cleveland until 1890, and ultimately Governor of the State of Maryland from 1904 to 1908.

Aside from editing THE TIMES, his ventures into the business world were equally numerous and just as successful. In 1886 he originated and organized the meeting that resulted in the establishment of the Patapsco National Bank of Ellicott City. He served as director until 1890 when he resigned due to the pressures of other enterprises. In 1887 Mr. Warfield purchased the MARYLAND LAW RECORD. In 1888 he changed it from a weekly to a daily paper, calling it the DAILY RECORD. He made of it the leading legal and real estate journal in the state. Mr. Warfield was also one of the founders and organizers—and eventually president—of the Fidelity and Deposit Company of Maryland, first organization of its kind in the South. His many other accomplishments, too numerous to enumerate here, may be found in many books covering the history of the state.

Meanwhile, from 1886 until the turn of the century, a series of successive owners and publishers including Emory Hill, John B. Morrow and James Fisher Melvin shaped the future of THE TIMES.

*　　　*　　　*

Little is known of the early location of the office of THE TIMES. The first reference found by the writer was noted in the reminiscences of Doctor J. R. Bromwell Branch of Crescent, Georgia, a former resident of Ellicott City. Says Dr. Branch: "In the late 80's and early 90's, the ELLICOTT CITY TIMES occupied the second floor of a building. This was on a level with the railroad platform." Dr. Branch's statement coincides significantly with that issued by the late H. L. Mencken, who claimed THE TIMES as his alma mater. On the occasion of the 100th anniversary of the paper's founding, Mr. Mencken's comment read in part:

> The TIMES office, in 1889, was on the second floor of an old stone building (now rebuilt) alongside the B. & O. station platform, and it was reached by a sort of porch that made off from the platform.

Despite much inquiry and research, to date the writer has been unable to definitely identify the building thus described if, indeed, it still stands. However, it is a matter of record that train service directly to the Patapsco Hotel where the passengers alighted at the second-floor level, via a porch adjoining the train platform, did exist. Since the old hotel was the only "rebuilt" building "alongside the B. & O. station platform" and was reached by "a sort of porch that made off from the platform," as described by Mr. Mencken, it seems definite that at one time THE TIMES did indeed operate from the second floor, as is suspected by the writer. Furthermore, the Century edition yields still another affirmative clue in an article written by Mr. J. Edwin Kroh in which he states that the old stone building on Main Street, adjacent to the B. & O. Railroad, when first known by him was occupied principally by the printing office of THE TIMES and partly as apartments.

Finally, Mrs. James F. Cole, the former Katherine Fort Heine, who grew up in Ellicott City and lived there as a young girl at the turn of the century, after admitting to no positive knowledge of the location of the first office, went on to add:

> ...But I do know that they were in what we used to call the Old Hotel Building at the lower end of town, and that at one time a man they called Cousin John Schofield either worked there or had something to do with it.

One undisputed fact concerning THE TIMES of the '90s was released by the Commercial & Industrial Review of Northern and Western Maryland during that decade. Rewritten for the 125th Anniversary Issue of the paper in 1965, it reads:

> THE ELLICOTT CITY TIMES is thoroughly Democratic in its proclivities, and its editorial columns teeming with the topics of the times. It is a clean spicy sheet of thirty-two columns. The sheet is circulated through Baltimore City, Baltimore County, Anne Arundel, Howard, Montgomery, Carroll, Frederick and Prince Georges Counties.

This might well be a description of THE TIMES today but for the fact that the original 32 columns have since grown to a newspaper of considerable size. It has been known, on occasion, to consist of as many as 40 pages!

*　*　*

THE TIMES was not without competition during the early years of its existence. Other newspapers were founded and enjoyed moderate success. But of all the old papers, only THE TIMES survived.

For a number of years a second paper known as THE INDEPENDENT, heretofore referred to, was published in Ellicott City.

A third paper, THE COMMON SENSE, was also published here in the 1860s by Mr. P. Unger. This paper's coverage of the great flood of July 24th, 1868 was of such detailed accuracy it was quoted by Dawson Lawrence in his "History of Howard County" which was included by G. M. Hopkins in his Atlas of 1878.

Still another paper, THE AMERICAN PROGRESS, was also offered the people of the same area. Published and edited by a Mr. Wolfersberger, it appeared on the streets each Friday. THE PROGRESS office was at one time located next to Hermann & Carr, Insurance Agency. Rates were $1.50 per year. But again, as with a number of other newspapers, the PROGRESS did not survive.

*   *   *

Undoubtedly one of the most dynamic and colorful editor-owners of THE TIMES was Colonel William Sotheron Powell who purchased the paper in 1904. Born in Alexandria, Virginia, in 1853, he was a member of the well-known Powell family of Loudon County, Virginia, as well as a descendant of the Sotheron family of St. Mary's County, Maryland. Although most of the men in his family, both maternal and paternal, were professional men, young William chose to become a merchant.

At the end of the Civil War, like so many other Southern boys, he found himself entirely dependent upon his own resources. Arriving in Baltimore at the age of fifteen—penniless—he was unable to raise the funds to pay the freight charges on his trunk. But a cheerful determination to work things out and cooperation on the part of the stationmaster soon overcame this first challenge. There followed a period of meager living. With a starting salary of $12.00 per month and a floor for a bed, plus modest meals prepared on an old gas stove, he overcame his financial problems in an unbelievably short time. Within six months he was on his way.

After serving an apprenticeship with Wm. H. Brown & Co., chemists, he was soon admitted as a partner in the firm, eventually becoming manager and treasurer of the organization. He later served as president of the Chemical Exchange. His formulas for fertilizers "in the early days of reclaiming worn out lands with chemical fertilizers," as well as a patent medicine known as "Brown's Iron Bitters," were both financial and practical successes, marking him as a man of wealth and achievement.

After many years of continuous activities in the field of commerce, Col. Powell decided on a home in the country choosing first Llangellen, a large farm at Annapolis Junction straddling Anne Arundel and Howard Counties; then Wisteria, later known as the Holton place; and finally the house on Church Road in Ellicott City, still referred to as "the Powell house."

As a resident of Howard County he contributed with characteristic energy to its betterment. He originated the first poultry show and subsequently backed all "farm shows," the forerunners of the present-day County Fairs. The idea of community Christmas trees and treats for the children also originated with Col. Powell.

Although a registered Democrat, he enjoyed the respect of members of both parties, and served on various state boards under appointment by several Governors of Maryland. While a resident of Howard County he served on the State Board of Education and was a director of the Merchants Club. The Maryland Academy of Sciences also benefited from his services, as did various other social and scientific societies.

His first days as editor of THE TIMES were best described by his son, Edward Burr Powell, in the Century edition of the paper:

> When my father acquired THE TIMES in 1904 it consisted of one sheet of paper, two pages on each side. It only had to be ground through the press twice. Everybody took a hand at folding it. It contained about a third of a column of editorials, a column or so of "locals," a column and a half of legal advertisements, a few local commercial advertisements, one or two correspondents' letters, and about a page of boiler plate. The balance was filled with electrotype advertisements of St. Jacob's Oil, Sloan's Liniment and kindred nostrums....
>
> After my father arrived THE TIMES got some action. Within a year he had developed a fine corps of correspondents and part-time reporters throughout the county, systematized the gathering of news from the Court House, added feature article series, established the Sykesville and Laurel departments, appointed sales

agents at a dozen places in Howard, Carroll and Prince
Georges Counties, and conducted a subscription-getting,
voting contest that jumped the paid circulation three or
four times over. THE TIMES went to town....

He was a world traveller, having circled the globe in 1901,
and as such, brought "the knowledge resultant to such travel to the
direction of the paper," thus introducing a cosmopolitan flavor into its pages. Purchasing the old DEMOCRAT which was then still
in existence, he merged it with THE TIMES. He remained as editorial head of the county's only newspaper from 1904 until 1913.
During this period he was instrumental in reorganizing the defunct
Democratic Editors Association, later known as the Maryland Press
Association.

In 1913 Col. Powell sold his interest in THE TIMES to A. P.
Gorman, Jr., principal stockholder of the Maryland Printing &
Publishing Company. For a brief period John E. Raine assumed
management of THE TIMES, leaving the detail to Edward Powell
who stayed on with the paper. Shortly thereafter Mr. Powell was
assigned the post of editor. In 1919, following the death of Senator
Gorman, Col. Powell repurchased his original holdings, selling
them again within a few months due to a change in personal plans.

Upon his death in August, 1931 THE TIMES paid Col. Powell a lengthy, informative, and warm tribute, calling attention to his
great capabilities as editor and business man through the columns
of the editorial page. Further insight into his colorful and humane
individualism was rendered in an additional article by Michael J.
Sullivan. It read in part:

> Always a fastidious dresser Col. Powell was invar-
> iably garbed for the weather. In severe winter weather
> a fur coat, on hot summer days a complete suit of white
> ducks, topped off with a bamboo helmet of the same im-
> maculate color, was worn. Usually he carried a cane.
> In Germany he learned that gentlemen had their cloth-
> ing remade by the simple process of having their tail-
> or turn them inside out. He adopted the custom and
> took keen enjoyment in showing his friends that the but-
> ton-holes in some of his clothing were in the left facing
> of the coat, instead of the right, the side usually pre-
> ferred in men's garments. Nothing gave him more
> pleasure than to present a friend with a suit of white
> duck clothes, or an order on his hatter for a hat.

With a kindly heart and his ear ever ready to listen to a charitable appeal, Col. Powell was never known to fail to respond to a worthy cause. Churches, charitable organizations and many individuals in this county will remember his liberality. He detested shams and admired an honest adversary. Aristocratic in bearing the humblest citizen was his friend.

Since his retirement and removal to Washington 11 years ago no single individual has had the temerity to set himself up as a leader of public thought in this community or attempt to organize enterprises in the wholehearted and convincing manner of Col. Powell. His place has not been filled and it is doubtful if Howard Countians will ever look on his like again.

*   *   *

1968 window display in the new TIMES Building. The sign reads: "Howard Countians have been reading THE TIMES 127 years. We're Older than Howard County."   – Courtesy of THE TIMES

Following the death of his father Edward Burr Powell, who enjoyed a keen sense of humor, had this to say of his own experience while associated with THE TIMES:

> THE TIMES newspaper press in those days was a two-man-power Babcock cylinder. There was a crank on the side of it (not the editor) and at press time two husky colored men went to work somewhat like two men hauling buckets of dirt out of a hand-dug well. Later, we installed a temperamental gasoline engine that would run for nobody around Ellicott City but Gene Keith. We sold it eventually, while it was in a good humor, to Lou Randall, but none of the mechanics he hired to start it could get it to budge.
>
> It was not until I, personally, was running THE TIMES that we got an electric motor. Ellicott City progressed in my time... I was also the prime mover in having a linotype installed, which I hope is paid for by this time.....

These comments appeared in the Century edition of the paper, along with many other reminiscences of days long gone.

In 1919 when Judge James Clark and Edward Talbott became the new majority stock holders, Edward Burr Powell resigned his post as editor, taking a position with the American Ice Company in Washington, D.C. He was later employed by the government in the Department of Internal Revenue, from which he retired in 1952.

For a time he made his home at Woodley on St. John's Lane, where he operated a 122-acre farm on a temporary basis. Having purchased the site from Dorsey Williams in 1935, in 1937 he sold 107 acres to Natwick's Dairy Farm "across the road."

After commuting to and from Washington for six years, he finally sold the dwelling and remaining acreage to a Mr. Byrne in 1941 and moved to Newark Street in the nation's capital, where he has resided ever since.

* * * * * * * * *

When Judge Clark and Mr. Talbott chose Paul Stromberg to succeed Mr. Powell as editor of their newly acquired paper, little did they realize just how far his editorial and managerial abilities would carry him. Neither could they have foreseen this assignment as Mr. Stromberg's first step toward his ultimate goal, the Stromberg Enterprises. They knew only that he was an exceedingly fine newspaper man and, as such, could help make their paper one of the leading weekly publications in the state.

Paul Griffith Stromberg, better known to his associates as "Pete," was born March 21, 1892 at Clarksville, Maryland. The son of Antony P. and Mary Ellen Flanagan Stromberg, he was one of twelve children. The old stone gatehouse of Doughoregan Manor became his home early in life. Here he spent most of his youth, attending school in Ellicott City, for the most part walking the three-mile distance in good weather and bad.

In 1911, following his graduation from high school, young Pete took a job with THE BALTIMORE SUN starting as a copy boy. In later years he became associated—in both editorial and advertising work—with papers all over the country including the CLEVELAND PRESS, CLEVELAND PLAIN DEALER, PITTSBURGH PRESS, PITTSBURGH LEADER, INDIANAPOLIS STAR, CHICAGO TRIBUNE, OMAHA WORLD-HERALD, and the ST. PAUL PIONEER and DISPATCH. His career was interrupted by World War I, during which period he entered the first Officers Training School, receiving a commission as Lieutenant. He rose to the rank of Captain in the U.S. Field Artillery.

Being a strong believer in the importance of the weekly newspaper, he finally returned to his home in Howard County to accept the job of editor of THE ELLICOTT CITY TIMES, as it was then known.

On the occasion of the newspaper's 100th anniversary Mr. Edward Powell commented:

> Mr. Stromberg took over THE ELLICOTT CITY TIMES just as it was beginning to convalesce from the World War battering. I am not going to belabor his readers with a detailed description of the development of THE TIMES to its present high standard, not only as a progressive business enterprise but also as a most important constructive influence in the community. These are the kinds of things which speak for themselves. But I do not hesitate to say that THE TIMES is a far better paper than when I ran it and that Ellicott City is a far better town than it was.

Little by little Mr. Stromberg purchased stock in the company, gradually gaining the controlling interest. No longer hampered by restrictions, but retaining the respect and confidence of the remaining share holders, he put the little paper on its feet, to the delight of all parties concerned.

By 1926 THE TIMES, which had operated in cramped quarters ever since its inception, felt the first real pangs of growing pains. A new building with more floor space was constructed on the north side of Main Street. During this period of construction THE TIMES occupied temporary quarters on the second floor of an old building on the southwest corner of Main Street and Columbia Road opposite the Howard House. It is thought by many of the senior citizens and one past editor that the site of the new "1926 building" was that of the original TIMES office, although no positive proof has been uncovered.

Shortly thereafter additional floor space was needed. Thus the editorial and business offices were moved to a rented building on the south side of Main Street and, until early 1966, the problem was solved.

In 1928 the first two papers heretofore published outside the county were acquired by the owners of THE TIMES. They were THE CATONSVILLE HERALD and THE COMMUNITY NEWS (Reisterstown, Baltimore County). Stromberg Enterprises was born. In 1932 THE MONTGOMERY SENTINEL was purchased, followed in 1938 by THE COMMUNITY PRESS (Dundalk).

By 1939 Paul Stromberg became sole owner of the newspaper chain, liquidating the company the following year, just a few months prior to the publication of the famed Century Edition of THE TIMES.

Considered one of the finest sources of local and county history, this edition consisted of ten sections, totaling eighty pages. Five thousand copies were printed. Today scholars and historians alike refer to this issue when little known or forgotten bits of information are needed.

Despite the pace he had set for himself in the newspaper field, Mr. Stromberg also maintained a regular schedule of civic activities. He was a member of UNESCO, a charter member of the Ellicott City Rotary Club, and a member and ultimate president of the Maryland Press Association (now the Maryland-Delaware Press Association), which he reactivated.

An example of the deeply humane approach used by Mr. Stromberg in his political editorials can be gleaned from the following quote which appeared in THE TIMES in 1936 when Franklin D. Roosevelt conducted his campaign for the presidency against Governor "Alf" Landon. Under the heading "Current Comment," Mr. Stromberg wrote:

The election is over. The great American elector-
ate has spoken in a way that leaves no doubt of the public's appreciation of sincere effort to govern by action
—to battle by aggressive attack. As between the two
major candidates the people showed that they loved
President Roosevelt MORE rather than Governor Landon LESS.

Despite political affiliation or party loyalty, a less understanding man could hardly have paraphrased the heartbreaking de-
feat suffered by Governor Landon as did the courteous and sympathetic editor of THE TIMES.

In 1938 Paul Stromberg relinquished his job as editor, as-
signing Charles L. Gerwig his successor. He spent his time and
energies in building up the Stromberg Enterprises, now known as
Stromberg Publications.

With the outbreak of World War II he again served his country in the capacity of Captain of Company F, 7th Battalion of the
State Guard. Then from 1946 to 1950 he served as State Senator
for his native Howard County, winning out over Thomas O. King.

A summary of his contributions in the field of journalism can
hardly be noted in a few words, but a well-deserved honor was bestowed upon him when he was singled out for special notice due to
his exceptional talents and numerous achievements. Listed as a
publisher and editor of seven weekly newspapers in Maryland, a
past president of the Maryland Press Association, and a member
of the National Editorial Association, at the peak of his career he
was named as a member of WHO'S WHO IN THE FIELD OF JOUR-
NALISM.

Not unlike a number of his predecessors, Mr. Stromberg
was a civic-minded and patriotic man. Love of country and home,
and a deep regard for his friends and neighbors dictated his pattern of life. Of the many men who guided the destiny of THE TIMES,
he was possibly the best loved.

Although a man of great foresight and a natural born leader,
he remained to the end just plain "Pete" to all who enjoyed the privilege of knowing him. He earned and held the respect and admiration of his many competitors in the newspaper field, as well as the
loyalty of all his employees for whom he was never too busy to extend a helping hand.

He has not been—nor will he be—easily forgotten.

* * * * * * * * *

As has been noted, the late Charles Lee Gerwig held the position of editor from 1938 through 1957. It was during this period that further changes were made by the publishing company. In September, 1951 Stromberg Publications founded still another weekly paper, THE STAR, which serves the people of Glen Burnie (Anne Arundel County) and the surrounding area. Then following Mr. Stromberg's death THE MONTGOMERY SENTINEL was sold by his survivors.

Ten years later THE EASTERN BEACON, serving the people of Essex and vicinity, was added to the chain of newspapers published by the Ellicott City company. Then in February, 1968 THE COLUMBIA TIMES came into being, to be followed in April by THE TOWSON TIMES. Simultaneously with the publication of the Towson paper all Stromberg papers adopted the same name—THE TIMES—with each paper designating the area it now serves. Thus it is that as of this writing Stromberg publications reach the people of seven counties, namely, Anne Arundel, Baltimore, Carroll, Frederick, Howard, Montgomery, and Prince Georges, as well as three major cities, Baltimore and Washington, and the new city of Columbia.

*   *   *

Charles Gerwig, son of Mrs. LaRue R. Gerwig and the late Arthur L. Gerwig, was born at Pine Orchard, Howard County, September 17, 1913. Upon his mother's marriage to Paul G. Stromberg, publisher of THE TIMES, he was adopted by the Senator although he retained the surname Gerwig.

Educated in the Howard County elementary schools, St. Paul's Catholic School, Mt. St. Joseph's High School and the Strayer Business College, he also took correspondence courses in advertising and offset printing, the latter becoming a specialty in which he pioneered in the publishing of weekly newspapers in Maryland.

As a boy Mr. Gerwig worked as a clerk in Howard County grocery stores. As a young man he served eight years of apprentice training in the old ELLICOTT CITY TIMES printing plant, then advanced to advertising solicitation and layout work.

Aside from his duties as editor, from 1945 to 1952 he also served as mechanical superintendent of the Stromberg Publications printing plant. In 1953 he was appointed vice-president and general manager of Stromberg Publications. His guiding principle in newspaper production was:

We cannot do today's job with yesterday's
tools and be in business tomorrow.

As general manager of the company, Mr. Gerwig installed
one of the first full-scale offset printing plants for weekly newspapers in Maryland March 9, 1960. His knowledge of the offset printing process, which revolutionzed weekly newspaper publishing,
was profound. He became a recognized authority in the field. After installing the new equipment he added many innovations of his
own to improve the quality and appearance of the Stromberg papers.
Finally, after much careful thought and consideration, in October,
1965, Stromberg Publications initiated the twice-weekly publication program.

Somehow, in his personal life Mr. Gerwig also managed to
include public service to the people of his home county. He served
as Clerk and Custodian to the Howard County Board of Supervisors
of Elections from 1938 to 1952. In 1954 he was elected a director
of the Commercial and Farmers Bank of Ellicott City. He was active in civic and service club affairs and in newspaper publishing
circles. He held offices in many clubs including the Hoplite Ath-
letic Club of Howard County; the Kiwanis Club of Ellicott City, of
which he was a charter member; the Ellicott City Business Men's
Association, of which he was also a charter member; the presidency of the Ellicott City Little League, which he helped organize,
and director and former president of the Maryland Press Association. He was also a member of the Association's Advisory Council; a stockholder and director of the Howard County Fair, and a
member of the Advisory Council of the Maryland-Delaware Press
Association.

Like his immediate predecessor, Mr. Gerwig's interests
and contributions to the county as a whole knew no bounds. And
like Mr. Stromberg, who undoubtedly encouraged and influenced
him in his chosen field, he will be remembered for many many
years to come.

*   *   *

From 1958 through 1961 F. Otis Smith served as editor of
THE TIMES, to be followed in 1962 by Jean Holmes, the first woman to hold this position. Upon her resignation in 1964 the editorial
responsibilities again reverted temporarily to Mr. Gerwig, after
which he was succeeded by still another member of the Stromberg
family, Mrs. Doris S. Thompson, Mr. Gerwig's sister and daugh-

ter of Paul Stromberg.

Like her father and brother before her, Mrs. Thompson has won the respect and admiration of the people of the county. Her qualifications as a newspaper woman cannot be challenged. Nor does she rest on her family's reputation. Her ideas are clear and precise, and they are her own. As a member of a journalistic family, she has inherited an innate sense of perception and good judgment, which qualifications she uses to advantage.

Since Mrs. Thompson has assumed the post of editor, the publishing company has undergone another series of changes. The first move was made in July, 1966 when the main office of Stromberg Publications, including THE TIMES, was relocated at a new address—99 Main Street. Although completely remodeled, the "new" building has an interesting background of its own.

*   *   *

In 1870 Henry Christian Buetefisch came to Ellicott City and opened a tailoring business at 99 Main Street, which building had then been standing a number of years. Here, above his shop, he reared his family. (One daughter, Mrs. John B. Loughran, who was born there, still makes her home in Ellicott City at 302 Main Street.)

Mr. Buetefisch operated his business for many years, buying wool from farmers in Howard, Carroll, and Montgomery Counties. He also purchased raw furs including raccoon, muskrat, opossum and occasionally mink "for trim work." He taught the business to his son Charles who was also born on the premises. Charles later opened a shop of his own farther west on Main Street.

Mr. Buetefisch retired in 1912. He died July 5, 1916, leaving the property to his daughter Bertha who, prior to her upcoming marriage to John B. Loughran, completely renovated the entire building. The living quarters were redecorated and the old tailor shop, which had become a landmark, was modernized and offered for rent.

Three weeks before the impending marriage, on Easter Monday, 1917, the Buetefisch property was gutted by fire, as was the adjoining building—the old Patapsco Pharmacy.

Within a year both properties were rebuilt. The Patapsco Pharmacy, having located elsewhere, was replaced by Johnson's Drug Store, whose proprietors published Ellicott City's first postcards. The first floor of the Buetefisch property was rented for a time as a restaurant. Later it was leased to the Atlantic & Pacific

Tea Company. Then in 1925 Mr. and Mrs. Loughran converted it into a bakery shop which they operated for many years. Finally, in the early forties, both the Bakery Shop and Johnson's were purchased by Samuel H. Sachs. The present generation remembers the building only as The Economy Shop, owned and operated by Mr. Sachs, from whom Stromberg Publications purchased it.

*   *   *

The ground floor of "the new Stromberg building" was remodeled to include offices for the editorial staff, advertising staff, circulation department, classified department, art department and bookkeeping department of THE TIMES. Additional offices were also set up for members of the out of town newspapers belonging to the Stromberg chain.

Another first in company history was recorded when Stromberg Publications again expanded, taking over a third location in Ellicott City, the former Parlett Building on the corner of Columbia Pike and Old Frederick Road. This building housed the camera room, printing press, paper rolls, and mail room. Meanwhile, the old building on Main Street, built in 1926, continued operations as the composition department expanded. Machinery and equipment were installed on the first floor where pages were made ready for the press. Upstairs, type-setting continued as usual. Thus another chapter in the history of Howard County's oldest paper was written.

Then in early January, 1969 announcement of still another move for Stromberg Publications was made. Having acquired the former Miller Chevrolet Building, all departments formerly located in the three Main Street buildings were to be moved to the new location at 175 Main Street. To quote Mrs. Thompson: "Once again the production of our papers will be under one roof—as will the management offices." Only the editorial office will not share this central location. Having been established in Columbia shortly after the new city was opened to the public, it will remain there in the heart of the ever-growing community.

*   *   *

As of January, 1969 THE HOWARD COUNTY TIMES is staffed by the following people: LaRue R. Stromberg, president; Phillip S. Thompson, vice president and general manager; John E. Blitz, managing editor; Doris S. Thompson, editor, and James F. Myers, advertising manager.

In the increasingly competitive world of the weekly newspaper business, Ellicott City's original newspaper has not only survived for more than a century, but has, instead, grown into a large and far-reaching publishing company.

The tiny sheet that first saw the light of day in 1840 has grown as part of an expanding enterprise. Its future is assured. THE TIMES, one of Maryland's oldest newspapers, is here to stay!

*   *   *

2003 UPDATE

Phillip St. Clair Thompson became owner of THE HOWARD COUNTY TIMES in 1953, following the death of "Pete" Stromberg. For many years the newspaper remained located in the building next door to "The Rock" on Main Street. THE TIMES owned this building until 1960. Expansion occurred first into another Main Street building, when the pressroom and mailroom were moved into the structure at the corner of Columbia Pike and Old Frederick Road. With the growth of the city of Columbia, editorial offices were moved first to the Wilde Lake Village Center, then to the Columbia Mall, and finally to its present home in the Patuxent Publishing Company building in Columbia.

Doris Stromberg Thompson served as editor of THE HOWARD COUNTY TIMES and its sister paper, THE COLUMBIA TIMES (now THE COLUMBIA FLIER) until her retirement in 1978. In October, 1975, she received the Emma McKinney Award from the National Newspaper Association, recognizing "her civic leadership as exemplified in contributions through her newspaper editorship, her services as a public servant.... [and] gratifying home life with her family."

By 1973, when Stromberg Publications sold the newspaper business, it published a chain of twelve newspapers serving various areas of Howard and Baltimore Counties, all including their geographical location followed by TIMES in their mastheads.

Phillip Thompson followed his publishing career by entering the real estate business, while Doris found a new life in volunteer activities. This mother of five daughters was the first Chair of the Board at Howard County General Hospital and also served as Head of the Volunteer Auxiliary at the hospital. Following Phillip's death in 1998 after 53 years of marriage,

Doris Thompson sold the family farm and moved to a retirement community in Ellicott City. Until recently she remained active in such groups as the Historic District Commission, the Ellicott City Restoration Foundation, and Historic Ellicott City, Inc.

Following the departure of THE HOWARD COUNTY TIMES, the original Times building served as the headquarters of the Department of Vocational Rehabilitation for the State of Maryland. Later it housed an antique shop. In 1981, its present owners, Alan and Brenda Fishbein, purchased the building. At that time the first floor of the building and the exterior were fully renovated. In April of 1988, the second floor was renovated and converted from commercial use to offices. The law firm of Fishbein and Fishbein, P.A., comprised of five attorneys and support staff, now utilizes both floors of the building.

2003 photo by Charles Kyler.

ELLICOTT'S COUNTRY STORE
The Walker-Chandler House

In 1789 the first general store in Ellicott's Mills opened its doors to the public. Located on the east bank of the Patapsco River, it was known simply as The Ellicott Store. Here, according to Heinrich Ewald Buchholz, "fashionable ladies in the closing days of the eighteenth century looked over a stock of fine linens, brocades, silks, satins and India china, and here their beaus and husbands and fathers, equally critical, examined the offerings in liquors and wines."

About the same time (circa 1790) another building—destined to eventually outshine The Ellicott Store—was erected, its three full stories making it one of the most impressive buildings in town. Located on the north side of Main Street west of the river and half way up the hill, it became known as "the Walker-Chandler house." Having built it as a permanent and private residence, the two men had little reason to suspect what the future held in store for them.

The customs of the day being what they were, they were in no position to turn away transients who sought food and refuge from the night air after a long day's ride, particularly when there was

100

no room at the inn. Because of the size of the building, the Walker-Chandler home became anything but private. Many weary travelers passing through the small mill town immediately headed for "the big house" when the inn was full, knowing the smaller residences could yield no help.

Keeping in mind their personal desire for peace and privacy, it is not too difficult to visualize the sometimes-questionable courtesy and hospitality with which these men must have received some of their guests. But regardless of feelings they could not bring themselves to refuse sanctuary to the footsore and weary. For to do anything contrary to custom would have cost them the respect of their friends and neighbors, their most prized possession.

Then, as sometimes happens to those of good heart and intention, one of the two old friends, Mr. Walker, met with disaster and was killed instantly. A particularly attractive feature of the house, a front porch running the width of the building across the second-floor level and approached by outside steps, proved to be the killer.

Exactly how the accident occurred remains a mystery. Whether he was alone at the time or escorting one of his house guests to a room is not known. But one moment the victim was approaching the second floor and the next, his battered body which had crashed through the front railing lay still and lifeless on the sidewalk. Since then the place at 108 Main Street has been known simply as the Chandler house.

Although the present owner, Mr. Samuel Caplan, maintains that no one is certain which man died, when questioned, old-timers who had learned much of the town's history at their mother's and grandmother's knees remained adamant on the subject. Having never heard the name Walker connected with the building until recently, they insist that 108 Main Street was "definitely Mr. Chandler's old home."

After Mr. Chandler, the next man to own the property was Mr. Wilbur Kinsey who operated a bootmaking shop. Mr. Kinsey made each pair of boots by hand, his excellent skill manifesting itself in the finished product. Although he could have marketed them in many places, he chose to make them exclusively for the young students of St. Charles College, just a few miles west of Ellicott City.

There is no record of anyone else sharing the building with Mr. Kinsey. From all indications he operated his shop on the first floor and reserved the upper floors for living quarters. His son chose another profession and moved to Baltimore where he became the manager of the Lyric, one of the city's finest theatres.

According to G. M. Hopkins, the Kinsey Building was still family property as late as 1878 when it belonged to a Mr. T. Kinsey. Later it changed hands several times and ultimately was converted into an office building. But despite the change in ownership, the name "Kinsey Building" lingered for many years.

Eventually, after the turn of the 20th century, Charles A. Herrmann, insurance broker and outstanding member of Emory Methodist Church, became the owner. Mr. Herrmann deeded part of the land adjoining the building which ran from Main Street to Ellicott Street (now Church Road) to his beloved church. He also served as Superintendent of the Sunday School for forty-six years. A memorial window in the church building attests to his generosity.

In 1929, during Mr. Herrmann's ownership, the Chandler House became the Higinbothom Funeral Home. Operated by Mr. Frank C. Higinbothom, a native of Ellicott City who had just returned from five years of practice in Weston, West Virginia, the Home remained at this address until 1932 when the need for larger quarters became apparent. For a time Mr. Higinbothom located on the south side of Main Street, eventually moving to his present location on Columbia Road—the completely renovated home of the Kraft family, former owners of Ellicott City's oldest and best known meat packing plant and market.

Following Mr. Herrmann's death in 1936 the Chandler House was sold to Caleb Dorsey Rogers, an enterprising real estate broker who, at one time or another, had owned, if only for brief intervals, many of the properties in the small town. He in turn sold the old home to Isaac H. Taylor who offered it for rent. The new tenant converted the house into a tavern, the outcome of which no one foresaw—least of all Mr. Taylor.

There are those who remember only too well the dismal deterioration of the grand old building. Cleanliness became an unknown virtue. And the proverbial brass rail soon resembled a cast iron pipe, there being no one interested enough to keep it shining. It is said that things went from bad to worse until stray animals, wandering into the building, no longer distracted or disturbed the customers, so intent were they on "downing another."

For a time it appeared certain that the once-beautiful Walker-Chandler House would soon be completely destroyed. Having rented the building "as is," Mr. Taylor was unsuccessful in his attempt to break the contract. But shortly before the outbreak of World War II Mr. and Mrs. Samuel H. Caplan, members of a family associated with Ellicott City for more than seventy years, persuaded him to sell the property to them. The new owners took possession of their building and proceeded with the business of restoring it to its former condition. This represented a costly investment, and only someone with unfaltering faith in the future of the little town would have undertaken such a task.

*   *   *

Extensive repairs were made. The entire house was stripped to the stone walls and replastered to guarantee cleanliness. The two original fireplaces were restored; scarred and worn woodwork and flooring were sanded and refinished or replaced where necessary; and paint and stain were generously applied until at long last the lovely old home was once again one of Ellicott City's finest structures.

During the War and for a number of years thereafter, two proud flags—one of the United States, the other of the State of Maryland—proclaimed the occupancy of the building by the American Red Cross. A modest rent was charged, which in turn was used by Mr. Caplan primarily to keep it in good repair.

After the Red Cross vacated the property the Chesapeake and Potomac Telephone Company signed a five-year contract and opened a business office here after having completely remodelled it to suit their needs.

Although by this time telephones were taken pretty much for granted, it had not always been so. An interesting story is told of the early days when the Citizens Telephone Line (owned and operated by the Maryland Telephone Company) was built around the Ellicott City area. This company was located above James Gaither's Livery Stable and served those customers west of Ellicott City. The Howard Telephone Company served another section. Thus, two phones were needed if one cared to talk to his friends across the dividing line. Then came a third company and complications. Confidences were not exchanged for, to quote Mr. Edwin F. Hanna, Jr. who remembers well the early years of this century, "the operator often did the talking as a go-between relaying messages from one line to another!"

In his reminiscences Dr. J. R. Bromwell Branch, formerly of Ellicott City, tells of another interesting and equally amusing story. In the eighties when Ross Martin ran his drug store on Main Street, he also operated this first telephone company over Gaither's Stable. Furthermore, he was the owner of the first talking machine in town which he enjoyed sharing with his friends.

Thus it was that "in the early days he would have some of his friends connected up to the switchboard and give a gramophone concert!" Ellicott City's "hello girl" at the time was a Miss Josie Ray.

In 1902 there were less than fifty phones in the Ellicott City area. In 1907 there were approximately one hundred and seventy-five. Then in 1910 the C. & P. Telephone Company purchased all the lines in the area, paying one dollar a pole for everything west of Ellicott City, thus adding a hundred stations and offering services to such "distant" villages as Clarksville, Dayton, Glenelg, Guilford and Highland. By today's standards this achievement seems barely worthy of note. But at the time Dr. Bell's invention was still in its infancy. Today stations and sub-stations are to be found throughout the county. And calls are placed at such a fast pace that even if they chose to listen in, today's operators could not possibly relay messages as they once did as part of the "excellent service."

* * * * * * * * * *

When the Telephone Company moved its headquarters to another location, once again leaving the ancient Chandler House vacant, three enterprising women of remarkable foresight approached Mr. Caplan with a plan that must have made him raise his eyebrows a bit. For everyone then believed that Ellicott City was a dying town where it was no longer wise to spend money on improvements.

They requested the owner's permission to tone down somewhat "the newness and modern look of the building," to be permitted to create once again a more authentic background for their carefully thought out venture—a new kind of business, a combination antique shop and country store. Mr. Caplan listened attentively, envisioning his property as his prospective tenants spoke. The old Walker-Chandler House...the Kinsey Building...another shop?

With all the necessities of life provided by surrounding merchants, including himself, could Ellicott City support still another enterprise? Or was it the other way around? Would such a place help support Ellicott City?

Mrs. Mildred Werner spoke for the group. This would not be "just another ordinary store." Nor would it be "merely an antique shop." It would be something extraordinary, something to attract the casual shopper, and gradually something to attract customers from near and far.

When the list of suggested merchandise was presented to him Mr. Caplan was undoubtedly second only to the three women most involved in recognizing what such an attraction could do for his home town. An antique shop of exceptional character in the center of one of Maryland's oldest mill towns! But more than that, an outlet for truly unusual items, rare and appealing. Why not? How could it possibly hurt the current effort to restore the little town? Indeed, it might well prove the finest attraction the town could offer, provided the merchandise was as represented and the prices were right.

Thus it was that in September, 1962 Mrs. Mildred Werner and her two daughters, Mrs. Enalee Bounds and Mrs. Barbara Provenze, opened the doors at 108 Main Street and with tempting flyers advertising their wares, introduced the public to Ellicott's Country Store. Once inside, the year might well have been 1789.

The list of merchandise available would have given Ellicott's first store some genuine competition. There was china and glassware, brass and copperware, hand-woven towels and woolens, hand-made quilts and aprons for the ladies; then came the wooden dolls and toys for the children as well as penny candy; and for the "beaus and husbands and fathers, equally critical," there was the old cracker barrel, New England Clam Chowder, cheese, buckwheat pancake mix and other flour mixes from an old grist mill in Virginia where Thomas Jefferson had his grain milled, home-made jellies and the never-to-be-forgotten Indian pudding. There were three floors to delight the shopper, the second and third floors yielding fine furniture for the home, most dating back a century or more, the rest painstakingly reproduced from satiny old boards of pine, cherry or fruitwood. Tomorrow's antiques...

None but the expert could distinguish the difference. But as promised, Mrs. Werner and her daughters have made it their policy never to misrepresent any of their merchandise to their customers. Because of this they keep returning and spreading the word among their friends.

It is said that in the beginning, with commercial advertising rates being what they were, the three women decided to depend primarily on word-of-mouth publicity. Today, through this medium, they are as well known across the Potomac in upper Virginia as they are in nearby Washington and Baltimore, from where busloads of people come each Sunday—the newcomers, just to be convinced (which they are in short order) and the others, regular customers, to shop again and again for the old or the unusual.

So well pleased are the ladies with the results of their enterprise that young Enalee Bounds has been heard to say that indeed she would work there "even if she didn't make any money," just for the joy of handling such fascinating items. And in fact, for a time all three women did just that. But perseverance and determination to "abide by the rules" have won for them a much-envied reputation in surrounding areas.

In this day of exorbitant prices and over-estimated values it is a unique experience to shop in such pleasant surroundings, where cheerful conversation supplants the usual high-pressure salesmanship, and where selecting the correct gift or accessory is both a joy and a challenge, thanks to the vast assortment of unusual and fascinating items offered by three scrupulous women of superb taste.

When Ellicott's Mills was first founded and the original Ellicott Store was the meeting place for most of the little village's shoppers, to receive honest value for prices paid was an accepted policy. Today it is an experience, and a rare one at that. But here at Ellicott's second country store, the buyer can indeed make a purchase and come away convinced that in fact he has gotten more than his money's worth, all things considered.

The writer knows of no more fascinating way to spend a Sunday afternoon—or any afternoon for that matter—than to visit the ancient building in the ancient town at 108 Main Street. Aside from browsing around and seeing things such as you may not have seen in years, you will also meet a number of fascinating people through whom you will learn a great deal about the small mill town and its past.

Thus it is that at long last through the efforts of three women —Mrs. Werner, Mrs. Bounds, and Mrs. Provenze, and one compatible landlord, Mr. Caplan, the old Walker-Chandler House has recaptured much of the stature and dignity with which it was endowed so many years ago. For once again it is occupied by people who love it, as did the original builders. There is no "created" atmosphere about the place. It is real, as is the rest of the little town. And because of this it carries the tourist back to the 18th century when home-made candles and soap were actual necessities and not just unusual items.

So once again, in seeking out the unusual, one finds instead a truly authentic Early American Country Store in a truly Early American country village, Ellicott City—Mill Town, U.S.A.

* * *
2003 UPDATE

In 2002 Enalee Bounds celebrated forty years of operation in Ellicott's Country Store on Main Street, the second oldest continuous business in the Ellicott City Historic District. Although the store remains true to its country roots, it has evolved into much more. Keeping up with the times, Mrs. Bounds offers design services as well as antique and attractive decorative elements scattered throughout the four floors of the shop.

Following the deaths of her mother, Mildred Werner, in 1998 (who worked at the shop into her ninetieth year) and her sister, Barbara Provenza, in 1999, Mrs. Bounds continues as the guiding light of one the most popular enterprises in the Historic District.

Mrs. Bounds and her husband, Roland, purchased the building in 1967 and gradually expanded the shop to include all four floors of the building. Mrs. Bounds enjoys relating that in the early days of operating the store, the family received freight from the Baltimore & Ohio railroad station until the flood of 1972 caused the B & O to board up the station. Today's merchandise arrives via the less nostalgic freight trucking companies, although its selection undergoes the same careful scrutiny. Now the challenge, according to Mrs. Bounds, is to find suppliers of the cottage industry type goods she features.

The building has undergone major renovations in the last 30 years, some preceded by tragic events. Two fires have caused varying degrees of damage. In 1972, the building caught fire and the damage repair evolved into a restoration, with friend Andrew Cascio working to uncover original kitchen fireplaces, wood flooring, and old window paneling. This restoration also included replacing a set of inside stairs. A second fire in 1991 destroyed the second, third, and fourth floors, and closed the shop for seven months.

Although working full-time at the store, this lady of many talents has also used her energy in preservation efforts in Ellicott City. For 15 years she edited the preservation newspaper, THE HERITAGE, and has worked vigorously for such events as Historical Ellicott City, Inc.'s annual decorator show house and other fundraising activities. In most of these ventures she has been joined by her husband, Roland, a local attorney who was the first chairman of the Historic District Commission, a president of the Ellicott City Restoration Foundation, and is currently president of Historic Ellicott City, Inc. Ellicott's Country Store is but one charming example of this family's contribution to their cherished community.

The Howard House today

The Howard House in 1850 shortly
after it opened. – Courtesy of Mrs.
John B. Loughran

THE HOWARD HOUSE

On the north side of Main Street facing Columbia Pike, there stands another of Ellicott City's many fine landmarks. Built of local granite and boasting handsome iron grille work, the old building was once known as The Howard House.

Many years ago when Ellicott's Mills was popular as a summer resort, the Howard House, or Howard Hotel, was a favorite meeting place for visitors from all walks of life. For the Howard House was noted for its lavish parties and unsurpassed cuisine.

A breakfast typical of the times would include such succulent foods as ham, farm-fresh eggs, broiled chicken with cream sauce, an assortment of buttered hot breads, tea and coffee—such as would have been served by the Ellicotts themselves when hosting visitors. For food was plentiful and delicacies easily come by due to the knowledge and efficiency of the neighboring farmers. Beef, pork, poultry, butter, cream, and eggs—the necessary staples for so luscious a menu—were to be found within a short distance of the hotel itself, while delays in shipment and the use of cold storage foods were unheard of.

Although Ellicott's Mills was founded in 1772, until 1794 "the village consisted only of the proprietors of the estate and their clerks, millers, coopers, blacksmiths, wheelwrights, millwrights, farm hands, and day laborers." Travellers depended upon the stage coach inns which dotted the rough and sometimes impassable roads between Baltimore and points west. Highway hotels, as such, were unheard of. Ellicott's Mills was hardly more than a dot on the map.

But the first half of the 19th century saw many changes in the little town. The heretofore limited population swelled to approximately 3,000 people by 1825. A commercial district started crowding itself along the narrow passage west of the river known as "the valley," and the beautiful scenery surrounding the small village beckoned the people of neighboring Baltimore and Washington. The heat and humidity of the summer months gradually drove the city dwellers to the surrounding counties where they enjoyed cool breezes and the pure luxury of good, clean, fresh air. Sykesville, Lisbon, and Poplar Springs offered much by way of scenic beauty and country living. But Ellicott's Mills was closer, just an enjoyable buggy ride from the heart of Baltimore, and a not-too-distant ride from the nation's capital.

From Washington stage coaches started arriving on a daily schedule. Then before long the railroad made its appearance. Many prominent men are said to have passed through or spent the night in the small resort town. Among those known to have done so were John C. Calhoun, Henry Clay, William C. Preston, Andrew Jackson, Daniel Webster, Robert E. Lee, and Roger Brooke Taney. One historian, Marietta Minnigerode Andrews, refers to Ellicott City as part of George Washington's country in her book of the same name. Although Miss Andrews makes no claim that "Washington slept here," she does point out the number of times he passed through the little town while serving as Commander-in-Chief of the Continental Army, and again later during his travels throughout the nearby countryside.

Local legend tells us that on one occasion when Andrew Jackson passed through the mill town on his way to visit his friend Roger Brooke Taney, there being no suitable lodgings available, he was forced to spend the night in a small home on Fels Lane. The next day he was taken by coach to his destination.

It was following this incident that a German couple, Mr. and Mrs. Christian Eckert (she, the former Christine Will) decided to open the Howard House. Built in 1850, it contained fourteen well-lighted and ventilated rooms, a bar on the first floor stocked with a large assortment of choice wines, liquor, and cigars, an ice cream parlor, and a second floor dining room for the hotel's patrons.

Later when Mr. Eckert built the adjoining building west of Howard House (where Paul's Market now stands) he added a lunch room for the townspeople and transients, as well as a banquet hall on the second floor. His capacity for handling food and serving was such that on a number of occasions he catered to as many as one hundred and fifty people at a time. The addition proved a success, attracting not only local clubs and groups, but also many from Baltimore and Washington who wished to hold special affairs and banquets at the now-famous inn.

Mr. and Mrs. Eckert brought with them not only their knowledge of hotel and restaurant management, but also their typically German recipes for fine food and drinks as well. Oddly enough their specialty was ice cream, a product not yet known in their native land. According to Mrs. John Loughran, a niece of the Eckerts, they supplied all the ice cream consumed at the annual Clarksville picnic, one of the county's largest social functions. It is said they produced upward of 2500 gallons per season.

Opposite the old hotel where once stood Parlett's Garage and parking lot, and including a part of the store now occupied by Taylor's (Jewelry-Furniture-Appliances), Mr. Eckert made soft drinks including soda, sarsaparilla, and ginger ale in great quantities. He also maintained a livery stable in the rear for the horses and carriages of his clientele.

As late as 1890 Ellicott City was still credited with having first class hotels where tourists were extended every courtesy and their needs and desires were anticipated. Howard House undoubtedly came under this classification even though Mr. Eckert was now serving as Mayor, the village having become an incorporated town.

In 1905 Emily Emerson Lantz of THE BALTIMORE SUN published this version of the hotel at the turn of the century:

> There are numberless old men passing to and fro, hale and hearty old men who speak to every passerby or sit in groups on the hotel porch discussing politics. It was this hotel, The Howard House, where a stranger once arrived after nightfall for lodgings and was shown to a room upon the third floor. The next morning, upon looking out of his window, he perceived that the bedroom was apparently on the ground floor, with happy children passing gayly on their way to the village school. The astonished traveler could not imagine under what optical or mental delusion he was laboring until he was told that the third floor of the hotel, if entered from the lower street, was level with the second street in its rear.

Two years later Heinrich Ewald Buchholz made the following observation regarding the Howard House in a series of articles on Maryland County Seats:

> The habitues of the courthouse and also regular visitors to the hills lying around about have long been accustomed to use the hotel instead of the public highway as a means of mounting the hill.

Ellicott City has many houses built directly on a
hillside, and such is the case with the hotel. What is
the 4th floor front is about on a level with the ground
floor rear, and the pedestrian wishing to go to the
courthouse or any place in its neighborhood may enter
the Main Street door of the hotel, climb three flights of
stairs and walk out into the back yard, mount another
pair of stairs, and he is on the level of the rear street.

This courtesy, extended to the people of the town
by the proprietor, paid big dividends. For the rich
tempting odors of good things to eat lingered in the
halls, tempting many a welcome trespasser to linger a
while and partake of the good food and drink to be obtained in the hotel dining room.

Although there is an obvious discrepancy in the two accounts
regarding "street levels" from respective floors, the two articles
do bear witness to the courtesy extended both local people and
house guests alike. They also suggest the Eckerts' subtle form of
attracting customers, what with the aroma of luscious foods filling
the air!

Upon the death of Mrs. Eckert, Howard House was run by
Catherine Louise and John Reichenbecker, sister and brother-in-
law of the deceased. Following reverses, the newer building was
sold and became the home of the Masonic Lodge of Ellicott City.
Members of the Eastern Star soon established their headquarters
on the top floor. The once-famous restaurant was closed and the
older building operated only as a hotel.

On June 28, 1927 Christian Eckert died. The Reichenbeck-
ers retired from the part they had taken in maintaining the hotel,
and Howard House was sold to William Kerger.

Julius A. Kinlein of Ellicott City was the next owner.

*   *   *

There have been a number of alterations made in the outward
appearance of the old hotel, as well as the interior, since the days
when Mr. and Mrs. Eckert were proprietors.

Unfortunately the elaborate second-floor grille work has been
removed, exposing the double door which once led from the dining
room to an outdoor eating area. The iron work atop the mansard
roof, resembling a speared fence, has also vanished, as have the
two T-shaped chimneys and a central cupola of rather large pro-

portions, all features of particular interest. Much of the ornamental and lacy black metal trim has been modified to the simplest
possible design, and gone are the picturesque hanging flower con-
tainers that seemed to add a note of warmth to the welcome extended to visitors.

Additional doorways have been cut through the thick granite
walls where once there were windows. This was done to accommodate the people who made Howard House their home for so many
years.

It is interesting to note that the original entrance, as well as
the second-floor doorway, has been preserved. Undoubtedly some
of the fine old sand glass windowpanes still remain in the sashes
of the five-story building. The shutters have also disappeared—
possibly as an economy measure—and the twelve-pane windows of
the upper floors gleam and reflect the rays of the sun.

For reasons best known to the builder, the windows of the
top floor of Howard House differ from the rest in that they are
four-paned. But they are crowned with pediments of simple but effective design. Over all, the original cornice still remains intact.

The building itself is one of the finer examples of 19th century architecture to be found in the little mill town, resembling as
it does, the original structures erected in the last half of the pre-
ceding century. It is truly distinctive with its huge granite walls
long-since smoothed by time and the elements. Despite the loss of
so much of its picturesque grille work, Howard House is still a
building worthy of preservation.

Having been converted into an apartment house by Mr. Kinlein, one might say that for a time it still served the same purpose
intended by the Eckerts. For it offered shelter and warmth, as
well as security, to those who made it their home.

As for its 20th-century cuisine, all the writer can guarantee
is that it was undeniably varied, depending upon the likes or dislikes of its individual tenants. For one thing remains unchanged.
Within easy distance of the front door, the beef and pork and poultry, as well as the butter and cream and fresh eggs needed for a
luxurious menu are still available. For despite the gradual development of Columbia, Ellicott City remains fundamentally the heart
of a farming area.

But...what next for Ellicott City's Howard House?

*   *   *

Today there is little doubt but that it will survive. For in

September, 1967, according to the records in the Clerk to the Court's office, the old "hotel-turned-apartment-house-with-twelve-units" was purchased by Samuel A. Caplan, local business man and owner of several other parcels of Main Street property.

According to the new owner, aside from the antique shop already operating there and known as The Iron Rail, future plans include artist studios, and conceivably another good restaurant—depending upon the outcome of present negotiations.

While talking to Mr. Caplan, one of Ellicott City's most active preservationists, the writer could not help but be touched by the contagious enthusiasm with which he is approaching this new venture. Needless to say, the people of Howard County and all persons interested in the preservation of this quaint town sincerely hope Howard House will once again regain its former prestige; if not as a hotel, at least as the headquarters of appreciative tenants, and perhaps in the future, the home of another equally fine dining room.

Surely this is as the Eckerts would have had it.

*   *   *

2003 UPDATE

In 1986, local attorney Robert C. Brown and his wife, Paula, purchased the property from Samuel A. Caplan and so began a labor of love, honing the skills they acquired during the earlier restoration of The Old Emporium.

Comprised at the time of small apartments served by a heating system with mammoth pipes running through the building, the building had major structural and lead paint problems. The Browns hired a structural engineer who provided drawings and recommendations, but much of the work was hands-on.

Mr. Brown related with pride that he personally used an electric saw to remove gas pipes. They stripped nineteen or twenty layers of lead-based paint from the walls, thereby removing all traces of work done in the 1930's. The resulting interior features fewer, but larger apartments on the top four floors with space for retail businesses on the street level. Currently it is home to two art galleries.

The exterior of the building, with its intricate wrought iron railings decorating the front porch, remains one of the most striking facades in the Historic District. The Browns' restoration of the interior has assured its continued status of historic significance to the Historic District.

HOWARD COUNTY FIRE DEPARTMENT

Within the angle formed by Church Road and Main Street there is a small triangular building which once served as the home of Ellicott City's first Fire Department. Built in 1896, it housed all the Department's meager equipment which consisted primarily of leather buckets and ropes.

Although sponsored by the Mayor and City Council, Fire Company No. 1 was hardly more than a slight improvement over the earlier citizens' bucket-and-axe brigade, and certainly less than adequate to meet the needs of the growing community. But it was a beginning.

A call for volunteers brought immediate response from such men as Charles Buetefisch, Charles A. Herrmann, Edward Hilton, J. Edwin Kroh, Philip A. Laumann, Richard Talbott, Charles Werner and Julius Wosch, Jr. To summon them when needed, a bell was installed bearing the inscription: "Presented by the Mayor and City Council of Ellicott City to Volunteer Fire Company No. 1— 1896."

As time passed, the people of Ellicott City realized that despite the gallant efforts made by the men of the Fire Company, there was little they could do when disaster struck. Criticism mounted and it was generally agreed that better protection and more modern equipment were urgently needed if the little town was to survive.

On July 4, 1898 tensions were further aroused when a fire

115

cracker exploded and set fire to a stable owned by Thomas H. Hunt. The attempt to save the structure was unsuccessful, but it did lead to a campaign to buy a bright red Howe man-powered pumper, mounted on wheels, to be used with a two-wheeled hose reel.

The new equipment proved cumbersome and less than perfect. The men were hard-pressed to pull it up and down the steep hills. Two men manned the pumper which produced an uneven stream of water, and fire-fighting, as such, remained limited. But it was an improvement over the buckets, and had to do until better equipment became available and additional funds could be raised with which to purchase it.

Ten years passed before the fire company was provided with a hand-pulled two-wheeled truck supporting a gasoline engine. This supplanted the old see-saw pumper which, in itself, was an improvement. But it exceeded it in weight and therefore was still more awkward and heavy to handle. Fortunately the pitch of the road outside the firehouse—so typical of Ellicott City's hilly terrain—proved an advantage for it gave the men that much-needed "good running start." The present entrance to the building and single window have long since replaced the large double doors which once swung open facing west.

A few years later man-power was replaced by horse-power when the town invested in a horse-drawn gasoline pumper. The starting mechanism of the gas powered pumper was, however, very temperamental and unreliable, and it is a matter of record that Mr. Herrmann was the only man in the brigade capable of getting it started. Yet despite this problem, the gas pumper equipment served Ellicott City for more than fifteen years, until it capsized on Main Street on the way to a fire and was completely demolished. While still in operation the old pumper had fought many devastating fires including those at St. Charles College, Rock Hill College, the Gambrill Manufacturing Company, and one on Main Street which destroyed the old post office building.

In 1920 a move to modernize the department got underway with Commissioner Milton Easton taking an active part. Exclaimed Mr. Easton: "It takes anywhere from half an hour to an hour and a half for fire fighters and equipment to be gotten to the scene of a fire. A motorized outfit would put us on the scene up to a distance of five miles within a few minutes." Shortly thereafter a Model T Ford replaced the horses, and again a drive was on to update the Department.

Finally, in 1924 a modern fire engine, as well as a building in which to house it, were purchased by the county commissioners.

The building was located west of Talbott's store on Main Street. The name of the company was changed to the Volunteer Firemen of Howard County until it was incorporated, when it became known as the Howard County Volunteer Firemen's Association.

* * *

The first 24-hour protection plan was put into effect with a man stationed in an apartment above the garage at all times. B. Harrison (Harry) Shipley, a life-long resident of Ellicott City, was appointed Chief Engineer.

Mr. Shipley's career was varied and fascinating. Starting as a blacksmith, he later became a carriage maker, then an automobile mechanic, a trade he followed until his retirement in 1956. After his retirement he served the people of Howard County for eight years as a full-time Committing Magistrate under the Magistrate's Court System. In 1964 when the People's Court replaced this system, Mr. Shipley became its first Bailiff. But his major interest remained the volunteer fire service.

As a small boy he helped pump the bars on the local "hand tub." Many years later while serving as Chief Engineer (1924-1958) he also held the post of Fire Chief (1935-1958). One of the founders of the Howard County Volunteer Firemen's Association, he was elected their first president in 1944. He was also a member of the Maryland State Firemen's Association and served as president of this organization in 1937.

During World War II and for many years thereafter Mr. Shipley served as Fire Coordinator for the local Civil Defense organization. But throughout the state he was most widely known for his outstanding work in helping to establish the present fireworks law in Maryland.

B. Harrison Shipley, Howard County's first Fire Chief, died Monday, September 25, 1967.

* * *

Before his death Mr. Shipley spoke frequently of his many years as a member of the Ellicott City Fire Department. He recalled vividly the circumstances leading up to the purchase of "the new equipment in 1899"—the Howe pumper, the ladder wagon, and the hose reel. He also remembered well the day when the first mechanized unit drawn by the Model T Ford replaced the horse-drawn vehicle in the early '20s, only to be wrecked on Main Street en route to a fire at White's Hospital (now Taylor Manor). Needless to say, the Ellicott City Fire Department never reached its destination and the hospital was destroyed, but fortunately there were no casualties.

Reorganization of the Department followed. Benjamin Mellor was named Fire Chief. He served in this position until 1934. Then in 1938 a new building was erected on the corner of Main Street and Fels Lane. Today it houses not only the new and streamlined equipment of the present day, but the old hand-pumper as well. The history of the department is also available, as are all the reports filed since the reorganization in 1924.

The Company, which serves many areas of Howard County as well as nearby sections of the surrounding counties, now has four engines, the oldest being a 1941 American La France; the newest, a $30,000 1966 American La France triple pumper. The Company also operates two ambulances on 24-hour call. There are three men on duty during the day and one at night. As of this writing, more than 3000 missions have been completed by the ambulance corps.

Meanwhile, the old building where it all began has seen service as headquarters for the Howard County Welfare Board, the Health Department, and the Sanitation Department. It is currently being used as a branch of the Ellicott City Public Library.

The little building on West Main Street, with its cupola and weather vane still intact, warrants a second look. For although it has been altered slightly in general appearance to serve modern needs, the basic lines remain unchanged, offering mute testimony to the fact that in the old days, the slant of the road did indeed offer the men of Howard County's fire-fighting brigade that much-needed "good running start!"

*   *   *

2003 UPDATE

Fire Chief B. H. Shipley's extraordinary service to the community was continued in the person of his son, Benjamin Harrison Shipley, Jr., who was appointed Howard County's first part-time Fire Administrator in 1968. With charter government came a reaffirmation of public trust in Mr. Shipley's stewardship as he was again appointed Fire Administrator, a position soon enlarged to include service on the area-wide Regional Planning Council's Emergency Medical Services Committee. Mr. Shipley declined a full-time position as Fire Chief in 1979, and the department celebrated Mr. Shipley's career at several events. He was succeeded by Captain Henry L. Long III, who served for three years, and later by George E. Massey who retired in 1984.

Deputy Chief John J. Klein was next appointed Fire Chief and has served the community admirably and progressively to this day. The venerable Benjamin Harrison Shipley, Jr. passed away on February 1, 2002, at age 88, a mere two and a half months after being honored with a two-hour tribute at the annual Ellicott City Volunteer Fire Department banquet, November 16, 2001, having served 71 years with the department.

Fires in the old town have made their own history. In the late 1960's Ellicott City suffered only one major fire, when the administration building of Taylor Manor Hospital burned. It took 50 firefighters three hours to contain the blaze with no loss of life. In May, 1972 a fire broke out in Ellicott's Country Store on Main Street. Most of the building was saved, and a 90-year-old tenant in the top floor apartment was safely evacuated.

Firefighters offered a variety of services to the community during the flooding caused by Tropical Storm Agnes in June, 1972. They assisted with evacuating people from Main Street and restored electric power to the street using a generator. They also helped pump out basements. On November 14, 1984, one of the worst fires in the history of the town broke out behind Leidig's Bakery on Main Street, destroying six buildings and causing financial losses of approximately $1.3 million.

In 1974 the Ellicott City Fire Department opened its second station, Bethany Fire Station Number 8, situated on Route 99 at Old St. John's Lane. This building was appropriately dedicated to the memory of Edward T. Clark, Jr. one-time president of the Ellicott City Volunteer Fireman's Association. By 1975 the number of career firefighters had increased to eighteen. That same year the volunteer fireman's association purchased a boat, which was pressed into action soon thereafter during Hurricane Eloise.

In 1998 the fire station on West Main Street in Ellicott City was vacated as the Ellicott City Volunteer Company Number 2 moved to a newly constructed station at 4150 Montgomery Road, giving the company easier access to the expanding community. The vacated station has been remodeled for retail space. With the new station's immediate access to major arteries, response time to a fire has been reduced.

This response time was tested with the unfortunate fire on Main Street on November 9, 1999. The fire began behind the

Main Street Blues Restaurant and spread to destroy six businesses and nine residences. The Rosenstock building had to be
removed, and a new building to replace it is scheduled to open in
2003.

Meanwhile the unusual little building at the corner of
Main Street and Church Road is once again dedicated to the
interest of fire protection. On September 21, 1991, after restoration of the building to its original 1889 design, it was dedicated
as The Fire Museum, housing fire-fighting equipment and memorabilia from over 100 years. The Museum can be visited by
appointment.

*   *   *

2003 photos by Charles Kyler.

EMORY METHODIST EPISCOPAL CHURCH

On Church Road a short distance from the old Howard County
Fire Department Building, facing Emory Street, there is a lovely
little church of stone and frame construction known as "old Emory."
It is the small town's original Methodist Episcopal Church and, as
such, holds a place of honor in the town's history.

Standing on a piece of ground acquired by deed "from Samuel
Ellicott to John Forrest and others," it is one of Ellicott City's
many fine landmarks. Since the Ellicotts had so generously donated a number of sites for the erection of churches of all denominations, and since no price is quoted for the land received from Samuel in the church records, it is assumed it was given and not sold
to the new congregation. If, indeed, a charge was made, it was
probably for the nominal fee of five or ten dollars, as in the case
of St. Paul's Catholic Church and other places of worship. However, the deed did specify that the property must be used specific-
ally "to preach and expound God's Holy Word." (Although this historic paper was lost for a number of years, it was recovered in
1855 in the home of the first pastor.)

Despite the liberal gift given by Mr. Ellicott, old Emory
faced many financial difficulties. But ultimate triumph over seem-
ingly endless trials came after years of hard work, disillusionment and, at times, almost complete frustration. For funds were
hard to raise and despite the continued effort on the part of a few,
there were days when their hopes seemed futile and their goal—the

121

erection of a new chapel in the thriving mill town—doomed. But unfaltering faith and sheer determination are unbeatable qualities, and the good people of old Emory were gifted with both.

*   *   *

Although meetings were held in the homes of the parishioners and resolutions were offered "to get on with the building," money was not easily obtained either through private loans or the local bank. Every available source was tapped, but it was primarily through personal contributions and pledges that the majority of the money was raised.

Despite the financial embarrassments that plagued the small congregation, ground was finally broken and the construction of the new church got underway. It was completed in 1837 and proudly proclaimed one of the finest houses of worship in the area.

Then on November 27, 1837 "in pursuance and by the authority of an Act of the General Assembly entitled 'An Act to incorporate certain persons in every Christian Church, or Congregation in this State,' the 'per white male' persons above the age of twenty-one years, residing in Baltimore and Anne Arundel Counties met in Oella to elect Trustees in the name of and on behalf of the Methodist Episcopal Preaching House called Emory Chapel located in Ellicott's Mills."

The necessary qualifications for those elected specified that they be sober and discreet, above the age of 21 years, residing within eight miles of said Chapel in Anne Arundel County, and "being for at least twelve months in full membership of the Methodist Episcopal Church."

Possessing these requisites, the following men were selected: John Forrest, Isaiah Mercer, James Martin, William Fort, Joshua H. Hynes, William Hughes, David Emmart, William J. Timanus and Thomas Jenkins. The Baltimore Annual Conference appointed Rev. Richard Brown preacher-in-charge.

The first meeting of the Board was held December 5th, 1837 at the home of Isaiah Mercer. David Emmart was elected Secretary Pro Tem. At a meeting held later that month William Fort succeeded Mr. Emmart as Secretary and a resolution was adopted to elect by ballot a "standing secretary." At a subsequent meeting David Emmart was re-elected by a majority vote to this post while James Martin became old Emory's first treasurer. At this same time Rev. Brown was appointed Pastor.

*   *   *

It was not until June 7th, 1838 that the first sizable loan of five hundred dollars was negotiated by Mr. Mercer who obtained the money from William Matthews. Additional loans were made and repaid only to be followed by more loans.

Repeated meetings were held in the hope of finding other sources of income but the necessary money seemed almost unattainable. Benefits were arranged, including sacred concerts. Special collections were held outside the little mill town, and talks by men like Bishop Waugh and Reverend Thomas Sewell were given. All the proceeds from these affairs were applied to the existing debt.

As late as 1845 the Reverend William Halmead of Rock Hill College and Mrs. Almira Lincoln Phelps, then Headmistress of the Patapsco Female Institute, were both approached for support. No stone was left unturned. And no effort was left completely unrewarded.

Finally toward the end of the year 1853, under the pastorate of Reverend John Guyer, the debt was fully liquidated. The church cost $6,181.34 to build, plus the interest paid over the years amounting to $1,946.54, making a total of $8,127.88.

The stone work was done by Jake Timanus, the carpentry by W.S. Harrison, and the plastering by Jesse McKinzie. Lumber and other materials were furnished by W.E. Fell, and by Coates and Glennin.

*   *   *

Meanwhile the business of running the church went on. Regular meetings were scheduled to submit and pass resolutions for the good of the new congregation. For the most part they represented serious thought on the part of the Board members. However, the minutes of one of the first meetings, that of February 1st, 1838 yield a touch of humor although the problem in question was fundamentally of genuine concern to the parishioners, as shall be seen. The resolutions adopted at this session read as follows:

1. That James Martin be responsible for organizing a choir "and conduct same at all functions and future meetings in Emory Chapel."
2. That "our preachers request the congregation not to leave meeting until regularly dismissed."
3. That the President (or Pastor) "respectively request all persons using tobacco to discontinue it while in Emory Chapel."

The first resolution having been duly adopted was carried out, thanks to Mr. Martin's cooperation and willingness to comply with the request. The second resolution, although not complied with at all times by all members of the congregation, was for the most part generally adhered to. But the third resolution was another matter! It was not passed for more than fifty years, there having been placed under each pew or bench on the male side of the church "square wooden boxes, filled with sand, for their convenience." It was not until 1887 that the boxes were finally removed, undoubtedly to the chagrin of at least a few members, and the use of tobacco during services was finally prohibited!

Meanwhile in December, 1838 William Fort offered another resolution which was also adopted and followed by more serious consequences. It read in part: "...the use of Emory Chapel shall not be granted to any person or body of persons, but by the official sanction or consent of the Board of Trustess." This resolution ultimately led to the rental of the Sunday School room to the Trustees of Primary School No. 45 for a four-year term at $60.00 per annum. In this instance the basic terms of the original Ellicott deed were totally disregarded.

Over the next few decades request followed request, and all decisions were handed down by the Board, many of which were also contrary to the specifications set forth by Mr. Ellicott. In 1854 the Young Men's Christian Association of Ellicott City was given permission to use the building for its general program, although Miss Mary Thompson had been refused the right to conduct a "select school for females" on the premises on the grounds that such an institution did not constitute a "house of worship" as specified by Samuel Ellicott. Then on September 1st, 1865 the Board reversed its decision, permitting a Captain McCreary to use the facilities for a day school.

These conflicting rulings finally led to a special meeting on July 10th, 1867 when it was resolved that the lecture room could "not be used for any purpose other than the regular religious purposes of the Church, such as Sabbath School, Prayer Meeting, Etc." Thereafter the use of the room for "meetings for the dissemination of moral and religious principles was never refused," but "political and other similar organizations were always denied the use of the Church."

On June 19th, 1861 the house which had been used as the parsonage was purchased from Mahlon Falconer for a little less than two thousand dollars. It was enlarged in 1870 and served the needs of the pastors until recent years when it was torn down to make room for a parking area. A new parsonage has been provided at 8 Autumn Hill.

*   *   *

Emory Church overcame many hardships and setbacks during its first fifty years of existence. Aside from the fact that it was constantly "beset by financial depressions, the Civil War and the flood of the year 1868," it also suffered from the fact that periodically, with the exodus of many of the younger parishioners, the remaining congregation sometimes found the pressure of pastoral support and physical maintenance of parish buildings an almost unbearably heavy burden.

But the founding fathers and a goodly number of their descendants proved themselves equal to the challenge. Although old Emory did not enjoy the luxury of extravagant appointments, it did enjoy the loyalty and unselfish sacrifices of devoted parishioners. No better heritage could have been established.

*   *   *

Following the example of their predecessors, as part of the observation of the golden anniversary of Emory's founding, the church was "rebuilt" in 1887 at a total cost of $3500.00. Under the pastorship of Reverend R.R. Murphy the contract was awarded to C.W. Grimes. The windows, including the large "sunflower" back of the pulpit, were designed by William J. Robinson, Superintendent of the Sunday School.

The old seats (backless benches) were replaced by the present pews with back rests and racks for the necessary prayer books. A stone wall at the rear of the church was erected, and for the first time since its completion, seating arrangements were changed, permitting husband and wife or mixed groups to sit together. Heretofore the men sat to the right and the women to the left. The "new" church was dedicated Sunday, January 23rd, 1888.

Hitching posts were installed in the church yard in March, 1892 and electric lights followed in May. At the turn of the century water was installed and room for the Sunday School was made in the basement. A pipe organ was purchased and once again the entire church was redecorated.

*   *   *

The one hundredth anniversary of the founding of Emory Methodist Episcopal Church was celebrated in 1937 and was marked by the following events:

Nov. 21—A sermon by Rev. Frank R. Isaac and dedication of memorial windows in memory of Charles A. Herrmann; his wife, H. Lizzie Herrmann; and John W. Brian;

Nov. 28—Holy Communion and sermon by Rev. Dr. A. H. McKinley, District Superintendent, in the morning, and sermon by Rev. Dr. J. M. Gillum, former District Superintendent in the evening;

Dec. 2—Homecoming of former pastors with Rev. William A. Carroll, the Dean;

Dec. 3—Church banquet, with Mr. Linden S. Dodson, Ph. D., University of Maryland, as guest speaker;

Dec. 5—Sermon by the Rev. Fred P. Corson, D. D., Litt. D., L. L. D., President of Dickinson College in the morning, and sermon by Rev. Allan F. Poore, former pastor, in the evening.

An additional memorial to Mr. Charles Herrmann who had served as Superintendent of the Sunday School from 1890 to 1936 was placed in the church.

*   *   *

On November 25th, 1962 the 125th anniversary of old Emory was celebrated. Dr. Edwin Booth delivered a discourse on the life of John Wesley, founder of Methodism. The following evening Reverend Edison Amos of Washington, D. C. spoke on the life of Bishop Francis Asbury, the illustrious churchman of the 18th century, who is said to have ridden the hills of nearby Carroll County on horseback. He was referred to as "the Prophet of the Long Road."

*   *   *

Emory Church continues to progress. Although total membership is still limited to approximately four hundred persons, the old church is fortunate in having men and women of vision and good conscience to help forward its program.

Mr. G. Lee Burgess who, as of this writing, serves as Historian and Custodian of Legal Papers, and to whom the writer is indebted for the wealth of information made available to her, is a true son of old Emory and a true son of his father who also contributed greatly of his time and energy many years ago.

The Secretary's Record Book, which covers the entire life of the church, includes entries showing that Samuel F. Burgess "was elected to the Board of Trustees at the meeting held in February, 1877." Ten years later, in August, 1887, he was chosen Secretary of the Board.

Almost forty years later, on June 19th, 1923, G. Lee Burgess, son of Samuel, was also elected Trustee, having been voted Treasurer on May 29th, 1923. Six years later on May 15th, 1929 he, too, became Secretary, filling the post occupied by his father so many years ago.

On November 27th, 1966 Emory Church celebrated its 129th anniversary at the annual home-coming Anniversary Service. Reverend Watson Holley was guest speaker and many former members and friends came home to join in the celebration. Music was provided by both the Junior and Senior Choirs under the direction of Mrs. Margaret Owens and Mrs. Ruth McComb, respectively.

A special memorial was dedicated to still another outstanding member of the congregation, the late Mr. Lionel Burgess, Sr. Mr. Burgess, who had only recently been elected a member of the House of Delegates, died suddenly before having had an opportunity to serve in this capacity. Despite his many activities in both politics and civic affairs, he still found time to devote to old Emory. The men's class, which he led and taught for many years, honored his memory by contributing "two gifts to be used in worship."

* * *

Emory Church is fortunate today in having as Pastor the Reverend Robert Mitzel. An educated and knowledgeable man, he came to Ellicott City in 1960. He received his Bachelor's degree from Ohio Wesleyan College and a degree in theology from Wesley Seminary.

A native of Baltimore, he is married to the former Doris Justice of the same city, and is the father of three children: Donna, 22; Glen, 18; and Patricia, 15.

An insight into the character and thinking of this dedicated man can be gleaned from a glance at the Annual Report issued March 11, 1966. Reverend Mitzel's opening phrases on various topics are both enlightening and inspiring.

Says Reverend Mitzel: "We pray regularly 'Thy Kingdom Come,' but we seldom pause to think through what it would be like if that kingdom would really come on earth as it is in heaven." He adds: "When a church is really dedicated to building the kingdom, it is a redemptive fellowship." Then: "A kingdom-building church will nurture the lives of those who are a part of the fellowship, seeking to bring them into a deeper understanding of the truths of God." He further reminds us that "A kingdom-building church is one that is lifting up its members into the presence of God through worship." And finally, "A kingdom-building church is a fellowship that is concerned for those in the community around us."

Emory Church has always contributed to the welfare of the people of the small mill town in which it is located. May the future members, those who are today but small children or young adults, continue in the path laid out for them by their founding fathers.

And should faith or progress falter, may the members of this historic congregation remember the words of the Reverend Mitzel. For to be a "kingdom-building church" is indeed the goal of every Christian denomination, and the true incentive back of Emory's century and a quarter of continued success.

*   *   *

A visit to the little stone and frame building which hugs the side of one of Ellicott City's many hills is an inspiring experience. Still to be seen are the beautifully pedimented doors which cut through Mr. Timanus' symmetrical stone work; the "new and comfortable pews" installed before the turn of the 20th century; the memorial window dedicated to the Herrmanns who gave of themselves for more than forty years; and above all, Mr. Robinson's beautifully designed "sunflower" window, now serving as a colorful and significant backdrop for a handsome pipe organ.

Much of the traditional charm remains in this 19th century mill town gem which, from all indications, promises to survive for many years to come. Because of the work and sacrifices of the small but active congregation, future generations will also be privileged to see and hear for themselves the part played by the little church in the history of this area.

Nor will its members be forgotten. For in preserving their quaint chapel, they have, in fact, preserved their own memorial—"old Emory," today one of Ellicott City's best known landmarks.

*   *   *

2003 UPDATE

In November, 2002 the church celebrated its 165th anniversary. On Homecoming Sunday, the weekend after Thanksgiving, the church marked this milestone by dedicating new pew cushions, for what Celia Holland had called "the new and comfortable pews" installed before the turn of the 20th century—then in celebration of the church's 50th anniversary in 1887.

With a congregation currently numbering about 170, this small church continues to thrive and serve in the Historic District. The church reaches out to its community in a number of ways. In 1971 a Head Start program was held at the church. In 1987 Mother's Day Out was formed, which has evolved into the current Creative Child Enrichment Program for preschoolers. In 1988 the church's social hall began hosting the local senior center and continued to provide this service for twelve years.

Carillon bells were purchased and installed in 1989, and in 1996 the organ, originally purchased in 1907 in honor of the 70th anniversary, was refurbished for the second time at a cost of $10,000. The pipes were stripped, "goldened" and realigned, taller pipes to the side to show off the lovely sunflower window, one of the church's two stained glass windows.

Music Director Lois Hunter, who has been with the church more than ten years, has founded the Nightingales, a female vocal group of about a dozen singers from different area churches, who offer a yearly Christmas concert. Currently the church has its first woman pastor, the Rev. L. Katherine Moore, who has made her own special contributions. Rev. Moore has instituted children's ministries, strengthened the Vacation Bible School, and encouraged an active youth group.

With a wide range of members, increased attendance and continued commitment to the community, Emory United Methodist Church should continue to prosper in the 21st century.

*   *   *

34 CHURCH ROAD

On Church Road across from The Old Manse and next to the Emory Methodist Church, there is still another of Ellicott City's fine granite houses, known for years as the Macgill House. The lovely old home consists of the main wing, believed to be the original structure, and a small addition of slightly less than two full stories, plus a basement. Hidden today by a beautiful and sturdy growth of ivy, the lines indicating additions and alterations are no longer visible.

Although the writer has found no record or concrete evidence verifying the date of construction or name of the builder, according to the guide book for the Howard County House Tour of April 27, 1955, the original wing is thought to have been built in 1775 by Jonathan Ellicott, son of Andrew. Young Jonathan was but nineteen at the time. (Later, in 1782, as has been noted elsewhere in this book, he built another home for his wife and family which he occupied until his death.)

The guide further states that various members of the Ellicott family remained in the first house for approximately seventy-five years. Whether or not the original house was enlarged during this period remains a matter of conjecture, although credit for the alterations is given a subsequent owner by many of the town's older citizens.

In the mid-1800s the house at 34 Church Road became the property and personal residence of Marion P. Macgill who lived

130

there until his death. It is he who is credited with having enlarged the old home. Mrs. Macgill outlived her husband by a number of years. The Hopkins Atlas of 1868 lists her as the owner, as does another lesser-known map published approximately ten years later.

According to Mrs. Norman Betts, a lifetime resident of Ellicott City, upon the death of Mrs. Macgill a daughter, Grace, became heir to the old home and the final Macgill occupant. Upon her death Caleb Dorsey Rogers, one of Ellicott City's most active real estate brokers, purchased the home from the estate as an investment.

*   *   *

In the meantime Mr. and Mrs. J. Carroll Jenkins, the present owners, decided to make Ellicott City their home, coming here in the early 1930s. Mr. Jenkins was one of the founders of the Commercial and Farmers Bank, with headquarters in the former Washington Trust Company Building, Main Street, Ellicott City.

On November 1, 1934 the new bank opened its doors for the first time, starting with assets amounting to $320,000. As of this writing, Mr. Jenkins serves as president; Mr. James R. Rogers, as senior vice-president; Vernon P. Kraft, vice-president and cashier; and Melvin H. Weiderman, assistant vice-president and branch manager. As of 1965 the assets had increased to well over $5,000,000.

On Saturday, September 16, 1967 "a branch" of the bank was opened on the corner of Rogers Avenue and Route 40. Much of the heavier equipment from the main office had already been moved to the new site which then became the official home of the Commercial and Farmers Bank. In turn, the old building on Main Street became the branch office and business was resumed as usual.

Mr. and Mrs. Jenkins are members of St. John's Episcopal Church, where he serves as a member of the Vestry. He is known for his strong and decisive moves in matters pertaining to the advancement of his parish. Both members of the family are active in civic affairs as well as charitable enterprises. They are also members of the county's three historical societies—the Howard County Historical Society, Historic Ellicott Mills, Inc. and the newly-formed Friends of the Patapsco Institute.

*   *   *

The Jenkins House, as it has since become known, has undergone a number of changes since its erection. Aside from the addition of the southeast wing, the roof of the main house was raised to resemble a mansard roof from the front only. The third-story twin-dormered windows are crowned by a modified pediment, while the rest of the windows on the front of the house are accented by white louvered shutters.

A beautiful recessed doorway, showing the full thickness of the granite walls, is probably the most outstanding feature of the house. Boxwood, flowering shrubs, and the foliage of large trees help set off the rugged beauty of this old and historic home.

To the writer's knowledge, the house was opened to the public on but one occasion, during the 1955 Howard County House and Garden Tour. At that time special attention was called to the lovely interior with its original poplar floors, brass hardware, and deep eighteen-inch sills.

Mr. and Mrs. Jenkins, who purchased the old home in 1947 from Mr. Rogers and restored it to its present condition, are to be commended for the beautiful and exacting restoration they have achieved. Unfortunately, for many years the story of this lovely home remained confused and all but lost to the public, it being referred to merely as "a private home thought to have been built about 1840." In actuality, from all indications, 34 Church Road is, at least in part, far more than that. It is now believed to be one of Ellicott City's original landmarks. As such, it warrants special recognition.

Without the foresight of the Ellicott family, this little mill town might well have died many years ago, its buildings crumbled to dust, had they been built of less sturdy materials. But this was not to be.

Today the people of Ellicott City are proud of 34 Church Road, and are grateful to Mr. and Mrs. Jenkins for their contribution to the mill town's restoration program. Their preservation and beautification of still another of the town's earliest structures will be noted for years to come.

*   *   *

2003 UPDATE

Although we were unable to gain entrance to this home, located next door to the Emory United Methodist Church, from the exterior it seems to be quite well maintained and appreciated.

*   *   *

CASTLE ANGELO

In 1831 when Ellicott's Mills was receiving nationwide recognition as a town of significant importance, due to the construction of the first B. & O. Railroad terminal within its limits, a Frenchman, Monsieur Samuel Vaughn, decided to make the little mill town his home. Choosing a site overlooking the Patapsco River on a spot known as Tarpeian Rock, he built in miniature a tiny chateau fashioned after a French castle known as Castle Angelo, or The Castle on the Rocks.

Constructed of native granite and imported lumber, in which a knot has yet to be found, its original turrets and low parapets, as well as its Gothic windows and octagonal brick chimneys, immediately became objects of curiosity and constant observation.

Monsieur Vaughn, an artist of fair repute and designer of his own unique chateau, called the place Angelo, after the immortal Michelangelo. Today it is referred to simply as "the castle" or as "Angelo Cottage."

When completed the structure was in the shape of a cross, but subsequent small additions now conceal the original sharp lines. Although the rooms are small, the studio boasts a vaulted ceiling two stories high, with a huge Gothic window forming one entire wall. There is a balcony overlooking the studio room as well as

133

the river. Despite the few alterations and minor additions, the interior remains much as it was upon completion.

However, the exterior has undergone several more pronounced changes. The little castle which was originally finished in yellow stucco or rough cast, as it was known, is today covered with stained cedar shingles. The main entrance which was once protected by a miniature portico has also been altered. The portico has been removed and the chapel-like entrance is now fully exposed. Framed by the branches of numerous trees, the effect is both picturesque and reminiscent of its French influence.

According to the book MARYLAND—A GUIDE TO THE OLD LINE STATE, published in 1940 by the Works Progress Administration, the castle "aroused such curiosity that the Baltimore and Ohio Railroad ran excursion trains from Baltimore in 1831" just to view this phenomenon.

Following a trip to France and upon his return to the vastly expanding town, Monsieur Vaughn was both startled and completely dismayed by the utter lack of privacy and the over-crowded conditions of the once-peaceful little country town. He sold his beautifully designed castle to Mr. Andrew McLaughlin who, in turn, "held a great lottery of his estates, and Angelo Cottage was one of the first prizes." All this took place within a mere two years of its existence.

The original lottery poster, which includes a woodcut of Ellicott's Mills during the early 19th century, is still well preserved and is, on occasion, put on public display. (A past owner of Angelo Cottage, Mrs. Frank Hazel, holds a duplicate copy of this rare item.)

A print entitled "Patapsco Female Institute—Ellicotts Mills, Maryland," published in 1857 by Charles Koehl, Professor of Fine Arts, also includes the castle in all its charm. A number of years ago a copy of this print, once the property of Marion Meade, Jr. of Ellicott City, was reproduced in the local paper along with an article including this statement: "Down the hill from the female academy and slightly to the right is the building known as the Angelus." (Either a typographical error or misunderstanding accounts for the misnomer.) The article further states that it was once used as a home for Civil War veterans.

Although verification of this statement has as yet to be uncovered, the claim seems reasonable when one recalls that during the War Between the States the old Quaker Meeting House was in fact used as a hospital following the Battle of the Monocacy. Other local homes and buildings were also pressed into service.

According to the Atlas compiled and published in 1878 by G. M. Hopkins from actual surveys of Howard County, the owner of Angelo Cottage at that time was one William Lawrence. Whether he acquired the property by inheritance or by purchase remains unknown.

The Gothic Revival house located on Church Road (formerly known as Institute Road) served as a chapel during the building of St. Paul's Catholic Church. Masses were said here on Sundays for members of this denomination, and for a period of at least two years, it was also used as a rectory.

Today Angelo Cottage still stands in an exceptional state of preservation. It perches serenely on the side of a hill and over-looks the small but active little town with an outward display of cool detachment. Although the Baltimore and Ohio Railroad no longer runs excursions to view the little castle, it remains one of Ellicott City's best-known landmarks.

After many years and many occupants, Castle Angelo became, once again, the home of another artist who, like the builder, made the most of its many picturesque and novel features.

Mrs. Virginia Watkins Hazel, whose father Samuel H. Watkins purchased Angelo Cottage from the heirs of John T. Ray in 1912, lived here all her life until mid-summer, 1968. Always a gracious and kindly lady who was generous with her time when questioned concerning the Cottage, Mrs. Hazel had many interesting tales to tell.

Possibly the most humorous of these was the one concerning her sister's tour of France in quest of the chateau which served as model for Monsieur Vaughn's miniature here in America. Having been emphatically assured that such a castle did indeed exist—Castle Angelo by name—she and her party decided to accept the energetic plea of a young but impetuous bus driver who was certain he could find it. He proceeded at great rate to seek it out. However, he succeeded only in getting lost and having to retrace his steps over and over again. His accuracy did not match his enthusiasm for the hunt, nor did the latter spare him his final embarrassment. After a full day of searching—the last half of which was spent in awkward silence—he was forced to deposit his frustrated passengers at the original point of departure. Offering to return again the next day with more definite information he left, his shoulders sagging. For obvious reasons he was not heard from again. A Castle Angelo in France there is! But its location remains to this day the secret of Monsieur Samuel Vaughn.

Of further interest to even the most casual tourist is the fact that during his many visits to Ellicott City, the late H. L. Mencken (who spent considerable time at the Vineyard, an estate close by which has since disappeared) was drawn to the Cottage on numerous occasions. It held a particular fascination for him, a fact not too difficult to understand.

However, Mrs. Hazel's courtesy was not limited to persons of rank or prestige alone. She was equally courteous to amateur history "buffs" as well as curious students from nearby colleges. She was known on many occasions to willingly forego her privacy for as much as several hours to show her treasures to genuinely interested visitors. It was not uncommon for her to extend the invitation to a warm cup of tea as she fondly repeated the history of her quaint home.

As might be expected, legend tells us that Castle Angelo harbors a ghost of its own in the basement who, if antagonized, "will drag you down a narrow hole into the river." The origin of this story remains unknown, but a number of the town's senior citizens offer this explanation. Having built his home in the shape of a Christian Cross, the builder returned, in spirit, to protest the changes made by a Rev. Moor who is said to have been the first to "hear the sounds emanating from the basement."

Despite the fact that others also claim to have heard the strange noises, Mrs. Hazel never complained of any such disturbances. Perhaps she was spared since she, too, was a gifted and appreciative artist, separated from her ingenious predecessor only by a matter of years, but forever united through a mutual respect and admiration for this, Monsieur Vaughn's fascinating creation.

Although the Cottage is not generally open to the public and has seldom been included in the County House and Garden Tours, it can be seen from many vantage points. Any of the local people are more than happy to guide the tourist to the closest one, for pride in their Castle has never diminished.

So it is that today Angelo Cottage still stands, much as it stood when first erected—looking out over the historic and picturesque little town which attracted its builder more than a century ago. It was then, and remains today, one of Ellicott City's most unique attractions.

It is to be hoped the new owners will find here what Mr. Vaughn failed to find—peace and contentment and satisfaction, secure in the knowledge that neither change nor progress will reach their door only to obliterate the unobstructed view of the Patapsco and its eternal Tarpeian Rock.

*   *   *

2003 UPDATE

"Almost sliding down the hill" is the way Nathan Kealey, son of Castle Angelo's currents owners, described the precarious condition of the building when purchased by his parents nearly two decades ago. However, the property was about to be rescued by a family who, with a lot of love and a great deal of hard work, has returned the 1830's era building to glory.

In 1984 Castle Angelo, on an acre and a half of mostly vertical land, was purchased from the Peter van Rossum family by Louise and James Kealey, who moved in with their five children, then ranging in age from infancy to twelve years old. The children are now grown, and Louise and her second husband, Archie Minneman, have spent the past few years on assignment in Europe while son Nathan and his wife have made Castle Angelo their home.

Over the years the changes this family has accomplished have resulted in a home greatly altered from the building they purchased. The immediate changes were necessitated by the fact that they learned soon after moving in that the house was threatening to literally slide down the hill; it had to be shored up. Next, they acquired extra space for five children by remodeling the basement, which originally had a dirt floor.

In 1986-87 they gutted the basement level; only one room on this level was not demolished. They set steel in place and rebuilt the house from there. They jacked up the house and removed the roof. The lower level is now decidedly not basement-like, with windows several stories above the dramatically steep slope offering sweeping vistas of the town and the river valley. A modern bathroom incorporates a stone wall around which the house is built. Hand painted Delft tiles (a specialty of the former owners) surround the basement's stone fireplace. These tiles, designed by Delft Gallery, were created for the summerhouse of Historic Ellicott City, Inc.'s second Decorator Show House, MacAlpine.

On the first floor, the family made more fine improvements. The front entrance hall features a cathedral ceiling and a new custom-made staircase. The current kitchen, remodeled around 1991, was formerly the dining room, while the current laundry room was fashioned from the former kitchen. In all the work, they made every effort to retain existing moldings and trim.

Wilson's Lumber Company did the custom work of restoring interior windows and replacing exterior ones. They stripped and saved other windows where possible. In 1994/95, the family gutted and rebuilt the library, with its beautiful Gothic window, retaining the carved wooden fireplace and moldings.

Exterior renovation was equally extensive and even more challenging, with the family doing most of the work themselves. In the 1980's they removed the aluminum siding and the underlying rotted wood. They removed two old roofs and replaced them with new plywood and shingles, making improvements to the interior during the winter and to the exterior during the summer. Amazingly, they accomplished much of the exterior work on scaffolding that extended 30 feet above the sloping ground on which the house sits.

The family found a product called "Dryvit" that is stucco-like and durable to cover the outside. They created new walls with plywood and fiberglass. They covered joints with mesh, followed by two to four coats of "Dryvit." They began this work in 1995 and completed it in August, 1998. After several years of tarps on the roof, family and local residents alike celebrated the completion of Castle Angelo's exterior.

Inside, the family added central air conditioning and heat in 1999. Prior to that time two wood stoves provided the primary source of heat. And the work continues. There are plans for new gardens and for sturdy exterior stairs with a handrail leading to the home, to replace the set of steep steps now leading from a paved upper parking area.

As far as is known, Castle Angelo hasn't hosted any unearthly visitors and has no ghost stories to tell, but then, the family has been a bit too busy to notice!

*   *   *

LINWOOD

At the terminus of Church Road, there rises an immense stone house known as Linwood. Based on its many outstanding architectural features which bear a distinct similarity to those executed in the last half of the 18th century, the older section is believed to have been built shortly after the founding of Ellicott's Mills, possibly in the 1780s, while the newer wing is known to be well over one hundred years old. Constructed of granite quarried locally, the original house was erected by slaves who had quarters near the old barn. (The latter building still stands, although it is in a badly deteriorated condition.)

Over the years Linwood grew from a comparatively small house to its present size of seventeen rooms, an attic, full basement, and an outstanding "great hall." The double-door entrance opens into the hall which runs the full depth of the house. A magnificent spiral stairway, rising from the first floor to the attic, is perhaps the most remarkable feature of the entire structure, although the woodwork, fireplaces, floors and various types of windows—many with inside shutters—are of handsome design and workmanship.

Many of the window panes are the original sand glass. Age has made them brittle and easy to break. However, scratched lightly into one of the panes in the newer addition is the date 1865. It is signed "Martha."

The huge basement at Linwood is of particular interest, divided as it is into numerous rooms by walls of stone. There is much speculation as to its original use. It is known that part of it consisted of the first kitchen which was located beneath the dining room. Here we find a gigantic fireplace and a dumb-waiter which conveyed the food to the waiting servants on the floor above. Another room, with earthen floor, was used as a storage bin for potatoes, onions, and other rooted vegetables, as well as a shelved locker for home-canned foods. However, there appears to have been no provision made for the proverbial wine cellar.

The remaining rooms, cavernous in size and appearance and without light or ventilation of any kind, are paved with bricks set in sand. Eerie and unbelievably depressing, these chambers impressed the writer as being of ominous origin. The sight of them invariably raises questions in the minds of spectators. Local legend declares they were once used as slave dungeons for unruly offenders. However, upon inquiry, the writer was informed that no one wishes to admit to this possibility, although neither will anyone familiar with the history of Linwood deny it.

*   *   *

Linwood stands in the center of a four and one-half acre tract of land dotted with trees of tremendous size and ancient vintage. One unidentified species, of lacy foliage, but shaped like a huge Christmas tree, has been dubbed "the long fingerleaf tree." It is said that no other tree of its kind has as yet been located in the country. Until proven otherwise, it claims the distinction of being "one-of-a-kind." Other specimens include black beech, tamarack and linden. Many of these trees are at least two hundred years old. They alone are worth seeing, whether or not the visitor is granted admission to the great house.

*   *   *

Believed to have been built by a Mr. Hare whose family occupied it for several years, Linwood has changed hands a number of times since its erection.

In the mid-1800s, Major Washington Peter of Tudor Place, Georgetown, bought the beautiful estate so his daughters could attend the exclusive Patapsco Female Institute. The house grew in size and prestige until it became one of Ellicott City's most impressive mansions.

The Peters were related to several of this country's leading families including the Washingtons, the Balls, and the Lees. There were five children: George, who was the last to survive; Parke Custis; Gabriella (or Ella), who became Mrs. George Mackubin of MacAlpine; Emily, and Mildred Lee.

At one time Linwood was famous for its boxwood gardens. Slips were taken to Tudor Place from Mt. Vernon and when firmly rooted, brought to Ellicott City in saddle bags. However, over the years the grown plants have disappeared. Their destination remains unknown.

The days of the Civil War were difficult ones for Major Peters and his family who, as might be expected, shared the sentiments of his Virginia kinsmen. Ellicott City being divided in sympathies but remaining primarily pro-Union, had little or no understanding of the Major's position.

Although there is no evidence that the Major ever spoke out in defense of either the Union or the Confederacy, it is a well-established fact that following the war, General Robert E. Lee, cousin of Mrs. Peter, refused to recognize any member of the family who had fought in the Union ranks or who had been in any way sympathetic toward them. It is also a matter of record that in 1870 General Lee visited the Peter family in Linwood. According to Douglas Southall Freeman, author of R.E. LEE—A BIOGRAPHY, on June 30th, 1870 General Lee set out for Baltimore alone, to consult doctors concerning his failing health. One leading physician, Dr. Thomas Hepburn Buckler, recently returned from Paris, was to be seen. The General stayed with relatives, the Taggert family, until the preliminary examinations were completed on July 4th. He then went to visit Major Washington Peter of Ellicott City. He returned to Baltimore for a second examination by Dr. Buckler, then retraced his steps once more to the Ellicott City area where he visited with another cousin, Charles Henry Carter of Greenwood. He remained here more than a week after which, on July 14th, he recrossed the Potomac for the last time.

While at Linwood, General Lee is believed to have slept in one of the two rooms across the hall from the master bedroom, although no notation was made of the event.

*   *   *

Linwood was later sold to Judge Richard Merrick of Washington, D.C. He and his family made it their summer home, but maintained a permanent residence in the nation's capital. Miss Mary Merrick is well-remembered by a number of Ellicott City's outstanding citizens. She was described to the writer as having been "a true aristocrat and a devout Catholic." The Merrick family is also mentioned in Brother Fabrician's book, ST. PAUL'S CHURCH AND PARISH, ELLICOTT CITY, MARYLAND, as an exceedingly good and generous family.

While still a very young girl, Miss Merrick suffered a severe accident which left her crippled for the remainder of her life. Thereafter she spent her days in a wheelchair making layettes for less fortunate children. Upon her return to Washington, she founded The Christ Child Society, a Catholic charity organization, which is still extant. It is today being supported by the Archdiocese of Washington. Before leaving Linwood Miss Merrick built a small outdoor shrine to the Infant, the remains of which still stand on the grounds.

Upon her return to the District Miss Merrick also established Settlement House in Northeast Washington. She also founded the Christ Child Convalescent Home in Rockville, which now serves as a home for disturbed children.

Shortly before World War II a book and antique shop was opened in Georgetown to help finance Miss Merrick's many enterprises. It is known as "The Christ Child Opportunity Shop." Merrick Camp for Girls, at Annapolis, followed; then Merrick's Boys Camp. The latter is still operating.

Among Miss Merrick's workers was one Jeanne Simons of the Netherlands. She was destined to play an important role in the continuation of Miss Merrick's work. After the War a Christ Child Playground was established in the Hague. This was the direct result of the efforts made by Miss Simons during a visit to her home. It, too, is still operating, the funds being supplied by the American Embassy. It is open to children of all denominations. Another such playground was also opened in Cambridge, Massachusetts, and is believed to still be in existence as of this writing.

*   *   *

When the Merricks returned to Washington, Linwood was purchased by Mr. and Mrs. Frank Peach, the parents of eleven children. Following Mr. Peach's untimely death, his widow remained in the house, determined that her large family would be raised in the historic home. She was undeniably a woman of remarkable stamina and determination who met each challenge with great fortitude.

Finally in April, 1955, with her family responsibilities fulfilled, Mrs. Peach sold Linwood, reserving all but four and one-half acres of the original property. She now makes her home in a small house next to Linwood, within easy sight of the old landmark.

*   *   *

Shortly thereafter the beautiful estate became the Linwood Child Center, an incorporated school, described as a "miracle center for disturbed children." With the generous assistance of Mr. Milton S. Kronheim, Sr. of Washington, D. C., it opened its doors in June, 1955 under the Directorship of Miss Jeanne M. Simons, formerly of the Christ Child Society. She did not know at the time of her acceptance that her new assignment would take her once more to the home of her former employer and dear personal friend, Miss Merrick.

As a pioneer in the treatment of mentally disturbed children —not to be confused with mentally retarded children—Miss Simons has brought new hope and anticipation into the lives of many of her young students.

One child who entered the center in 1956, and who beforehand could not be "reached" by either public or private schools, a psychiatrist, or even his devoted parents, showed marked improvement in less than three years. Today he is doing well in school and can look forward to a normal and productive life. Miss Simons is convinced that without professional help during their childhood, eighty per cent of the emotionally disturbed children will undoubtedly become mental hospital patients by the time they reach adulthood.

Linwood students who show improvement resume their normal lives gradually. They oftimes attend Ellicott City schools temporarily, until Miss Simons feels they are ready to return to their homes and their own neighborhood schools. But the center continues to help through periodic consultations. Miss Simons' first experience in this field, even before her association with Miss Merrick, was in her native Brussels where she conducted a similar school with great success.

When this writer visited Linwood Center she was deeply moved by the sparkle in the eyes of the Director, as well as the enthusiasm in her voice. "There is much to be done to the house," she said cheerfully. "It was in a shambles when we came here. It will take time, but the children come first."

The down payment on Linwood was raised through the parents of the first children admitted. Then charitable groups gave additional funds and have continued to do so. As of March, 1964 contributions had been received from many organizations including the Altrua Guild, Amity, Beacon Chapter, Covenant Guild, Cristal Guild, Feldman Family Circle, Fidelton Guild, Freida Rosen Memorial Association, Friendly Hand Guild, Kiwanis Club of North Baltimore, and Liberty Guild, Inc. Also Liberty Hills Women's Club, Lions Club of Allview, Miriam Lodge, Royal Sisters Society, Sorority Guild, Triad Guild, Variety Club, Weinblatt Guild, and the Women's Club of Gaywood. Others, too numerous to enumerate, have followed since this list was made public.

*   *   *

Upon entering the house the writer noted the beautiful spiral stairway, heretofore mentioned. It was garlanded with ordinary rope from the main floor to the attic. "Why?" I asked quietly. Miss Simons smiled.

"When we first came here I discovered rather quickly just how fast little boys can slide down a bannister!" And looking up the steep stairwell she added thoughtfully, "There could be such a terrible fall..." Unfortunately the beautiful stairway will have to be sacrificed due to fire regulations. Either a firewall will be built concealing it completely or the stairway itself will be replaced by a closed staircase. Despite the obvious regret expressed at having to sacrifice a fixture of such rare beauty, "the children come first."

Already sacrificed is one of the earliest and most ingenious "air conditioning units" this writer has ever seen. A cupola atop the house, with an opening to the great outdoors and flues between the rafters leading to open and screened areas in each of the ceilings, offered a cool breeze throughout the top floor. These have all been sealed. Fire regulations dictated the necessary alterations, thereby minimizing the possibility of excessive drafts in case of a catastrophe.

The remains of an old ice pit to the rear of the house, "one of the deepest ever," was also filled and closed for safety's sake.

Today there are thirty-five students in all, ten in residency, the rest being day scholars. A new wing which will conform architecturally with the existing building is to be added to the rear and side of the old building. But even then, Miss Simons hopes to limit enrollment to forty.

On Tuesday night, March 1, 1966 particular honors were bestowed upon Milton S. Kronheim, one of the oldest benefactors of the school, at a dinner held at the Blue Crest Fordleigh, Baltimore, Maryland. Associate Justice of the United States Supreme Court William J. Brennan, Jr. and Mayor Theodore McKeldin of Baltimore were among those in attendance. Guest speaker was Dr. Leon Eisenberg, professor of psychiatry at Johns Hopkins, who praised Miss Simons for her untiring efforts and devotion to the center. He cited her methods of treatment as "highly effective."

The following day, March 2nd, an entry made upon the pages of the Congressional Record (House) included the following statements which speak for themselves:

> Mr. O'Hara of Michigan: Mr. Speaker, last night in Baltimore, an outstanding citizen of our Nation's Capital City, Milton S. Kronheim, Sr., was honored. One of the leading attributes of Mr. Kronheim is his foresight.
>
> It was he who, 11 years ago, helped make possible the establishment of Linwood Children's Center, a research and treatment facility and school for children suffering serious emotional disturbances.
>
> The large gathering—an overflow crowd of 300—was led in the tribute to Mr. Kronheim by Associate Justice William J. Brennan, Jr. Mr. Kronheim had the foresight 11 years ago to see that Miss Jeanne Simons, the director of Linwood, could successfully tackle the massive task of treating emotionally disturbed children. He helped raise the funds, recruited other interested citizens from the Baltimore and Washington areas to the board of directors and aided in the purchase of a decaying mansion on a hill above Ellicott City, Md. Linwood Children's Center has survived near-bankruptcy, lack of heat and water and electricity because of worn-out systems, a leaking roof and many other tribulations. The old mansion now is in good repair.
> ... Linwood is a community mental health center, of the type envisioned by the Congress in legislative actions in 1963 and 1965. It is pointing the way for other centers. Linwood already has given many emotionally disturbed children a chance to reach the world of reality.

Associate Justice Brennan's remarks of the evening before were also included. Two statements of fact bear repeating:

It's a pleasure to join with you tonight on behalf of Linwood Children's Center to honor my dear friend Milton Kronheim. I know of no work more wonderful than Miss Jeanne Simons' remarkable effort to break through the blur that is the world to an autistic child.

Toward the end of his address, Justice Brennan's comments included the following testimonial:

I have the testimony of Dr. Dann that Milton Kronheim's encouragement, vision, and unswerving support have been the prime ingredients in the promise that Linwood now holds for these seriously mentally ill children everywhere. Only recently Dr. Dann wrote Milton this: 'Thirty months ago Linwood was on the ropes financially. At a meeting then, you and I with Mr. James Kunen, Meyer Foundation; Dr. Francis Rice, Notre Dame; Mr. John King, General Accounting Office; and Miss Jeanne Simons, director of Linwood, agreed (and we were supported by the whole board, which, in part, you helped to recruit) that we should (1) make all the personal sacrifices necessary to keep Linwood going, and (2) have the Linwood treatment methods analyzed and made known.'

The last was most important, because outstanding scientific discoveries, once made, can otherwise be subsequently lost for generations.

Justice Brennan concluded his remarks with the following:

Milton, it is an honor for me to present, on behalf of all of us here, this small appreciation of our heartfelt thanks for what you have done to make possible the magnificent work that Miss Simons and Linwood are doing. Linwood is one of the, as yet, too few schools in the country for these severely disorganized children —and with your help it is the best.

On March 3rd, 1966 the public was advised that a grant of $250,000 had been set up by the Federal Government. This money was to be used to enable investigators from the Institute of Behavioral Research, Bethesda, to make an intensive study of Miss Simons' treatment methods.

*   *   *

And so it is that Linwood, originally the luxurious home of a number of distinguished families, has taken part in many aspects of our American way of life.

As the home of Major Peter, it offered security to a great and noble gentleman and soldier, Robert E. Lee, at a most crucial point in his life.

As the home of Miss Mary Merrick, it was the scene of tragedy. But despite her own distressing handicap, Miss Merrick found the remarkable courage to consecrate her entire life to those less fortunate than the members of her immediate family.

Finally, as the Linwood Children's Center, under the direction of Miss Jeanne Simons, this noble building has reached its peak of greatness. For where else can afflicted children find greater understanding and security than that offered by this world-renowned center? And who but this first lady of magnificent vision has introduced methods with such far-reaching effects?

Were there unlimited funds and ample space to provide for all, Miss Simons' desire to help as many as possible would best be described in a single sentence from the Bible: "Suffer the little children to come unto Me..."

So it is at Linwood. The little children do come, and they do leave—all better for the months or years spent in this truly beneficial institution.

From its beginning almost two hundred years ago, Linwood has been the scene of numerous historic events. Today, if for no other reason than its present-day humanitarian service, its contribution exceeds by far that of most other landmarks within the boundaries of this small town. It warrants the complete attention and respect of the residents of Ellicott City, as well as that of the county as a whole. For it has already earned not only the approval of knowledgeable men, but the moral and financial support of the entire nation as well.

*   *   *

2003 UPDATE

The lovely stone house known as Linwood stands at the terminus of Church Road, although access to the property is now via Martha Bush Drive, off Court House Drive, thanks to a new housing development that has grown up around the facility. The slave quarters are gone, the barn is now a ruin, but the house remains in remarkably good shape.

Visitors enter the granite structure, capped by the old

cupola, through impressive double doors, which open into a hall-way. Prominent in the entrance hall is the beautiful spiral stair-well, still festooned with rope, as it was thirty years ago—the rope there to keep ambitious children from falling as they attempt to slide down the banister. Original crown molding still enhances the rooms on the first floor, and fireplaces still feature their carved marble mantles.

The Linwood Children's Center continues its nationally recognized work with autistic children in the old stone house, serving approximately thirty children, with a staff of forty. Warren Sraver served as Executive Director for nearly thirty years, continuing the caring and progressive work begun by Jean Simons. In May, 2002, Bill Moss was appointed the new Executive Director and Karen Spence named Deputy Director. Miss Simons is enjoying retirement in Columbia.

Since 1970 the Center added a dormitory wing to one side of the building, and a ranch house is now on the other side. A state of the art playground stands proudly in the back yard of the now three-acre property. The school is equipped to handle all grades, but the average stay of Linwood students is five years. Funded by local, state and federal education moneys, the Linwood Children's Center has maintained its standard of excel-lence over the years and contributes a most valuable service to the community.

*   *   *

PATAPSCO FEMALE INSTITUTE.
Mrs. Lincoln Phelps, Principal.

- From the author's collection

THE PATAPSCO FEMALE INSTITUTE

When first the Ellicotts settled on their land in Upper Arundel, they erected a huge log building on the eastern bank of the Patapsco River to accommodate the mechanics and laborers who had come with them from Pennsylvania. The structure consisted of a number of units (apartments) as well as a boarding house. It served as temporary quarters until individual homes could be built.

They then turned their attention to the building of grist mills, sawmills, iron works, stores, a rolling mill for sheathing copper, and the necessary stables for draft horses, after which they erected their family residences. When all was in order Ellicott & Company built the first school for the children of the village, as well as those of neighboring settlers.

Although intended for all the youth of the area, Ellicott's first school was, in fact, a private school, as we speak of private schools today. A tuition was decided upon but the inability on the part of a parent to pay this fee did not prohibit the attendance of the less fortunate child. The arrangements set up by the founders are best expressed in the words of Martha E. Tyson who, in 1865, offered the following account:

> Into this school, all of suitable age were admitted irrespective of the means of their parents, and deficiency in this respect being supplied by the owners of the property. In this way many, who otherwise would have grown up in ignorance, received a fair amount of instruction in all the most useful branches of education.

As early as 1807 Henry Dearborn, Secretary of War under Thomas Jefferson, personally registered two sons of two of the principal chiefs of the Chickasaw nation in the school founded at Ellicott's Mills. They were "committed to the personal guardianship of the Ellicotts" as were others who followed—all members of peaceful tribes. The building was located east of the Patapsco River near the George Ellicott house.

150

Within a few years the increasing age and number of girls and boys "compelled a division of the school" so that in 1820 the male members were transferred to a separate building, being the small stone house beside the First Presbyterian Church on Church Road—then known as Ellicott Street. This building, which has undergone many alterations, now serves as the home of THE CENTRAL MARYLAND NEWS, Howard County's newest newspaper, founded in 1963. (See chapter on Ellicott's Second School.)

In 1824 the boys were again transferred, this time to a large stone mansion on a low hill across the Tiber Creek overlooking Wild Cat Branch, on a site known as Sam's Rock. Here the success of the school fluctuated. Finally, in 1857 the property passed into the hands of the Christian Brothers who, in turn, founded the famous but now extinct Rock Hill College.

Meanwhile the girls' school continued in the original building. With the population of Ellicott's Mills rapidly approaching one thousand, each new year yielded more and more enrollments and quarters became cramped and inadequate.

There were those who recognized the need of advanced learning for the adolescent female student, particularly in the field of teaching. But for the most part the general public clung to the theory that higher education for women was not only unnecessary, but in some respects even undesirable and detrimental to a peaceful and modest way of life, as prescribed by many members of the opposite sex.

Nevertheless, in 1829, prior to the announcement that a girls' seminary would be constructed within the town limits, the Ellicotts, who were firm believers in the advantages of a good education regardless of sex, "performed their last act on behalf of schools, being a gift of seven acres of their woodland forest, as a site for the Patapsco Institute." The ground, which lies 339 feet above sea level and overlooks the Patapsco Valley and all of Ellicott's Mills, was set aside until such time as it would be needed. Despite this generous gesture and obvious attempt to arouse interest in the theory of advanced education for young ladies, the land lay untouched for a number of years.

Gradually private discussions of the issue became public. This ultimately led to a hesitant but widespread curiosity. Men of high rank spoke to all who would listen and urged the local citizenry to take careful and intelligent note of the situation.

Finally, in 1833 the first two of a series of meetings took place at the Patapsco Hotel (August 1st and November 16th) which resulted in the formation of a committee to memorialize the state for a charter, which charter was granted in January, 1834.

On February 8, 1834 another meeting was held at the old hotel, the outcome of which resulted in the appointment of a Board of Trustees, namely: Charles Carroll, Isaac McKim, Edward Gray, Nathaniel Ellicott (Secretary-Treasurer) and Thomas B. Dorsey (President). Other men of prominence who took an active part in the program included John Ellicott, George Ellicott, Col. Charles Dorsey, and Dr. Allen Thomas. Edward Gray and George and Nathaniel Ellicott were appointed a committee of three to accept proposals from builders and architects. Before the end of the month Robert Cary Long, Jr. was chosen as architect, and Charles Timanus, Jr. as builder. The building was to be of a "chaste style of architecture" and "suitable for eighty students" ranging in age from twelve to eighteen years.

Additional land was needed and was soon acquired from John Butler, Enoch Clapp, and a Mr. McLaughlin. Including the Ellicott gift the tract now totalled twelve acres.

Thus it was that the Patapsco Female Institute was erected "in accordance with an act of the Assembly of January 18, 1834, with money raised by public subscription." Eleven thousand dollars was obtained through this sale at fifty dollars per share.

It was further supported by private contributions as well as annual grants by the state. The idea embraced in the original regulations of the Institute, which empowered the principal of that establishment annually to "educate eight poor girls, free of charge," for which they were to be paid eight hundred dollars per year out of the treasury of the State of Maryland, was the suggestion of George Ellicott, and conceivably the forerunner of today's state scholarship program.

This endowment was discontinued within a few years and in its place a lottery fund of $15,000 was set up with the same stipulation prevailing. The Institute was also partially financed through a mortgage held by the Patapsco National Bank, some of whose officers and depositors took an active part in establishing the school.

A tuition covering board, "washing, use of bedding, fuel, and other incidental expenses" was set at $120 per session," $100 payable in advance, the remainder of the charges at the close of each session." The school year consisted of two sessions of twenty-two weeks each, or four quarters of eleven weeks each.

Extra charges per quarter were: Piano, $15.00; use of Instrument, $2.50. Organ, $10.00; use of Instrument, $2.00. Guitar, $10.00; use of Instrument, $5.00. Drawing and Painting, $7.50. Oil Painting, $10.00. ' Latin, Greek, French, Spanish,

Italian, or German, $7.50. Dancing, $10.00.

Although the building itself took better than two and one-half years to complete (from October, 1834 to May, 1837) the school was officially opened January 1st, 1837. Built of a rare yellow-tinted granite, another gift of the Ellicotts, the handsome Greek Revival building was described by one historian as "so classically beautiful of architecture, so unrivaled in impressive site, so picturesque in forest environment and background as to recall Hellenic monuments of beauty."

Many years later Edward Paul Duffy of the staff of THE BALTIMORE SUNDAY SUN paper, in comparing the lovely old building with the ancient Parthenon wrote:

> The Parthenon looks down on Mars.Hill, where Pani preached to "ye men of Athens" on their superstitions which reared temples made by hands. The Patapsco looks down upon a church named after Paul, in which is a heroic figure of the great preacher, a patron of the congregation that worships within.

As recently as 1962 the Howard County Historical Society and the Ellicott City Rotary Club, in their Civil War Centennial souvenir program, THE RAID OF ELLICOTT'S MILLS, offered this poignant description of the once-beautiful Institute:

> With all of Ellicott City at her feet, stand the magnificent ruins of a once-famous seat of learning, the Patapsco Female Institute. Although partially dismantled and shamefully exposed to the elements, this fine Greek Revival structure majestically keeps watch over the town, as though hopefully waiting for good fortune to restore her to the happy and useful life she once knew.

Meanwhile, the small coed school from which this architectural phenomenon stemmed, was destroyed in the flood of 1868 and all but forgotten by many of its former students and by most of their descendants.

*   *   *

At the height of its glory the Patapsco Female Institute was approached by nineteen mammoth stone steps through a portico supported by four immense columns. A long central hallway with a beautiful winding stairway divided the building in two. There was a dining room to the right, a drawing room to the left, and a succession of other rooms, including library, recreation room, and classrooms, to the rear. In all, including the ground level and the top floor, there were fifty-seven rooms. Although there was from the beginning a small chapel, the large chapel wing (seventy-five feet long and forty feet wide) was added at a later date, as were the dormers on the top floor. From the grounds, the chapel was approached by way of a covered entrance, the outline of which can still be seen on the outside wall. A double portico is thought to have run across the rear of the building.

Such unexpected conveniences as steam heat (supplied by an early and temperamental system) and running water (from two huge water towers) were listed among the school's physical comforts. There were also two or more utility buildings to the rear of the main structure which have long since disappeared.

The grounds were beautifully landscaped and flowers grew in great abundance. Wisteria vines encircled the columns of the portico. Legend tells us that at one time the beautiful flowers seemed to spill over into the interior of the building, since wisteria-designed paper was used in at least one of the larger rooms on the second floor. Stately and colorful trees including magnolia, dogwood, flowering cherry, red leaf maple, oak, and even horse chestnut were to be found scattered over the grounds. Evergreens, including magnificent boxwood, encircled the driveway. There was little lacking by way of natural beauty.

* * * * * * * * * *

The first principal chosen for the Institute was Reverend J. H. Tyng, who opened the school in January, 1837. Although he had signed a lease for two years, he remained as principal only until August, 1838 when he decided that "$1500 was not enough to support a 'family' of twelve." He was succeeded by Mrs. Mary Norris of England, who agreed to operate the Institute as "a school or collegiate institution for the education of females." The curriculum, as set up by Mrs. Norris, included the classics plus modern history, chemistry, astronomy, and botany. Students were also permitted to study piano, guitar, painting, drawing, tinting, or wax work. Enrollments increased, but not at the expected rate.

Thus it was that in 1841, following Mrs. Norris' retirement and by invitation of Bishop Whittingham, Protestant Episcopal Bishop of Maryland, the Honorable and Mrs. John Phelps, parents of Judge Charles E. Phelps of Baltimore, agreed to conduct the school as a diocesan female school—he, in the office of Manager of Finances, and she, as Principal.

Before long enrollment reached three hundred including a number of students from such faraway places as Ohio, Illinois, Missouri, Massachusetts, Connecticut, New York, New Jersey, Delaware, Pennsylvania, Virginia, North Carolina, South Carolina, Georgia, Tennessee, Alabama, Mississippi, Texas and California. The District of Columbia was also well represented, as were Cuba and Nova Scotia, but the majority of students were from Maryland and the Southern States. Many became prominent during the harsh days of the Civil War, following their departure from their beloved alma mater. Possibly the best-known was Winnie Davis, daughter of Jefferson Davis.

Another celebrity of a different and romantic nature was also credited with having attended the Institute. She was Vesta Custis, heroine of George Alfred Townsend's intriguing novel, THE EN-TAILED HAT, and daughter of Judge Daniel Custis, an erstwhile fictional resident of Teackle Mansion, the most noted house in Princess Anne, Somerset County. It is upon her approaching marriage to Meshach Milburn, owner and custodian of "the evil head-piece," that Vesta recalls nostalgically her "happier days at the boarding school in Ellicott's Mills."

*   *   *

It was not long before Mrs. Phelps' abilities as Headmistress of the Institute became obvious. The report of the Trustees, dated October, 1842 and covering her first full year, stressed the confidence and esteem with which she was regarded. It reads:

> The Trustees of the "Patapsco Female Institute" in their Report of the preceding year, congratulated its founders and patrons on "the prospect of realizing the anticipation of its projectors, of its becoming one of the most distinguished Female Collegiate Institutions of our country." They have now the satisfaction of announcing that their hopes have been amply realized. Never since its foundation has this Institution exhibited the flourishing condition which it now presents. Its business concerns are successfully managed by Mr. Phelps, who devotes his time and talents to overseeing

the financial department, and providing for the comfort of the household; while Mrs. Phelps has the entire supervision of the educational department; and her literary and scientific character, as well as her reputation for ability to manage and preside over such an Institution have been fully sustained.

In the short space of six months, the whole interior of the college edifice has been remodeled—the discipline of the Institution changed and perfected—the accommodations and comfort of the pupils increased—and their number swelled beyond any former estimate. The original large dormitories have been, at great expense, subdivided into smaller ones, each capable of containing, with comfort, from two to four pupils; and these answer the purpose both of sleeping apartments, and of retiring rooms for study. They are comfortably warmed in winter, and well ventilated in summer. This arrangement is productive of many advantages. It precludes the many bad effects resulting from the practice of crowding together a large number of individuals into a single room; is promotive of order, delicacy, neatness and health, and gives to the pupils that strict retiracy, by which, alone, they are enabled effectively to pursue their studies.

The government of the Institution is established upon principles somewhat new in this quarter of the Union. Its grand secret consists in the establishment of inflexible and salutary rules, which operate upon all, from the Principal to the humblest dependent. Disgraceful or corporeal punishment is discarded, as, in an especial manner, repugnant to female refinement and delicacy. A sufficient stimulus for mental exertion is found in the weekly reports of the teachers, which are presented at the stated meeting of the Board of Officers, and read by the Principal before the whole school at the close of the term. In a brief address at the close of the examination (April 15, 1842), the Principal gave an explanation of her mode of government, the substance of which, in part, we here insert, as it will, no doubt, be highly gratifying to the public, to have, as it were, from her own mouth, an account of her system.

In the language of Mrs. Phelps, "the Conduct-list is the sum of the fault and credit marks received by each pupil during the term. Fault marks are given for violation of well-known and established rules, affecting the order and government of the Institution, or for the neglect of positive duties. Credit marks are given for the faithful performance of the duty of monitor." Mrs. Phelps farther remarked, "I consider the monitorial system, as modified in my plan, to have an important bearing on the character of my pupils, by leading them to weigh the consequences of actions, and accustoming them to a station of responsibility and duty. It is thus that every pupil thoroughly educated with me, will, herself, become fitted for the office of a teacher, should circumstances hereafter render it desirable or necessary for her to enter upon the profession. That kind of education which takes away from females their helplessness, and gives them firmness and decision, must commend itself to the judgment of the parent, whose anxious eye will often look to that future when he may no longer be able to support or protect his daughter."

The Trustess have found the heads of the Institution fully equal to the high anticipations which had been formed of their moral qualities and intellectual powers. The teachers whom they have chosen, are selected with the utmost skill and judgment. Ladies they are who would do honour to any society, and worthy examples to those under their charge of every thing which it is their duty to teach. Love, order, and harmony reign throughout the establishment, and each feels as though she were acting not so much for her own good, as for the general prosperity. All institutions are progressive. If such be the beginning of the "Patapsco Institute," what may we not hope will be its progress, and its eventual prosperity.

Upon the death of her husband in 1849, Mrs. Almira Hart Lincoln Phelps assumed the responsibilities of Director as well as Headmistress. In 1853 a brief but equally eloquent report was filed by the Trustees. It read:

The Trustees of the Patapsco Female Institute renew, with increased confidence, their assurance to the founders, patrons, and friends of this Institution, that it is now realizing all that was anticipated of it. That

158

Cover from an issue of The Patapso Ladies' Magazine

— Courtesy of Mr. Lewis Simpson

under the superintendence of the distinguished individual by whom it is now conducted, it has, we believe, justly acquired an eminence, as a Collegiate Female establishment, not only unequalled in the State of Maryland, but unsurpassed by any in the Union.

(Signed) Thomas B. Dorsey
President of the Board of Trustees
of the Patapsco Female Institute.

During this remarkable woman's administration two interesting innovations took place. Male teachers were introduced, although they remained in the minority, and a school publication, THE PATAPSCO YOUNG LADIES' MAGAZINE, was published. Although few copies of this publication are extant, the writer is happy to be able to present a reproduction of the front cover of one issue. (See illustration opposite page.)

Mrs. Phelps remained at the Institute until 1856. Following the death of her daughter Jane who had assumed some of the duties heretofore executed by her father, she retired to Baltimore where she died in 1884, having reached her 91st birthday.

It was written of her:

...She was a native of Connecticut and a sister of Emma Willard. Her long and active life was devoted to the education of young ladies, but she found time for the culture of literature and was the author of more than one book. Among her works may be named as worthy of special commemoration THE BLUE RIBBON SOCIETY; THE SCHOOL GIRLS REBELLION; CHRISTIAN HOUSEHOLDS; FAMILIAR LECTURES ON BOTANY; OUR COUNTRY AND ITS RELATION TO THE PRESENT, PAST AND FUTURE; THE FIRESIDE FRIEND.

A number of her text books became standard works, and it is said that over a million copies of her "Botany" were sold.

*   *   *

At Mrs. Phelps' own suggestion she was succeeded by Mr. and Mrs. Robert H. Archer who had conducted a similar school in Baltimore prior to this assignment. Ironically, during the first year of their residency (1857) the chapel wing, which had been envisioned by Mrs. Phelps for more than a decade, became a reality. Designed by N. G. Starkweather and built by William Allen, its shell still stands, a mute reminder of the best known of all the Patapsco's Principals.

Under Mr. Archer's supervision advertisements appeared in various newspapers including THE BALTIMORE SUN. One such notice was dated September 6, 1862. But because of the war, attendance dropped sharply and the school was forced to close its doors.

It reopened in 1865 with the Archers still in charge. This lease ran through 1872 when the new lease was made out for Mrs. Mary Archer only (1872-77). There are indications that Mrs. Archer's final year at the Institute presented problems, since the records reveal that she was served with an eviction notice, although no mention is made of the nature of the issue.

Following Mrs. Archer's departure, the school was conducted briefly by the Misses Annie Matchett and Amanda Taylor.

Then in 1879 Miss Sarah Nicholas Randolph, great-granddaughter of Thomas Jefferson, became Principal. Under her supervision conditions improved until the Institute was, once again, considered "a school of the highest order." New hopes were aroused and there followed a brief interlude of moderate success. But despite Miss Randolph's complete dedication and valiant efforts, old Patapsco's days were numbered. For lack of public support, the doors were closed permanently in 1885.

After leaving Ellicott's Mills Miss Randolph opened a small private school at 1214 Eutaw Place, Baltimore, where she died April 24th, 1892.

In June, 1934 a group of former students of the Institute met at the home of Rebeckah and Eleanor Harrison, which was located on land once a part of the Institute's grounds, and formed the Sarah N. Randolph Patapsco Alumnae Association. The first reunion was held at the Institute in 1935 when it was serving as a Summer Playhouse. Mrs. John P. Breckenridge of Ellicott City was present at this meeting as an honored guest. According to Mrs. Breckenridge, there were between twenty and twenty-five members present.

There were six reunions in all, with the number of members steadily diminishing until none remained to recall life as it had been "on the hill." Twice they had journeyed to Miss Randolph's grave at Monticello and there, in silent tribute, placed a laurel wreath on her tomb. The first visit was made in 1935, exactly fifty years after Miss Randolph had closed the school.

* * *

Of the faculty members several are still spoken of, for each in his own way achieved success. Miss Polly Carter, one of the best-loved teachers at Patapsco, joined her sister, Miss Sally Randolph Carter, who conducted a private school in Catonsville, formerly known as Stevenson. This school is today called St. Timothy's and is considered one of Baltimore County's finest schools for young ladies.

Reverend Alfred Holmead, erstwhile Chaplain of the Institute, was later appointed first pastor of St. Peter's Episcopal Church, Ellicott City. He served at the historic little church, which was later destroyed by fire, from April 20, 1842 through 1847.

In 1861 Mr. Alfred F. Toulmin, music instructor, wrote a stirring march which he dedicated to Jefferson Davis, "President of the Confederate States." Calling it the "Confederacy March," Mr. Toulmin offered it for publication in Baltimore. George Willig accepted the challenge and the front cover, a photograph of Jefferson Davis by McClees of Washington, D. C., was lithographed by E. Sachse & Company of South Charles Street, Baltimore, one of Maryland's most famous lithographers. Although the composition was accepted by Southern sympathizers in this state, it was not as well received here as in Georgia and the Deep South.

*   *   *

Sheet music written in 1861; by Alfred
F. Toulmin, instructor at the Institute.
   – From the author's collection

Life was good at the Institute for, despite the rigid requirements, there were lighter moments when these girls of gentle
breeding knew joy and happiness. Nevertheless certain standards
and regulations applied to all who enrolled. They were not permitted to read newspapers, magazines, or novels, without permission
of the Headmistress. Visitors and off-campus visiting privileges
were limited and for many years not allowed at all on Sundays.
Discipline was strict and consistent. However, as was the custom, those girls who had personal maids were permitted to bring
them. They were housed in one of the service buildings to the rear
of the main building. There was, of course, an additional charge
for their board.

It was customary that the students march to the dining room
in orderly fashion for their meals. They were taught to modulate
their voices. Never was one permitted to call out or holler in boisterous tones. According to their age they spoke when spoken to.
Personal opinions on public matters, openly expressed, were considered in poor taste. Politics were left to the men. Strenuous
exercise was considered unladylike, but the girls were required to
walk around the small circle of lawn in front of the main entrance
each day, in good weather, until the distance of one mile had been
covered. This was considered both ladylike and necessary exercise.

Although the Institute was equipped with a heating system,
the basement remained cold. Neverthless, during the winter
months modified gymnastics and calisthenics were conducted there
to "promote the free circulation of the blood, call into exercise the
various muscles of the body, and expand the chest..." The students
were further advised that they (the exercises) "...also improve the
pupils in the graces of motion, and inspire them with that cheer-
fulness and innocent gayety, so appropriate to the season of youth."

Dancing classes, keyed to the accompaniment of two pianos,
were also a part of the regular routine. Lessons in violin, piano,
cello, guitar, and voice were also offered in addition to the other
extracurricular activities.

At times, when the basement was particularly chilly, the
music students met with difficulties. Fingers would stiffen and
wrong notes would be struck, either on the keyboard or on one of
the stringed instruments. The teacher in charge would then—with
unerring accuracy—crack the knuckles of the unfortunate student
with a small stick or ruler, despite the chill that had stiffened the
fingers of the offending culprit! Perfection was the aim of all the
instructors regardless of talent or extenuating circumstances. The

thought of a gently bred young lady faltering during a musical interlude or concert, or during a social affair, was not to be tolerated under any circumstances.

Thus it was that the student learned not only the fine arts, but the fine art of self-control as well, plus quiet self-discipline. Many an unshed tear came to the eyes of those gentle girls only to be controlled or ignored, or gently brushed aside. Strength of character and poise were also stressed, thereby preparing them for the inevitable disappointments and disillusionments, as well as the joys, that lay ahead in the outside world.

Religious training was of the utmost importance. Although it was a rule of the Institute that all students attend services held in the chapel each week, the actual instructions in matters of creed were handled with a gentle and understanding approach. In their wisdom the instructors were fully aware of individual beliefs and respected them.

* * *

This, then, was the background upon which another of the Institute's more renowned students leaned when, in later life, she met tragedy and sorrow in its harshest form.

Young Alice Montague, kin of Governor Andrew Jackson Montague of Virginia (1902-1906) and later mother of Wallis, Duchess of Windsor, was a beautiful girl, endowed with grace and charm and a deep sense of humor. Her education at the Patapsco Institute not only prepared her to take her rightful place in Virginia's society, but also fortified her for the sorrow and trials she was destined to face. The story of her brief but happy marriage to T. Wallis Warfield is well known. But the courage and stamina with which she faced adversity following his untimely death, although inborn, had certainly been further developed during her formative years at the Institute.

* * *

But there was also a lighter side to life on the hill. At times when the girls did not wish to be disturbed for one reason or another, whether it be to rest or study, to write a hasty but secretive note to the dashing hero of the hour, or to answer with bits of mirror and the reflection of the sun (plus dainty white handkerchiefs) the messages sent them in much the same manner by male admirers at the Presbyterian Manse or other houses on the hill, they would hang a small sign reading "Posy" from the door-knob. The word was part of a code of their own creation and translated, meant "Positively No Admittance!"

A number of students inscribed their initials on the window-panes of the venerable old building, using the diamonds in their rings as cutters. Among those who indulged in this quaint but accepted hobby was the aforementioned Alice Montague. Before the building was gutted, when one of the county's more interested sons checked it from top to bottom, no trace of the famous initials could be found. Undoubtedly the much-coveted windowpane had long since been removed by another fascinated admirer.

Although the students were not encouraged to go home over the weekends, when they did, those who lived nearby often took with them those who came from greater distances. In bad weather permission to leave the campus was denied except in cases of emergency. On these occasions the big day was Saturday when "the candy man" with his baskets of goodies trudged up the steep hill, to be greeted with joy and laughter and the "unladylike" squeals of delight emitted by the excited girls. Candy, not being the commonplace food it has since become, was enjoyed as a very special treat, sometimes to the extent that having over-indulged, the girls themselves were the first to admit that "once a week was enough!"

Another well-remembered resident of Ellicott City was Mrs. Lizzie Curran, in later years known as "Everybody's Aunt Lizzie." As a small child she would watch her mother churn the butter and gather the eggs that were consumed by the students on the hill. Frequently she would go with her parent when deliveries were made, and in time, took an active part in preparing the required products.

Only the finest foods were served at this distinguished school. But this presented no problems despite the lack of electric appliances or freezers. For Ellicott City was, and still remains, the heart of one of the finest farming areas in the entire state. As such, fresh foods were available on a regular delivery basis and the importance of nourishing and substantial meals was stressed. Although the accent was on manners, delicacy of behavior, and proper attire, good health was also emphasized. Despite the fact that it was not anticipated that any of the attending students would be reduced to actual kitchen work, it being assumed that good fortune would always be their lot, they were instructed in the art of managing a home, which included the planning of daily menus as well as formal dinners and buffets. In many instances, where circumstances changed and necessity dictated, the practical training received at the Institute served its purpose.

* * * * * * * * * *

Graduation was a rather formal affair combining prayer, music, and readings by members of the graduating class. From all available information, it is evident there was little or no variation in the program. Nor were there public speakers, as we think of them today.

The ceremony opened with a prayer. This was followed by musical selections sung by a choral group, a piano duet, a vocal quartette or trio, and finally a vocal solo. A series of three compositions would then be read, to be followed again by more musical selections and readings. In all there were usually no less than fifteen or twenty musical selections interspersed by almost as many readings.

The music ranged from Verdi's "Traviata," to the march from "Tannhauser" by Wagner, to Gounod's or Schubert's "Ave Maria," to "Gypsy Life" by Schumann, to "Spring Song" by Mendelssohn, to the "Wedding March" by Liszt, giving a vivid indication of the range of musical knowledge imparted to the young ladies at the Institute.

Such topics as "Why Does Woman Write," "What's in a Name," "Woman, Her Sphere and Influence," "The Advantages of Education," "One Today Is Worth Two Tomorrows," "Farewell to School" and "Home Life" would be presented in the best possible form of the day.

Then followed the highlights of the occasion, the address by the top student, selected as Valedictorian, followed by the Conferring of Diplomas.

Closing with a Prayer of Benediction the humble but significant ceremony came to an end, and another group of genteel and well-trained young ladies became new members of the Alumni of "old Patapsco." As was to be expected emotions were mixed. There was the normal feeling of pride in accomplishment, intermingled with the natural regret of departure. But over-ruling all emotions was the knowledge that once again another year had ended and another group of hand-picked young ladies had been prepared, and prepared well, for whatever lay ahead.

*   *   *

Although there are no survivors left to give us a first-hand description of school life at the Institute, there are in the area a number of their descendants who remember well the events that took place atop Patapsco's Heights, as told to them by their mothers.

Perhaps one of the best known local students was the former

Miss Varina D. Herbert, daughter of Mr. and Mrs. John Henry Herbert of Grey Rock, and later mother of Miss Laura Hanna, Mrs. John Breckenridge, and Mr. Edwin F. Hanna, Jr., all of Temora. Miss Herbert attended the Institute in 1880-1881. While there, her room-mate was Edith Adams of Oak Hill.

Among Varina's closest friends was Miss Minnie L. Owings, the only member of Dr. Thomas B. Owing's family to survive the flood of 1868. (She was visiting her grandparents when the tragedy struck.) Varina's younger sister, Virginia L. Herbert, also attended the school at a later date.

Young ladies from prominent but more distant families were also numbered among the school's student body. As has been noted, Major Peter, kin of the Washington and Lee families of Virginia, purchased Linwood, the beautiful home now serving as the world-renowned center for disturbed children, so his daughters might be educated there.

Thomas Francis Bayard, Senator from Delaware, and later Secretary of State and Ambassador to England, enrolled all four daughters. They were Florence, Louise, Mabel, and Katherine Lee, all of whom attended a reunion at Monticello prior to the founding of the Sarah Randolph Alumnae Association. Luncheon was served and every girl present coveted the memory of a notable day spent at a notable mansion as the guest of Miss Randolph, the gracious and beloved Headmistress of the Institute.

Margaret Oliver Colt, granddaughter of Robert Oliver, one of the founders of the Baltimore and Ohio Railroad, also attended, as did Miss Ariana McElfresh of Frederick, who later became Mrs. Charles Edward Trail, great-grandmother of Senator Charles McC. Mathias, Jr.*

The Patapsco Female Institute, famous as one of the first schools of its kind in the country and a building of superb architectural beauty, lived on for a time serving in other capacities even after its doors were closed permanently as a young ladies' finishing school.

*   *   *

---

*A list of names of those who attended Ellicott City's famous Institute, now in the possession of the writer, is growing day by day. It is to be hoped that within a few years a comprehensive list can be compiled and printed as a final tribute to an outstanding institution, since time and space prohibit the immediate publication of even those names which are currently available.

For a few years the grounds of the Institute became "the nucleus of a summer colony glad to escape from city heat to the grateful shade of its wooded environment." So wrote Emily E. Lantz of THE BALTIMORE SUN at the turn of the 20th century.

Then in 1891 Mrs. A. Marshall Elliott (not to be confused with Ellicott) bought the magnificent estate for $8500 and restored it to its former glory, refurnishing it with beautiful antiques. She converted the chapel into a magnificent reception room, adding an immense and handsome fireplace.

Mrs. Elliott, the former Lilly Tyson, was indebted to her father, James E. Tyson, for his assistance in acquiring the property. Mr. Tyson advanced the money for his daughter and held a mortgage on the old estate amounting to $8,000. As a small gesture of gratitude, Mrs. Elliott is said to have had "at all times, and on the mantels of all the fireplaces throughout the house, appropriate holders for the numerous pipes used by Mr. Tyson" when on the premises.

Calling the place Berg Alnwick (or Burg Olynwyck), after the ancestral 12th century Alnwick Castle in Northumberland, England, Mrs. Elliott later converted her property into an exclusive summer boarding house and inn, "to rival the Red Lion Inn of Massachusetts." From 1905 until 1917 it was highly regarded and patronized. But with the decline in business, due to the outbreak of World War I, "when the United States entered into war against foreign aggression, Mrs. Elliott offered the building and grounds for use as a convalescent war hospital provided the women of Maryland would equip it and be responsible for an annual overhead charge of $1500 necessary to keep the property in repair." The medical women of Baltimore came forward and assumed this responsibility, calling upon every woman in the state to assist them in this undertaking.

The building then consisted of sixty rooms, including several of ample size to be converted into wards, and was able to accommodate one hundred and fifty beds. There were seven baths, two showers, all other necessary plumbing, heat, and electricity. Breezy corridors and porches and terraces of velvety green lawn were all conducive to speedy recovery. An artesian well supplied the hospital-school with ample water.

We are indebted to Miss Lantz for the balance of our story. In the July 6, 1917 issue of THE BALTIMORE SUN we find the following statement:

On Saturday, July 7, the United States colors will be

raised above the fair old Institute, indicating that once again the building is dedicated to the service of the country and, as a convalescent hospital and re-educational school, will take her place in war-relief work. It will be the first re-educational school to be established in the United States and most wonderfully is the building adapted to both purposes.

The hospital became known as the "Maryland Women's War Relief Hospital," and every woman in the state was asked to contribute one dollar a year toward its support. The people of Maryland responded generously. Aside from the dollar-a-year drive, rooms were equipped by individuals and by societies and churches. China, cutlery, surgical supplies, and other necessities were forthcoming. Financial, Re-educational, and Equipment and Supply Committees were quickly formed. Drives were launched, the Church of the Good Shepherd at Jonestown near Ellicott City being the first to take up a collection. St. John's and St. Peter's, both of Ellicott City, rose to the occasion and a chain reaction of contributions followed.

The following persons served as officers of the hospital: Dr. Anna S. Abercrombie, president; Mrs. Emerson C. Harrington, Mrs. Albert Sioussant, Mrs. Robert W. Johnston, Miss Emma Marburg, and Mrs. Edward C. Wilson, vice-presidents; Mrs. George R. Ellsler, secretary; Dr. Nellie V. Mark, treasurer.

Pride in this remarkable achievement is best expressed in Miss Lantz's final words:

On Saturday afternoon, when the Star-Spangled Banner is floated before the hospital upon the height, the building will be open to the inspection of the public and ready to turn over to the Government for war-relief uses. Automobiles will meet the trolley cars at Ellicott City, the military bands of the Fourth and Fifth Regiments will render a musical program and Col. William S. Powell, the Rev. Edward T. Helfenstien, Mr. Lawrence Clark and other prominent men will deliver the addresses of the occasion. And so, with earnest purpose and loving hope, the ancient school on Patapsco Heights will resume the activities of life and take its place in national service.

Following World War I and upon the death of Mrs. Elliott,

Berg Alnwick again changed hands when it became the home of her daughter, a Mrs. Parker. Little is recorded concerning the years of Mrs. Parker's occupancy except that it was of short duration. She was known by a mere handful of local people.

Although the property was put up for sale in 1927, it was not until the mid-1930s that it was purchased by four men: W. Greggs Gassaway, Kent Milliken, Arthur Nelson, and John Stanley. They, in turn, leased it to Donn Swann, Jr., son of the noted artist, who converted it into the Hilltop Theatre, the first professional summer stock theatre in Maryland.

The former ballroom was converted into the theatre proper which seated two hundred persons. A guest book of those who attended reveals the names of persons from at least thirty-eight states and ten foreign countries. Talent scouts from 20th Century Fox, R.K.O. Radio Pictures, Inc., and Metro-Goldwyn-Mayer were frequently spotted in the audience. Among those who sponsored the venture were: Governor and Mrs. Herbert R. O'Conor, Mrs. Charles Carroll, Judge and Mrs. William H. Forsythe, Jr., Rosa Ponselle, Herbert Bayard Swope, Jr., Col. and Mrs. Frederick A. Dale, William Gaxton, Dr. and Mrs. Adolf Meyer, Victor Moore, and Frank A. Vanderlip, Jr.

During the season the players and apprentices made the famous old landmark their home. It is said that even at this late date some of the ancient wisteria and ivy still clung to the outer walls, even as the interior bore the marks of its most recent restoration. One visitor recalls a wisteria-designed wallpaper in a front bedroom, a nostalgic reminder of the last owner's final attempt to restore the building to its original charm.

From 1938 to 1941 the Hilltop Theatre offered no less than thirty plays, some of which were Broadway hits and others, manuscript plays. It became known as a talent mine—a place to watch for new plays and new faces. One of its features, step singing between the acts by the audience, appealed to the public and added an air of festivity to an otherwise enjoyable evening.

Mr. Swann, the producer, presented such plays as "Stage Door," "Idiot's Delight," "Torchbearers," "Love From A Stranger," and "The Vinegar Tree."

With the outbreak of World War II, the shortage and rationing of many items including gasoline, forced Maryland's first summer stock theatre to close its doors. It has never reopened at this location.

*   *   *

170

In 1942 Mrs. Manola Brennan of Washington, D. C. purchased the building with the intention of turning it once again into a luxurious and exclusive "retreat." The plan never materialized. Instead, she rented it to Mitchell Gould who converted it into a nursing home for indigents (1953-56).

Upon the death of Mrs. Brennan the building was willed to her

daughter who, in turn, sold it to Dr. James J. Whisman, formerly of Ellicott City, who also used it as a nursing home for a short time. There were accommodations for approximately ninety women, most of whom were welfare patients. Within a few years the once-handsome structure became a dismal and depressing building. The financial situation went from bad to worse until the interior deteriorated and the beautiful rooms became faded and drab. As recently as 1960 the remnants of an old fire escape, erected under the terms of the fire laws, could still be seen. It was, in itself, an additional fire hazard, being constructed entirely of wood.

Portico of the Institute, abandoned and vandalized.
-Photo by Donald E. Fisher, M. D.

Finally, the home was closed as a safety measure.

*   *   *

Dr. Whisman, who made his home in Washington, died in 1965, leaving the old landmark and nine other substantial properties to the University of Cincinnati, his alma mater.

But even before his death, and before it became public knowledge that the property was to pass to the University and not to the people of Howard County, as had been hopefully anticipated, Louise Hawkins, the gifted and far-sighted editor of THE CENTRAL

MARYLAND NEWS, had already taken her first step toward a project that was to lead to honors for her paper and, happily, the prospect of a new life for the Institute. On May 21, 1964 under the heading "Is the Finishing School Finished?" Mrs. Hawkins published a brief article submitted by this writer. It read:

Ellicott City, county seat of Howard County, and center of the business and legal activity of the surrounding area, abounds in historic landmarks. Not the least of these is the shell of the once beautiful and impressive Patapsco Institute, a gutted building of eerie but fantastic charm.

Established in 1837, the gracious and stately building was situated on a seven acre tract of land, a gift of the Ellicott family. It was located on one of Ellicott City's more prominent hills and overlooked the town which was then alive with activities contributing to the history and heritage of this great nation.

The Institute, highly regarded by educators of the day, was well known throughout the country. Prior to the War Between the States a number of southern belles, including Winnie Davis, daughter of Jefferson Davis, were students here. Later Alice Montague, mother of Wallis, Duchess of Windsor, also attended and learned the art of being a genteel and gracious lady.

However, depending as it did upon grants from the State and private donations, the prestige of the Institute gradually diminished until in 1885, for lack of funds and "contributing" students, it was forced to close its doors.

Today nothing remains of the elegant splendor of yesterday. But the sun's rays slanting through the graceful portico all but blot out the shambles of the once-great structure. Brush and rubble literally conceal the landmark from the casual visitor. Arguments in favor of its restoration and preservation can still be heard throughout the state. But the fact remains that only as a state shrine can such a dream be realized. Perhaps if enough historians can be persuaded to seek out this ghost of the past and bring it to the attention of the general public, pride and determination may yet preserve it from total annihilation.

The Patapsco Female Institute, once one of Amer-

ica's truly fine finishing schools for gentle young ladies, shall always be recognized and remembered by
those of us who have learned of its early contributions
in the field of culture. Like the author of this brief account, there are those who rejoice (albeit nostalgically) in the knowledge that the walls still stand—and still
standing, defy the elements of time, nature, and neglect!

*　　*　　*

From all indications the article was well received and seemed
to draw public attention back to the prize that stood at the top of
the hill.

When Doctor Whisman's death was announced the following
year and the contents of his will disclosed, the people of Howard
County found themselves facing the possibility of losing their famous landmark. As in all such instances, there were arguments
"for" and "against" its preservation. A decision had to be reached
and a stand taken. Thus it was that once again THE CENTRAL
MARYLAND NEWS presented to the public a plea for its preservation and ultimate restoration.

On July 15th, 1965 the following Letter to the Editor, the first
of a long series, appeared in the columns of THE NEWS:

At the risk of sounding repetitious, and also of an-
tagonizing those people who are not in sympathy with
the program of preservation of our historic landmarks,
I wish to bring to public attention the possibility—and
probability—of the destruction of another of Howard
County's outstanding landmarks, the old Patapsco Female Institute.

True, there is little left today but the shell. But
there are among us a goodly number of people who literally remember the Institute as it was 30 or 40 years
ago. This was before it was used as a summer stock
theatre, and as it must have been when Winnie Davis,
daughter of Jefferson Davis, was in attendance here.

Since the writer has been active in other preservation and restoration programs, she knows only too well
that petitions to our Senators or Representatives (whether national or state) are of little consequence. For although they may be in complete sympathy with such a

project, they have no jurisdiction to halt the needless destruction of these old and significant buildings.

Therefore, if a town—or building—or room (as in the case of the Willow Brook oval drawing room which is being rescued and preserved at the Baltimore Museum of Art) is to be saved, it must be done by the people of the town or city or area.

In the case of the Patapsco Institute, both Historic Ellicott Mills, Inc. and the Howard County Historical Society are the logical groups to initiate a program of this kind. But unless they get the complete support of the people, both moral and financial, it cannot be expected that so few could accomplish so much.

The people of Howard County now have an additional incentive for staging an all-out drive to preserve this building. In the June 3 issue of THE NEWS, announcement was made that Mr. Lewis W. Simpson, renowned architect both here and abroad, has expressed a deep interest in Ellicott City, which he compares to a Swiss village, and the Institute itself, which he calls a "palatial old building." He has volunteered his outstanding talents and widespread experience to act as an advisor "to anyone who might want to do the great service of restoring it." Coming as it does from a man of such knowledge, this offer must certainly indicate to all the very real reason for preserving this architectural gem.

A benefactor may yet be found. But it is not enough to sit idly by and wait for such a streak of luck. A start must be made. Then, and only then, can we afford the luxury of looking around for help.

Regardless of politics, most people are in agreement with the idea that the first lady's program for beautifying the nation is an admirable project. Our natural wonders are truly magnificent and should be preserved at all costs. Also of benefit to the American people is the overall effort on Mrs. Johnson's part to beautify our cities and highways—whether it be by planting additional trees and shrubs or by cleaning up the slums and highways where our foreign visitors can observe the other face of America.

But in addition to these various projects, Mrs. Johnson is also interested in preserving our national and state landmarks. In a letter received by the writer a few months ago, Mrs. Johnson said: "...I share your distaste for the possibility that America could 'gradually become a land of make-believe' without visible touchstones of our architectural past."

On another occasion, from the Executive Department at Annapolis, Mr. Russell H. McCain, Executive Assistant to the Governor, wrote: "The Governor shares with you a deep concern in buildings with outstanding historical significance. However, the situation in question is one that is beyond the purview of the State government and is a matter that comes under the sole jurisdiction of the local authorities."

And so it goes...

If the Institute is to be preserved, it must be accomplished by the people of the county and those public officials who can be of some assistance. All this, providing the owners are willing to sell at a reasonable price, keeping in mind the cost of restoration.

In nearby Old New Castle, Delaware, town ordinances protect the old buildings and homes from wanton destruction. They also specify that new buildings within a given radius of the picturesque little town must be built in keeping with the existing type of architecture. These ordinances are now paying big dividends by way of the tourist dollar.

With a little thought and foresight, Ellicott City might well have developed into an eloquent example of another period. But with the loss of Mt. Ida, and now conceivably the old Institute, Ellicott City seems determined to commit architectural suicide.

Mr. Rouse, the proposed builder of the new city of Columbia, and a man from out of the County, has agreed to preserve the old homes and churches, etc. now standing on the land whereon the planned city shall rise.

Can the people of Howard County do less?

(Signed) Celia M. Holland.

Following the publication of this letter widespread interest was manifested, and concerned people spoke up through the pages of THE NEWS. Excerpts from a number of these letters follow.

Walter A. Henley, Director, Howard County Department of

Industrial Relations:

> ...Several people have discussed this old historic structure with me in the past month and have expressed hope that it can be saved. This certainly is one of our most valuable and historic monuments and every effort should be made to preserve it for our future generations.

Richard Higgins, President of the Ellicott City Jaycees:

> ...We feel that this building is a fine example of architecture which illustrates a past era in the history of our county. We would like to see this building as well as other historic sites in our community preserved.

Michael L. Grable of neighboring Baltimore County:

> ...perhaps no other single part of the State has so lavish an individual architectural legacy to squander. The Patapsco Female Institute is a magnificent part of that legacy. Discreetly screened by an overgrowth at the top of Church Road, this sadly neglected but still splendid example of Greek Revival architecture stands a symbol to Howard County's embarrassment. It remains, even in its presently crippled state, for those observant enough to find it, one of the most imposing treasures of Ellicott City. A community which loses touch with the past forfeits its power to realize the richness of the present. Does Howard County so carelessly condemn itself to blindness?

And a farmer-resident of Howard County for over sixty-five years, Frank Giampaoli, when raising his voice in protest against the increase in county taxes, ended his note on a thought quite foreign to his original complaint. Wrote Mr. Giampaoli:

> ...Speaking of these old landmarks or buildings which some people want torn down, if we need land for buildings, why not go out in the open country, say for instance Route 40. That ancient Ellicott City which is the remains of a dead volcano should be used as an antique and leave the old buildings stand. I agree with some of our leading citizens who say they should not be

Patapsco Institute

Ellicott City, Maryland

Restoration of the Institute as visualized by Richard Gucker

torn down. I know the future generation will be glad to
look them over.

And so it went. The battle was on. Before long, local people in public life spoke "for the press," and for all to hear. Senator James Clark, Jr. was among the first to speak openly in support of the preservation program. Stressing that he "would do everything he could to help preserve the old building," it was rumored that he might even purchase the property, rather than see it
destroyed.

Mrs. Phillip Hannon, president of Historic Ellicott Mills,
Inc. (which organization has within the past few years accomplished
much toward the restoration of the town) made it unmistakably clear
that she saw no justifiable reason for the destruction of the famous
building. Calling upon the county to buy in the remaining property,
once again she volunteered her services and those of her co-work-
ers where needed.

Thomas G. Harris, Jr., Howard County planning director,
and Howard G. Crist, Jr., head of the county's Park Advisory
Board, recommended that the Institute "be purchased with funds
from the county's park program."

Chairman Wilmer Sanner of the Planning Commission infor-
mally directed the staff to make a survey and give recommendation
on the possibilities for restoration of the Institute. Noting that the
General Plan for Howard County makes mention of historical sites,
Mr. Sanner argued that "it is within the Commission's province to
concern itself with the future use of the property." Said Mr. Sanner: "If we're the watchdogs of the county, we should look into it."

Mr. Lewis Simpson of Maidstone, England, one of a family
of world-renowned architects who, with Mr. B. Ingelow, was responsible for the restoration of St. Xavier's Church in London, now
known as the Southwark Cathedral, as well as the great Sherbourne
Abbey, also defended the motion to restore the "palatial old building." Calling the Institute "one of the finest buildings of its kind
in America...in all its glory still, a fine piece of stonework," he
declared: "It is powerful in its simplicity." Hoping to see it restored as a museum, he added: "It is one of the most beautiful
buildings I've ever seen." And he has seen many. His promise,
"I'll certainly do anything I can for it," is not to be taken lightly.
His years of great experience could prove a boon to those who strive
for its restoration.

Mr. Edwin F. Hanna of Temora, a beloved and respected old-
timer on the Ellicott City scene, and an accepted authority on the

county's most notable landmarks, commented: "The Patapsco Female Institute is one of the most beautiful architectural monuments to be found in the state of Maryland. The structure, purely Greek Revival in design, introduced by Thomas Jefferson... should not be merely a thing of the past, but should hold an important place in the present and future of Howard County!"

Judge John L. Clark, upon hearing that the Institute might be demolished, appeared before the Board of County Commissioners with a plea for them to "just leave it alone..." He added: "There is a rumor that you are thinking about tearing down the Patapsco Institute. You know, the people who built that building did a pretty revolutionary thing. They built a school for girls by public subscription in a time when people did not educate women... As long as it still stands, there is hope it might be restored. Once torn down, it is forever gone."

Charles E. Miller, then Chairman of the Board of County Commissioners, responded: "What's happened to us? If those people could build it, why can't we rebuild it now?" At a later meeting he further commented: "All those buildings in Europe, all the ones bombed during the war, have now been restored. Why can't we in America save the few we have?"

Robert E. Watson, associate editor of THE CENTRAL MARYLAND NEWS, summarized the general reaction of the public on Thursday, August 12, 1965, when he closed his coverage of "Ellicott City - A Granite Mill Town With An Architectural Treasure" with these words:

> ... It is as Judge Clark has said. Once gone it can never be replaced. And for those so oblivious to its glory and beauty as to say nothing would be lost, let this be their answer: That a part of an era and an attitude which daily shapes our very lives would be lost. That the presence of all that took place within its walls, the laughter of so many young women, the society of a century that we should every day be straining to understand would be lost. That a one and only, individual piece of master architecture would be irretrievably gone and lost. That the opportunity for future generations to see for themselves the power and glory of one of the giants of the American nineteenth century would be lost.

*   *   *

On September 30, 1965, THE TIMES, Howard County's original and highly respected newspaper, furthered the drive for restoration by sponsoring a mass meeting at Howard High School to
bring together those people who were interested in, and willing to
work for, the preservation of the building. The name, "Friends of
the Patapsco Institute" was adopted. Approximately six months
later the Articles of Incorporation were accepted by the state of
Maryland and a set of bylaws were written. The following persons were named to the Board of Directors:

Charles E. Miller	Doris S. Thompson
Sen. James Clark	Judge John L. Clark
Jean O. Hannon	Mrs. T. R. Whyte
Benjamin Mellor	Samuel H. Caplan
William S. Hanna	Patricia Sybert
Robert E. Watson	Richard Higgins
Henry L. Sandlass	David Buswell

Robert E. Watson was appointed chairman. Special advisors
and committee chairmen included:

James Vaughn, Legal Council
Lewis W. Simpson, Architectural Planning
Thomas G. Harris, Architectural Planning
Morton Hopenfeld, Columbia Advisor
Dr. Robert Schaffner, Federal Funds Advisor
Celia M. Holland, Historian

*   *   *

Thus it was that once again Ellicott City's famed Patapsco
Female Institute faced the probability of a reawakening and still
another life of constructive contributions. Certainly the most encouraging letter concerning the fate of the Institute was forwarded
to THE CENTRAL MARYLAND NEWS and published by them on
March 10, 1966. It read:

Mr. E. Holmes Hawkins, Jr.
Clerk
County Commissioners of Howard County
Ellicott City, Maryland
     Re: Offer to purchase Patapsco Female Institute Property

Dear Mr. Hawkins:

Your letter of February 28, 1966 submitting an earnest offer of $17,500 to the trustees of the University of Cincinnati for purchase of the Patapsco Female Institute property has been received.

This is to advise that officials at the University have indicated to me that the offer is acceptable and to request that the formal contract and deposit be sent as you have indicated. At the time the contract can be formally approved by the Board of Directors of the University of Cincinnati.

As to the formalities of the contract, to comply with the legal powers of the University, all documents should be prepared for signing by the Board of Directors of the University of Cincinnati by the Chairman and attested by the Clerk.

Your cooperation is appreciated and we shall be waiting your further advice.

Sincerely,

Alfred J. Tighe

Following by a week the announcement that THE NEWS had captured the first place Community Service Award at the Maryland-Delaware Press Association Convention in Frederick "for its efforts to save the historic Patapsco Institute," the members of the staff, as well as the gifted editor, Louise Hawkins, had reason to celebrate.

On June 16, 1966 it was announced that Charles E. Miller, Chairman of the Board of County Commissioners, had initiated the drive for funds with a generous donation of one thousand dollars. In less than a year, Mr. Miller further stipulated that his entire salary as county commissioner be turned over to the FPI to be applied toward the restoration of the town's famous landmark. His continued generosity should serve as a stimulant for all those who still hope to see this worthy project realized.

But a great deal of money will be needed (approximately one-half million dollars). Needless to say, so much cannot be raised by a mere handful of people. Nor should pride in such an architectural gem be limited to local people and local societies alone.

It is to be hoped that the state as a whole will share in both the honor and the expense of recreating this center which was once proudly proclaimed one of Maryland's outstanding Institutes, as well as one of its finest landmarks.

* * *

2003 UPDATE

The Patapsco Female Institute (PFI) has been saved, although its current stabilization looks nothing like the artist's rendering proposed in Mrs. Holland's earlier edition of this book—and retained here—which features the building restored to something more like its original state, including a roof. Preservation activist, former Friends of the PFI president, and continuing PFI champion Sally Bright described the restoration as "unique, open-air ruins...an attraction not only for tourists but for people seeking a memorable place to hold an outdoor event."

Several organizations have worked to restore and maintain the Patapsco Female Institute, including the Howard County Historical Society, Historic Ellicott City, Inc., the Howard County Department of Recreation and Parks, the Friends of the Patapsco Female Institute and the Upper Patuxent Archeology Group. The Friends of the Patapsco Female Institute group dates back to 1965. This band of determined preservationists worked hard to keep the structure from being totally ruined, and now maintains and coordinates activities for it. One of the original board members, Charles E. Miller, gave up a year of his Howard County Commissioner's salary to put a fence around the property to deter vandals.

Howard County purchased the Patapsco Female Institute in 1967. In 1976 the Institute was named to the National Register of Historic Places. It took nearly thirty years, but the County restored the facility as a stabilized ruin and opened it as a Historic Park in September of 1995. This commanding, roofless stone structure with its four Doric columns offers soaring views of the Patapsco River Valley at its feet. Elevated walkways lead the visitor through the 8,000 square foot structure. A spacious deck holds 125 people, and the portico holds up to 40 people and offers outstanding views as well.

Meryl Carmel, the first Director of the park after its restoration, wrote, "It is ultimately expected that the park will be a Mecca for lovers of gardens, historical interpretations, concerts, art shows...a place where our school children can come to learn botany, archaeology and history." An ongoing adopt-a-tree and memorial tree program ensures the continued enhancement of the grounds.

The site is now used as an active archeological site, a wonderful photo opportunity, and a unique setting for outdoor weddings. According to Sally Bright, one wedding featured the bridal couple walking to the site from Mt. Ida, accompanied by a bagpiper.

Musical recitals and movie presentations, plays, fun runs and summer camps occur there. A musician used the site as a backdrop for his CD cover, an artist had a video made there showcasing her costumes against the interesting features of the site. The annual Halloween ghost tour—"Ghosts of the PFI"—is always a popular event, featuring the participation of local high school students. Area Girl Scouts visit the site to work on their women's history badges. An annual Easter egg hunt on the grounds provides fun for younger children.

In 1999 the Friends produced a musical tribute to the PFI with an outdoor drama titled "Dear Old Patapsco," interpreting the beginnings of women's education in America, which has its roots in this girls' school. Most of the material for the play came from the original diaries and letters of the girls who attended the school.

Shakespeare came to the ruins in 2003, with the Chesapeake Shakespeare Company's production of 'Romeo and Juliet.' Despite weather that forced the cancellation of several performances, the event was very well received and planners hope to make it an annual occurrence.

The Friends of the PFI continue to pursue novel and interesting uses for the site, thus ensuring its vitality for the future.

2003 photo by
Charles Kyler.

Mount Ida, as it appeared in 1960
-Photo by Dr. Gerard F. O'Brien

MOUNT IDA

Until a few years ago Mount Ida, proud home of another member of the Ellicott family and one of the town's best-known landmarks, stood on a hill overlooking Church Road. Located as it was almost within the shadow of the famed Patapsco Female Institute, it was considered by some to be less historic and therefore of little consequence.

If the term historic is applicable only to those homes, churches, and buildings wherein outstanding events in the history of our country have taken place, or if it applies exclusively to structures dating from the 18th century or earlier, then indeed Mount Ida could not be included in this category. But this does not happen to be the case.

More often than not, buildings of another period—particularly those of architectural merit—are preserved primarily as specimens of that era, or as living monuments to an earlier American way of life. If for no reason other than this, the abandonment of Mount Ida represents a genuine loss for future generations and a break in the continuity of Ellicott City's unique history.

Although the Ellicott City landmark did not enjoy the same prestige as some of its more illustrious neighbors, such as Doughoregan Manor, Burleigh, Cherry Grove, or Oakdale, nevertheless it cannot be dismissed as insignificant and nothing more than a 19th century home. For Mount Ida had an identity of its own and a le-

183

gitimate claim to recognition. As part and parcel of the old Ellicott's Mills, and as the last home to be built by an Ellicott within
the town's limits, it warrants recognition.

*　　　*　　　*

　　Mount Ida was built in 1828 by Charles Timanus for William
Ellicott, son of Jonathan and Sarah Ellicott, and grandson of Andrew, one of the founders. It took two years to complete. Commanding in appearance, it was a remarkable specimen of the ante-
bellum period. Thus, in erecting it, William made his contribution to the growing town. However, Mr. Ellicott was not destined
to enjoy his home for long as death came at an early age. In 1838,
just eight years after the completion of this final Ellicott monument, William Ellicott died. He was forty-three years old.
　　In 1854 John Schofield of THE HOWARD GAZETTE published
an early print of Ellicott's Mills. This print reveals Mount Ida as
having three tall chimneys rising from the rooftop, two flights of
steps broken by a flat walk, and bordering thereon, rows of boxwood of considerable size. The main entrance boasts a large doorway with sidelights, and a narrow double portico crowned by an intricate railing, the only concession made to ornamental trim, other than the widow's walk atop the roof. Two-story columns flank
the doorway as well as the French door on the second-floor level
leading to a small balcony. The windows on either side of the entrance run from floor to ceiling and are many-paned, while the
second story openings_are of average size, having twelve panes of
glass and louvered shutters to close against the weather. (It is of
interest to note here that all early prints and pictures of Ellicott's
Mills include Mount Ida as a prominent landmark.)
　　At the time Mr. Schofield's print was released, William Ellicott was dead and Mount Ida had become the home of Judge John
Snowden Tyson, a member of one of Maryland's more prominent
families, and a man of exceptional talent and accomplishment. He
and his wife Rachel lived here until their deaths some time prior
to 1878 when the property was listed as belonging to their heirs.
Their only son, John, also an attorney, perished tragically in a
boating accident, but his three maiden sisters remained in the family home for the balance of their lives.
　　According to the will of Anna M. Tyson dated February 25,
1898, her share of the estate as well as all her worldly possessions were bequeathed to her sister Ida, after whom the house is
thought to have been named, and who, by rare coincidence, lived to

be the last surviving member of the family.

At the turn of the century, Edward Paul Duffy of THE BAL-
TIMORE SUN went to Ellicott City for one of his periodic tours.
Mount Ida was then approximately seventy-five years old and held
a special fascination for him. Miss Ida Tyson, a lonely but wist-
fully proud figure, still occupied the house, determined to "stay
on" in the home that had once known the happy echoes of laughter.

Mr. Duffy spoke of the house nostalgically in one of his fascinating articles calling it "the strikingly beautiful home of the descendants of General Tyson, of whom none remain to maintain the
dignity of their ancestral halls except one daughter. It is a solid
and imposing specimen of modest style of architecture, befitting
its setting of mighty oaks and emerald lawns."

In 1915 Adelaide Snowden Hodges, second cousin to Ida Tyson
and widow of George Addison Hodges, Sr., moved to Mount Ida with
her five children to care for their aged relative. Her sister, Marie Antoinette Snowden, accompanied them. Although in her late
seventies at the time, Miss Ida was spry and agile and surprisingly self-sufficient. She denied the need of anyone to look after her,
but the Hodges remained until her death.

*   *   *

Many stories are told of Ida Tyson who lived to be "ninety or
more." Judge John L. Clark, another cousin of the remarkable
Miss Ida, tells an amusing one about his venerable relative.

At the approximate and commanding age of ninety, Miss Tyson was extremely deaf and partially lame, depending upon an ear-
horn to catch as much of the conversation as possible, and a cane
"to get about."

Young John, both fascinated with and curious about the cane,
apparently enjoyed carrying it around the house, possibly mimick-
ing his ancient relative as only the very young can! On one such
occasion his childish curiosity led him to poke the cane into the
holes of the floor register. It slipped from his fingers, disappear-
ing from view, and before he had time to realize what had happened or to become even a little alarmed, the house was filled with
smoke.

Although Miss Ida may not have heard the cane fall, or both-
ered to question her visitor, the first signs of smoke were enough
to drive her outdoors, leaning heavily on young John, until the
house was cleared and normal breathing restored! A vivid imagination can easily conjure up the stormy session that must have

followed between the young and the old! Needless to say, John lost all interest in the cane and behaved admirably thereafter.

* * *

Despite the fact that Mount Ida did not boast a background as historically significant as some of its mightier neighbors, it did enjoy the undeniable characteristics of a real home for each of the occupants in turn, with the exception of the unfortunate builder.

Following the death of Miss Ida, the house was purchased by Mr. and Mrs. Louis T. Clark in October, 1930. Mr. and Mrs. Clark were no strangers to the people of Howard County, having made it their home ever since their marriage, and having lived in some of the county's finest homes including Walnut Hill and Font Hill.

This was the second time Mrs. Clark was to reside "on the hill" in Ellicott City. As a child—the daughter of Rev. Henry Branch, pastor of the First Presbyterian Church—she lived in the home on Church Road now known as The Old Manse for approximately twenty-three years. Undoubtedly she was happy to return to her former neighborhood. The Clarks remained at Mount Ida until June 22, 1959.

A tale is told of the elderly Mr. Clark who was well known and highly respected by the people of the community. To be appreciated, it must be remembered that Mount Ida was situated on one of Ellicott City's highest hills. Church Road is a winding, curving, all-up or all-down lane, without a level break whereon a man might stop to catch his breath. But for almost twenty-nine years Mr. Clark walked that hill, back and forth, each day at a given hour. It is said that one could almost set his clock by the sound of his familiar voice as he greeted each of his friends and neighbors in turn.

Then age took over and the cheerful greeting of the hardy old man was no longer heard. Something was gone. A part of the pattern was missing, and Mount Ida and its occupants were never quite the same. For the old man had added color and warmth to all that he touched, and over all who lived on the hillside. He was deeply missed. Indeed, he remains to this day a part of the story of Mount Ida never to be forgotten.

* * *

With the exception of a frame wing which was added at a later date, Mount Ida was built of rubble stone, stuccoed and painted yellow. The old house was outstanding in its simplicity of line, so characteristic of the town itself. According to professional architects as recently as 1965 when an effort was being made to preserve this noteworthy home, the building was declared as solid as the day it was erected almost one hundred and fifty years ago. Unfortunately, there were no town ordinances to which one could turn, so Mount Ida was doomed to annihilation.

*　　　*　　　*

A letter received by the author from Mrs. William Snowden Hodges, Jr., who lived there in 1920-21, reveals that the house boasted a lovely front hall, two parlors on the north side, both of which were filled with family antiques from the Tyson family, and a large kitchen which had all the bells from the bell cords throughout the house. (The original kitchen, with open fireplace, was in the basement.) There was also a fine dining room. The stairway, in Mrs. Hodges' opinion, was not too impressive, although there are those who would not agree. However, there were six bedrooms conceded by all to be beautiful. One opened on to a balcony over the front entrance, from which a wonderful panoramic view could be had of Ellicott City and its seven hills.

There was, of course, an attic. And according to Mrs. Hodges, "if lucky, one might meet Cousin Ida with her bunch of keys, and if it were her pleasure, she would escort you to the little widow's walk atop the house where the view was even greater."

There were formal gardens in the rear, terraced to the line of the Patapsco Institute grounds. Flowers, vegetables and fruit trees were plentiful. The carriage house, a miniature of the main house, was picturesque yet completely functional. In its day Mount Ida knew both dignity and security, such as can be known only in similar settings.

Today, a mere skeleton of the building remains, gaunt and bare and stripped of its identity. Despite the appeals of the local people, the order of condemnation still stands. The shell of the once-stately home is gradually disintegrating, the result of abandonment, poor planning and vandalism. Nothing remains of the mighty oaks or the orchards or the unique carriage house. In wet weather the "emerald lawns" are but a sea of mud.

More than three years have passed since the present owners acquired the property and the necessary zoning to erect additional and "much-needed" office buildings on the site. There has been a little action on the hill but that, too, seems to have ceased. Yet, before this book is concluded, the bulldozers will undoubtedly have completed their dismal job of total destruction.

Then there shall rise a few new offices and an eloquent marker reading "Tyson Square." Both will stand where once the old landmark stood, first proud and distinctive, then impoverished and mutilated. But the memory of Mount Ida's charm and background, as well as the delightful stories of the families who at one time or another were privileged to live there, will remain. For history is not easily erased.

*　　　*　　　*

For future generations, and for scholars of all ages, it is the hope of the writer that by including the story of Mount Ida in this book, it will not be forgotten or overlooked in years to come when the history of Ellicott City is finally given full recognition by a thoughtful posterity.

Hopefully, with the coming of Columbia this day is not far off. Already, with the influx of new people and homes, Ellicott City is once again becoming the focal point around which all this growth will revolve. At long last the little town is being carefully studied by an ever-growing group of "doers." And once again it is reclaiming its state-wide prestige as one of the last of the 18th century mill towns still in existence.

Rich in historic significance and architectural charm, Ellicott City cannot help but become one of this state's more remarkable examples of another era. Most of its 18th and 19th century buildings still stand and are gradually being restored. Unhappily, Mount Ida is not to be included.

In the restoration of notable centers such as Ellicott City, great vision and foresight are of crucial importance. The case at hand sadly illustrates what can happen without enlightened vigilance. Nevertheless, although destined to disappear visibly, Mount Ida will not be forgotten. For as long as the town stands, there will be those who will repeat the story of this significant building and delightful home.

*　　　*　　　*

2003 UPDATE

Charles Miller and the Miller Land Company purchased Mount Ida in the 1970's and had it stabilized. When Mr. Miller died in 1979, his son Paul Miller and Paul's wife, Valerie, became the current owners. The property went from private to commercial usage, serving as office space and most recently as the Visitors Center of the Friends of the Patapsco Female Institute Historic Park.

In 1995 Mount Ida became the site of the 11th Decorator Show House sponsored by Historic Ellicott City, Inc. The organization did a tremendous amount of work to restore the house to its former glory. Decorators for this show house uncovered some of the previously covered fireplaces; painters gave the entire building a new coat of yellow paint; and builders restored the old widow's walk to the roof. Landscapers created new gardens to enhance the property, and installed new stone walkways. The workers took care to upgrade the electrical system to handle the extra load.

Since then the Friends of the Patapsco Female Institute have used the building. The Friends greet tourists to their Historic Park at Mount Ida and use the facility for everything from summer camps for children to Victorian teas. They have furnished the house with fine antiques and lovingly maintain it.

After the devastating fire destroyed several buildings on Main Street in November, 1999, the Millers offered their assistance to displaced merchants, and local artist Bill Sachs and his wife, Carole, temporarily relocated their businesses from the fire-gutted Spring House Designs to the second floor of Mount Ida. In 1970 Celia Holland had predicted total destruction for this distinctive property; she would undoubtedly be delighted to have been mistaken in this case.

*   *   *

THE OLD MANSE

In Ellicott City on Church Road, there stands a tall three-story residence known today as The Old Manse. Described in the Howard County Tour Guide of 1959 as "a private home built in 1850," its history remains little known to the many tourists who admire it primarily for its unusual architecture and venerable age.

Built into a hillside and complimenting the town's rugged terrain, it has best been described by an early occupant who not only grew up in its environment, but who was the first child to be born there. He is Dr. J. R. Bromwell Branch of Crescent, Georgia, son of the late Reverend Henry Branch, one of the most revered pastors of the First Presbyterian Church of Howard County, when it was located in Ellicott City. Dr. Branch's minute description follows:

The Manse had a ground floor, a flight of steps above the roadway. This consisted of a small front porch, large parlor, and a small dug out cellar for storage. Above was a study, second floor front, but ground floor back, a small bedroom or winter kitchen, and a pantry and dining room. On this level also was a separate brick kitchen, connected by an open, though roofed, breezeway. Above this floor were three bedrooms, the front one over the study was on the 3rd floor, from the road. Yet one could jump out the rear bedroom to the

190

ground. (See photograph.)

There was another floor on which was a large dor-
mer-windowed sky parlor, the girls' bedroom. There
were also attic store rooms.

There being no plumbing of any kind, a well was drilled and
a pump installed on the kitchen level. Dr. Branch concludes his
description with this casual observation:

> Up the hill behind the house was a wood shed and
> what the Virginians call "The Garden House." We called
> it "Miss Jones."

The separate kitchen is no longer used as such, and "Miss
Jones" and the shed have long since disappeared, as have the old
pump and other 19th century conveniences. The house today is a
perfectly lovely home, its many fine features having been tastefully
restored by Dr. and Mrs. William Van Royen, former occupants.

*   *   *

The history of The Old Manse is, in actuality, the history of
the First Presbyterian Church of Howard County. Although the
church itself started as a mission chapel in 1837 and was located
at Thistle Mills (now Ilchester), as the congregation grew the Reverend J.B. Spottswood, pastor from 1839 to 1842, faced the need
of a larger building and looked to Ellicott's Mills for ground and
ample room to expand. However, in 1842 he was succeeded by Rev.
S. Guiteau, under whose pastorship the church was begun.

In 1844 the new church, located on Capitoline Hill across
from the courthouse, was completed. Rev. Joseph Smith was installed as pastor on November 10th of that year and served until
September, 1846, although there was no manse in Ellicott's Mills
at the time. He is said to have commuted from Thistle Mills during this period.

While the history of the church, as compiled by Miss Mary
Dorsey Clark, reveals only scattered bits of information covering
the years 1844-1849, there are a number of notations of interest,
indicative of the requirements of good, practicing members of the
faith. Among those of particular interest to the writer are the following: members who attended church on an irregular schedule
were visited by a committee appointed to investigate the reasons
for non-attendance. Others were admonished for such offenses as

intoxication, profanity, or continued absence from communion, etc. As can be seen, to qualify as a practicing Presbyterian one had to exercise much self-control and submit to strict disciplinary action, all of which contributed to the stability of the individual member as well as the congregation itself.

In 1850 when the Manse was built on Church Road, Rev. M. B. Grier, who had succeeded Rev. Smith as of December, 1847, became the first occupant. Rev. C. Huntington followed in 1852 and remained eleven years. He, in turn, was succeeded by Rev. B. F. Pittinger in 1863.

The church records reveal no evidence of Civil War incidents or effects upon the congregation. Nor do they treat with the lives of these men. But their accomplishments as pastors were numerous. They included the establishment of a systematic plan of giving, with certain dates designated for specific benefits including the local Sabbath School, Foreign Missions, Domestic Missions, and similar worthy causes. Prayer meetings were also initiated on Tuesday evenings—"one week at Ellicott's Mills and Thistle, the next week at Union and Grays."

Rev. W. A. Hooper was the next occupant of The Old Manse, serving as pastor from June 25, 1868, until 1881, when he was followed by the Reverend Henry Branch of Loudoun County, Virginia, possibly the best known and most colorful of all the men who served in this capacity. Installed on June 11, 1882, Rev. Branch remained as pastor until his resignation on October 4, 1909, a period of more than twenty-seven years.

Much was accomplished by the parish under the gentle but firm guidance of this man. The Sunday School was organized into a mission group; the study of the Catechism was introduced; pew rents were abolished, and in their place "the Church returned to its original and truly scriptural plan of worshiping God by offerings." Despite the economic depression in the 1870–1890 period, "the congregation maintained its numbers, in worship and financial support." Money was raised via a building fund to improve the church property and to enlarge the Sunday School.

Meanwhile, the Manse Society was formed. The members met once a month, combining meetings of a social nature with fund-raising affairs such as strawberry festivals, minstrel shows, or church suppers. Thus the necessary money to keep the lovely home in repair was generally forthcoming. The parishioners were both proud and humble in face of their accomplishments.

Then tragedy struck in April, 1894 as excavations were being made in the basement of the church for the enlargement of the

Sunday School. The front wall collapsed, followed by the entire building. During this period of trial, Sunday worship services were held in the courthouse and prayer meetings at the Methodist Church.

Upon the advice of George Archer, architect, a decision was reached to rebuild from the ground up. Grateful that no lives had been lost despite the complete destruction of their property, the stunned but determined members of the church started out anew, building the impressive edifice that now stands atop Mt. Misery.

Mr. Archer was retained as architect, and Frederick A. Wayland, as builder. The stone was quarried by Thomas Kirby from a local quarry owned by one of the elders. Razing of the original building began July 25, 1894, and dedication of the new church took place December 23rd of the same year, a truly remarkable feat.

In addition to the beautiful stained glass windows, of particular interest is the steeple which can be seen from almost any point in town. It reaches over one hundred feet into the air and is the tallest spire in the county today.

Despite the misfortune that had befallen the good people of the parish during that ill-fated year, in the July issue of PULPIT AND PEW, the official newspaper of the Presbytery, due recognition of the 50th anniversary of the establishment of the First Presbyterian Church of Ellicott's Mills was accorded them in these words:

> It has stood in its place with a pure Gospel and an excellent school, performing all the functions of a Parish School, in the best ways of the Church, sending forth young men and women, qualified for the highest duties in the church and state. The larger churches in Baltimore have recruited from just such little country churches.

*　　　*　　　*

Meanwhile, life went on at The Old Manse for Reverend and Mrs. Henry Branch and their growing family. The four older children, Harrison, Charles, Hardin and Desiree, were all born in Virginia. They were the first children to live in the Manse. None had ever been born there. But, to again quote Dr. Branch: "This sterility record was broken the next year, when on February 28, 1883, Bromwell arrived..." One other child, a daughter, was born to Rev. and Mrs. Branch while on a return trip to their native state. She was Eleanor Chinn Branch, born July 10, 1885, at Hamilton, Virginia.

Although the conveniences of the late '90s were not conducive to complete comfort, the Branch children accepted things as they were. Fireplaces and coal stoves supplied the heat. When electric lights replaced oil and kerosene lamps indoors, current was permitted only for a few hours each evening. However, gas lights continued to be in use on the streets of Ellicott City for some time. James E. Van Sant, popularly known as "Mr. Jimmy," was both town lamplighter and chief of police. Carrying his ladder from pole to pole, he soon had the little village bright and cheerful. And mid-winter often found the youngsters sledding on Ellicott's many hills, including Main Street!

The Branch family enjoyed a lifetime of happy memories despite the lack of present-day facilities. The youngest children seesawed out the second-story window of the old home, the elder of the two (Bromwell) permitting his little sister "the safety of the inside seat." However, a glance at the picture reveals little danger for either child since, as has been stated, the second-story window actually opened a little above ground level at the rear of the house.

The older boys had far more interesting pastimes. A signal system, set up through the ingenuity of this playful if mischievous group, using handkerchiefs, spy glasses, and bits of mirror, sent many messages—at least one way—to the young ladies then in attendance at the Institute on the hill!

Mount Ida and Miss Ida Tyson proved another diversion. Aside from using the Tyson lawn as their own private playground, on more than one occasion Miss Ida was persuaded to take them riding in her ever-popular buggy. Young Bromwell is known to have repeatedly used a subtle but successful approach on his old friend, when the urge to ride overcame his natural instinct to be quiet in her august presence.

"If I were Miss Ida," he would say shyly, "and you were Bromwell, you know what I would ask?"

"What?" would come the curt demand.

After a moment of planned hesitancy, the child would quietly reply: "I would ask... would you like to go for a ride?" And even the stern and aloof Miss Tyson could not resist the subtle diplomacy of this small child.

According to Dr. Branch:

The coming of this family made quite a change in the Old Manse which now resounded not only with the patter of little feet, but the shrill chatter of their voices. They were, however, well disciplined; this being the time and day of obedience. Rev. Branch was strict, though not stern; his coal black eyes flashed clear through one, and he seldom had to enforce discipline with his slipper, though he spanked thoroughly when necessary. Mrs. Branch was not above resorting to a "keen little switch" when the occasion arose.

Each morning the children assembled in the study for prayers before breakfast. But prayers were not said, nor breakfast served, until the entire family was present and each child had been duly inspected: face and hands, hair, teeth, shoes shined, etc. At breakfast Rev. Branch recited a verse from the Bible and each member followed suit. Guests were also expected to take part and were so forewarned. Then followed the Blessing. Dr. Branch continues:

Having just had family prayers, they [the Blessings] were brief and to the point. He told the family of one of his friends who, when he saw a nice juicy steak or chops set before him, thanked the Lord for this "fresh provision of His Fatherly Goodness," but, if perchance he was faced with a dish of hash, would say: "We thank Thee, Lord, for this renewed evidence of Thy Grace!"

Sundays were particularly quiet at The Old Manse, despite the six growing children. Dancing, cards, or theatre were forbidden. Tobacco and alcohol (as a beverage) were also outlawed, although a drop or two of the latter—in sauces or the like—was tolerated. The Westminster Shorter Catechism dictated how the day was to be spent. There was Sunday School, Church, Rose of Sharon Missionary Society once a month, Young People's Christian Endeavor before evening worship, and study of the Catechism itself.

Games were not allowed. Reading was limited to the BIBLE, THE SUNDAY SCHOOL TIMES, FOX'S BOOK OF MARTYRS or DAILY FOOD FOR DAILY NEED. This made for a rather dull day for six active children, but no one questioned the schedule since it "was regulated by the teachings and generally accepted customs of Presbyterian households in small towns." One was permitted a breath of fresh air, but only for a very short walk. But then, there was always Monday to look forward to!

The Branch children were all well educated. Having first attended Maupin's Preparatory School, the boys went on to higher studies, each according to his own particular interests and talents. Harrison, the oldest, graduated from Johns Hopkins. He settled in Hamilton, Virginia, where he died in 1956. Hardin also attended Johns Hopkins, then Princeton Seminary. Following in his father's footsteps, he became an ordained minister and spent most of his adult life in the state of Florida. He died in 1935 while still in his early fifties. Charles, who met a tragic death by drowning at the age of 23, had attended the Maryland Agricultural College (now the University of Maryland.)

Desiree, who later became Mrs. Louis T. Clark of Howard County, started school at Miss Thompson's, a private school next to The Old Manse. Later she attended Girls Latin School in Baltimore, after which she graduated from Goucher College. Mrs. Clark died in 1963, leaving eleven children, six boys and five girls.

J. R. Bromwell Branch, the first child to be born at the Manse, graduated from Johns Hopkins School of Medicine. He became a surgeon and gynecologist and spent many years in China, ministering to the needs of the less fortunate. He retired to Crescent, Georgia, where he still lives.

Eleanor, the youngest of the Branch children, attended Miss Thompson's School and then St. Timothy's at Catonsville. She married Mr. Lee O. Warfield of Sykesville and still resides in the area.

The Branch family occupied The Old Manse for approximately twenty-eight years, longer than any other family. For this reason it will always be associated with them and their descendants. Because of their warmth and congeniality, the old house became a real home for the first time in its history.

Recently an armoire, brought from New Orleans following the Civil War, was graciously donated to the Howard County Historical Society. The donor was Mrs. Lee Warfield, to whom the heirloom had been left by her grandmother. Used today for displaying exhibits, it once served as the hiding place for the Branch family silver which was stored beneath the removable top.

*   *   *

In 1910 Rev. S. M. Engle built a new Manse on Court Avenue. This newer building is said to have been constructed of salvaged lumber and other materials taken from an abandoned building on the grounds of the Patapsco Female Institute. Mr. Engle felt the need of being located closer to the courthouse, to make himself available for marriages. At the time Ellicott City had become another Elkton, where marriages were quickly arranged and waiting periods and tests were unheard of. The marriage business boomed.

In 1919 the new Manse was occupied by Rev. Wallace Fraser, who was followed by Rev. G.W. Mylne from 1920–1927. Today the "new" Manse serves as an apartment house.

From 1919 until 1928 The Old Manse on Church Road was rented. Then Rev. O. Hoyt Tribble and his bride moved in. He was succeeded in June, 1932 by Rev. Andrew Allan. Rev. I. Marshall Page followed, making it his home in 1939. Three days after he took possession a fire caused by a faulty fireplace resulted in considerable damage.

Mr. Page was succeeded by Rev. Cornelius A. Terhune, and in January, 1951 the last minister to occupy The Old Manse arrived. He was Rev. A.A. Johnston.

In 1956 the picturesque old home was sold to Dr. and Mrs. William Van Royen. Dr. Van Royen was a professor of geography at the time. It was he and his wife who restored the old house after many hours of consultation with Mrs. Louis T. Clark, who knew and loved the place so well.

Today this fine home is considered an outstanding example of the truly rugged type of architecture introduced by the Ellicott brothers which sets Ellicott City apart from other 18th century towns. It is the type of architecture the people of Howard County hope to see preserved in their mill town. And it can be said that Dr. and Mrs. Van Royen, who also identified the house by placing the sign "The Old Manse" over the doorway, did indeed do their part in contributing to the preservation program now overtaking historic Ellicott City.

The new owners of this famous home are Mr. and Mrs. Charles Higgins.

*   *   *

2003 UPDATE

In February, 1974, Mr. and Mrs. Charles Higgins sold the Old Manse to its current owners, Charles Edward Hogg, Jr. and his wife Ann Thompson Hogg. Both Mr. and Mrs. Hogg are from local families. Charles, known as "Ched," is the son of Mr. and Mrs. Charles Edward Hogg of Ellicott City; Ann is the daughter of Phillip S. and Doris S. Thompson, former owners of Stromberg

Publications. The Hoggs found the Old Manse a fine place to raise their children: Charles Edward Hogg III, known as Sam, and Julia St. Clair Hogg.

In 1989 the family embarked on a major renovation, primarily to the back of the home, assisted by Harford County architect James Wollen, known for his work with historic buildings. According to Ann Hogg, the projected ninety-day building project took fifteen months to complete, during which time the family lived with Mr. Hogg's mother. The renovation added a family room area to the back of the house as well as a large master bedroom with access to a generous screened porch stretching the entire width of the house and offering a panorama of Ellicott City and the surrounding hills.

The mantle on the fireplace in the family room is not original to the house, but the Hoggs saved it from a structure being dismantled on Fels Lane. They enlarged several bathrooms and removed superfluous closets, while keeping within the existing footprint of the structure. The original summer kitchen still remains on the grounds, now serving the family as a storage area for gardening equipment.

Over the years the family has dealt with storm damage, furnace replacement, and myriad other challenges. They have been rewarded with a fine old house that, according to architect James Wollen, is built "truer" than most products that come from a factory assembly line. Built into the side of the hill, the wooden flooring in places was carved to fit over the rock beneath, and the back of this unusual structure is a mere one-fourth inch wider than the front of the house. These are but two examples of the uniqueness of one of Ellicott City's finest old homes.

*   *   *

ELLICOTT'S SECOND SCHOOL
Home of THE CENTRAL MARYLAND NEWS

Standing by the side of the lane on Court House Road, next to the Presbyterian Church (the Historical Society), we find an old stone and shingle house. Having served for a number of years as the office of the Planning and Zoning Commission, it now serves as the home of THE CENTRAL MARYLAND NEWS, Howard County's second newspaper. The building is joined in the rear to a small frame bungalow facing on Park Avenue, which was used during World War II as Headquarters of the Selective Service Board.

The early history of the stone portion of the building, as pieced together by successive historians, leads the inquiring mind to but one conclusion.

In one of the earliest accounts of the town, written in 1865 by Martha E. Tyson, mention is made of the first school erected by the Ellicott brothers. As has been stated elsewhere in this book, it was located east of the Patapsco River. Later, according to Miss Tyson, the boys were "transferred to a stone building next to the Presbyterian Church, facing on Ellicott Street," now Court House Road.

In 1905 Emily Emerson Lantz, whose interest in Ellicott City led to further investigation of the building, stated in an article that "...close by the Presbyterian Church is the original stone building erected by the Ellicott family one hundred years ago for the instruction of their own and their neighbors' children." Although Miss Lantz did not specify that this was a school for male students

199

only, Miss Tyson's earlier history did.

Then in 1910 Brother Fabrician, author of THE HISTORY OF ST. PAUL'S CHURCH AND PARISH which includes an excellent history of the town itself, reiterated Miss Tyson's statement when he declared that in 1820 the original Ellicott school was divided, "the ages and numbers of the girls and boys" making this move imperative. The account continues: "...the male department was transferred to a separate building, the little stone house just beside the Presbyterian Church."

In his Atlas of 1878, G.M. Hopkins further noted that in this school "several of Maryland's distinguished men received the rudiments of their education." The Howard County House Tour Guide of 1959, in addition to identifying the building as a former school, also identifies it as having been "used as a hospital during the War of 1812."

Therefore, the house heretofore believed by most to have been built in 1840 or thereabout, gives every indication of having been erected much earlier, possibly dating back to the beginning of the 19th century.

When in 1824 the boys were again moved to another building atop College Avenue, the old property was sold. At that time the building was a simple stone structure, the outline of which remains visible to this day. The present building is considerably altered, having been added to and changed from time to time as needs dictated. Only the stone portion stood in 1820.

*   *   *

This same building, or at least that part facing on Church Road, is referred to by many of the older residents of Ellicott City as "the old Mayfield house." Just when William F. Mayfield first acquired the property is unknown. But a rare undated and unsigned map of the town, now in the possession of Mrs. Jean Hannon of Mackenzie Road, as well as the Hopkins Atlas (1878), identify him as the owner. It is generally believed that it was he who first enlarged the house to accommodate his growing family. He is said to have added a full second floor with Mansard roof, a distinct alteration which was noted in Miss Lantz's article. But it is doubtful that Mr. Mayfield made the other so-called "improvements" that followed. Nor did he "join" his quaint home to the small frame house facing on Park Avenue, heretofore mentioned.

Mr. Mayfield was at one time one of Ellicott City's leading merchants. Three of his daughters, Pauline, Maud and Nonie, were school teachers of excellent reputation. Pauline married a Mr. Harn. Maud chose for her husband, Montgomery Gambrill. Both men were also teachers. Nonie, the third member of the Mayfield teaching trio, remained an "unappropriated blessing."

Although the Mayfields were active members of the First Presbyterian Church, according to Brother Fabrician, one member of the family, Blanche, embraced the Catholic faith, becoming a nun in the Order of Carmelites at New Orleans, Louisiana.

*   *   *

When the county bought the property (to be used as the home of the Planning and Zoning Commission), the Mansard roof had been removed and replaced by the present pitched roof over the large front dormer which runs the full width of the house. The small pedimented attic dormer had also been added, as had the lacy grillework which encloses the front porch. The house bore little resemblance to its original appearance, but from all indications no one person was fully responsible for the many alterations.

The building was purchased from Mrs. John Weir, daughter of Louis Getz, former cashier of the Washington Trust Company, now known as the Commercial and Farmers Bank. Mr. Getz helped organize this bank and was an active member of the community.

The Planning and Zoning Commission, a comparatively new branch of the county government, was established basically "to supervise and control the orderly development of the County, that business may be located in the proper places, that industry should not encroach on residential development, the scenic beauty of the County preserved, and that the degrading of property into slum areas be avoided."

Today, Planning and Zoning are controlled by the following public servants: a Planning Commission; a Zoning Board; a Zoning Commissioner; a Board of Zoning Appeals; a Parkland and Watershed Advisory Board assisted by a Parkland Coordinator; a Planning Director and three appraisers; a Metropolitan Commission; a Building Engineer; a full-time Chief Plumbing Inspector and a Director of Industrial Relations. As may be seen, the duties and functions of the Planning Office are many and varied, but all are directed toward the betterment of the county as a whole.

The general long-range plan for Howard County (30-40 years) adopted in 1960 and including allowances for parks, highways, open spaces, public schools, churches and commercial centers had, of necessity, to be amended with the coming of Columbia. This is gradually being accomplished through careful planning and consideration.

In addition to their county-wide duties, the Planning and Zoning Commission must also be held responsible for the development and restoration of the county seat itself. It is to be hoped therefore that these man are always mindful of the following: despite the small town's prominence as county seat and heart of one of Maryland's most progressive counties, Ellicott City retains primarily its 18th century mill town atmosphere. With so much of the original settlement still in evidence, special protection is warranted against intruders who would alter the general plan. Piecemeal destruction can only result in general deterioration of a valued community.

As members of a fairly new organization, a few men have served blindly, but most have conscientiously endeavored to control the orderly development of the town as well as the county. They have striven to prevent "the degrading of property," albeit not always successfully. But keeping in mind that they have no ordinances to which to turn, they are to be commended for their untiring efforts.

*   *   *

When the Planning Commission moved to the new County Office Building on Court House Drive early in 1967, there was much speculation throughout the town as to the destiny of the picturesque old building. Before long Howard County's newest newspaper headlined the county commissioners' decision. A brief announcement in THE CENTRAL MARYLAND NEWS read in part:

> THE CENTRAL MARYLAND NEWS is tired of climbing uphill!
> The county commissioners, Thursday, June 15, leased the old Planning Commission building next to the Court House for one year to THE CENTRAL MARYLAND NEWS.

Thus it is that at least for the time being the old schoolhouse has become the headquarters of still another worthwhile enterprise. In doing so, it serves as a vivid example of an aged building serving modern-day needs.

This is as the Ellicotts would have had it.

*   *   *

2003 UPDATE

The CENTRAL MARYLAND NEWS published its weekly newspaper from the building once known as Ellicott's Second School for five years, moving in 1972 to Mount Ida. Subsequently the building was used as the central branch of the Howard County Library, until a larger facility was built in Columbia.

In 1988 the Howard County Historical Society purchased this small but charming building and moved its library from its headquarters in the old First Presbyterian Church around the corner. In January, 1989, the Society officially opened its Library. Volunteers greeting today's visitor describe the collection as consisting of extensive archives, books, photographs, and personal papers of many old Howard County families. It should be noted that the book holdings of the library have been expanded considerably in recent years with the addition of nearly the entirety of Celia Holland's personal Marylandiana collection, donated as a memorial to his parents by Dr. James C. Holland.

Archival holdings include manumissions of slaves, plus extensive government papers including land records, criminal and civil cases, voter registrations covering the years 1860 to 1930, and marriage licenses, including that of George Herman ("Babe") Ruth and bride Helen Woodford, who married at St. Paul's Catholic Church on October 17, 1914. Of particular interest is a 1784 survey of Doughoregan Manor.

A full-time Executive Director has been hired to enable the Library and its companion Museum nearby to extend their hours to be of greater service to the community. Visitors can sit at one of several long tables and feast on a wealth of information simply not available anywhere else, as volunteer workers offer their friendly assistance. Anyone curious about the County's history is welcome to come and explore.

This local treasure waits to be discovered by more of our citizens, eager to know more of the rich history of Howard County.

*   *   *

204

The Howard County Historical Society Building, formerly the First
Presbyterian Church.
    - *Courtesy of Miss Mary D. Clark*

THE FIRST PRESBYTERIAN CHURCH
Howard County Historical Society Building

On Capitoline Hill, across from the courthouse, there stands another of Ellicott City's well-known landmarks. Considered by many one of the town's outstanding examples of period architecture, it is well worth the steep climb up Court House Road to view this structure. Having been for years The First Presbyterian Church of Howard County, it is today the home of the Howard County Historical Society.

*   *   *

Although the history of Presbyterianism in Howard County began with the Harmony Presbyterian Church in Lisbon (1836), the First (United) Presbyterian Church of Howard County is the oldest continuing Presbyterian Church in the county. However, in 1837, in a little village known as Thistle Mills (now Ilchester), there rose a small mission church, the original First United Presbyterian Church in the county. It resembled a square Quaker Meeting House. The congregation consisted primarily of English and Scotch residents of the Patapsco Valley area. This chapel was built by the Morris brothers, owners of the mills, for the convenience of their employees.

At the time Reverend J. Pym Carter, who had served the people of the Valley even before the construction of the first church, ministered to them in the little chapel until April, 1838, when Rev. James Harper succeeded him. The following year a corporate body was formed "under an Act of the Presbytery of Baltimore on Feb. 13, 1839." Rev. J.B. Spottswood served as the new pastor until 1842 when he was succeeded by Rev. S. Guiteau.

In 1843, when it was determined that additional space was needed for the growing congregation, a new site was selected at Ellicott's Mills, which was then looked upon as the fastest growing community in the area. This second church was completed in 1844 and remained standing until 1894. Then tragedy struck when an attempt was made to enlarge the Sunday School room. The building collapsed and the idea of restoring it was abandoned. The ground was cleared and work on the new church—the present building—was started immediately. It was completed within six months, an almost unbelievable accomplishment. Perched atop Capitoline Hill, sometimes referred to as Mt. Misery, it looked down on the small village and welcomed all who chose to attend services there. (See article on The Old Manse.)

*   *   *

(Keeping in mind that Maryland was the cradle of Presbyterianism in America, it is of interest to note here that the first church of this denomination was erected at Rehobeth in "Old Somerset County" in 1691. Built by the descendants of Sir Robert King, Baronet, it still stands—a living monument to the memory and zeal of Rev. Francis Makemie, the acknowledged founder of the sect in America.

Before coming to upper Anne Arundel County the Presbyterians settled on the lower Patuxent River, having as neighbors the Puritans at Providence (Annapolis) and the Quakers at West River. At the time the three denominations shared a common grief—endless persecution—making settlement in this area a necessity. Here they found security and shelter, along with members of all faiths, and for a number of years gratefully accepted the protection of this sanctuary.)

*   *   *

In 1960, when the Ellicott City parish once again outgrew its facilities, the lovely old church was offered for sale. Mrs. James Clark, Sr., recognizing both the picturesque and historic value of the structure, wished to see it preserved. Considering it an appropriate memorial to her late husband, the esteemed Judge, she purchased the building and presented it to the members of the newly-formed Howard County Historical Society for use as its permanent headquarters.

To many the rugged features of the building are, in effect, truly reminiscent of the man himself.

*   *   *

The First Presbyterian Church, which was built during the pastorship of the Reverend Henry Branch, is of distinctive architectural design. Although difficult to photograph (because of its location), it has been sketched many times by artists of some repute, as well as by amateurs, with varying degrees of success.

Original in design with a few neo-Gothic characteristics, the handsome old building is constructed of huge rock quarried locally. The bell tower, one of its outstanding features, is of unusual height and is slightly reminiscent of the spires of European cathedrals, as are the jewel-toned stained glass windows.

A unique feature is the front or main entrance. The door is hung at an angle at the base of the tower. The approach to this part of the building, which once served as the church proper, is from one corner. The pews are set in a semicircular fashion, with the speaker's platform or podium partly encompassed by the audience. There is an additional all-purpose room, used by the Society for social functions, art shows, and various other programs.

The interior of the church is considered by most to be singular in appearance, as is the exterior. Although the floor plan is unlike any ever viewed by the writer, it is much to her liking. As one sits by a friend in this architecturally unusual but appealing structure, there is a feeling of being a part of the whole.

As the home of the Howard County Historical Society (which society Mrs. Clark had also founded), the building houses books, documents, and records pertaining to the history of the county. An excellent library is gradually taking shape. Items of historic significance—both county and state—are being catalogued as they find their way to the doors of this depository. For so young an organization and so small a group, this accumulation of "Marylandia" is encouraging.

Meetings are held four times a year and attendance is growing. As befits her generous gesture, Mrs. Clark was unanimously elected first president of the Society and today enjoys a lifetime membership. She was followed in office by Louis Dorsey Clark who was succeeded by S. Tracy Stackhouse. As of this writing, Charles E. Wehland is serving as president.

With the preservation of the First Presbyterian Church in Ellicott City assured, and the purpose it is serving of a permanent nature, another of the town's "obsolete" buildings has been rescued and put to good use. Thanks to Mrs. Clark's foresight, the old church now enjoys a new life in the community. A more appropriate future for so venerable a building would be hard to conceive.

*   *   *

2003 UPDATE

The tall spire rising skyward from the top of the former First Presbyterian Church continues to dominate the skyline of Ellicott City's Historic District, making this, the home of the Howard County Historical Society, an easy place to find. Aside from serving as headquarters and meeting place for the Society, the building also houses its museum, featuring a permanent exhibit of clothing, furniture and other memorabilia of times past in Howard County. Special exhibits enhance the permanent collection throughout the year.

A recent acquisition is proudly featured at the Society's headquarters. On March 15, 2003 the Society unveiled the newly restored portraits of Almira Hart Lincoln Phelps, famous headmistress of the Patapsco Female Institute, and her husband, Judge John Phelps.

Incorporated in 1958 with goals, as articulated in its Articles of Incorporation "to investigate and study the history of the County of Howard...to provide for the collection, preservation, and disseminating of knowledge and information thereto, and to provide for the collection and preservation, or display of papers, books, records, relics and other things of historical interest..." the Society continues to provide an invaluable service to Howard County residents. In addition to the director, the Society is well served by many volunteers who welcome visitors and maintain the Society's many collections.

*   *   *

ELLICOTT CITY'S JAIL, CONSTABLES,
SHERIFFS, AND POLICE FORCE

Directly behind the courthouse at the junction of Park Avenue and Emory Street, there is a small granite building known as "Willow Grove," Howard County's official jail. Built in 1878 when Ellicott City was still an incorporated town governed by a mayor and town council, it is the second building to serve the community in this capacity.

Minute by today's standards, the present jail was looked upon as more than adequate at the turn of the century. When compared to the building which then served as the original jail—an erstwhile private home in the Fels Lane area—it is easy to understand why the present structure was considered a maximum-security installation. For the first prison was not only inadequate, it was highly vulnerable to the escape artist.

Although built of stone, for unexplainable reasons it was later covered with siding and was reminiscent of earlier days when facilities were unbelievably crude. Ancient ovens were used to prepare food, and diets, as such, were not only limited and unappetizing, but at times, nearly non-existent. Health problems developed. The prisoner, whether male or female, was given only what was available, irrespective of bodily needs. Life as an inmate was indeed intolerable.

As in most such quarters, the floors were of rough planks,

ungrooved, while the stone walls were covered with only a thin coat of plaster, offering little or no protection against dampness or the bitter cold of winter weather. Rough bunks were provided with straw mattresses which, of necessity, were also used as covering. When the jail was overcrowded, loose straw thrown on the floor frequently served as bedding.

Depending upon the availability of such items, during the winter months prisoners were provided with small coal oil or kerosene stoves. When these were unavailable, additional straw to cover the floor and a blanket of sorts were issued. By pacing back and forth in his restricted quarters, a determined prisoner did what he could to ward off the bitter cold. Others, sometimes too weak to indulge in even this limited form of exercise, simply perished. The number of deaths caused by lack of heat in the first jail remains unknown.

Although the Ellicott brothers undoubtedly made provisions for criminals once the town was settled, to date no record of a public jail has come to light. Nor are there any existing records of crimes committed in or near the mill town prior to the turn of the 19th century.

*   *   *

During the building of the Baltimore-Frederick Turnpike, and before the construction of the present jail, men who had been tried in the courts of law and convicted of minor crimes were sentenced to work for the county or district wherein they had committed the crime. They were known as "wheelbarrow men" and moved from place to place. The nights were spent in well-guarded depots built of logs, located several miles apart. These depots have long since disappeared.

The offenders were kept under strict surveillance, the overseers being highly skilled in the handling of muskets. At times they were overly demanding and abominably cruel. But the convicts did not quickly forgive or forget. When an opportunity presented itself they took their revenge, occasionally bludgeoning their overseers to death.

Lack of hygienic facilities also contributed to the deaths of many prisoners. Jails, such as they were, were poorly constructed and the physical well-being of the prisoner was of little concern. Ellicott's Mills was no less guilty of these practices than were other American towns of equal size.

*   *   *

Ever since the founding of this country, police protection in one form or another was recognized as an indispensable necessity. Our earliest villages were generally protected by men known as constables or sheriffs. Both were considered petty officers and were held responsible for law enforcement. In his book CITIES IN THE WILDERNESS, Carl Bridenbaugh points out the range of duties which confronted a peace officer as far back as 1646. Typical of early colonial legislature is the law which read in part:

> Evry cunstable... hath, by virtue of his office, full powr to make, signe & put forth pursuits, or hues & cries, after murthrers, manslayrs, peace breakrs, theeves, robers, burglarers, where no magistrate is at hand; also to apphend without warrant such as are ovr taken with drinke, swearing, breaking ye Saboth, lying, vagrant psons, night walkers, or any other yt shall break our lawes; ... also to make search for all such psons... in all houses licensed to sell either beare or wine, or in any other suspected or disordered places, & those to apphend, & keep in safe custody...

In 1696, based on the practices of the earlier colonies, the Assembly at Annapolis appointed men in good standing, including His Excellency Sir Francis Nicholson, Edward Dorsey, Major John Hammond, Hon. Nicholas Greenberry, and others, a commission "for keeping good rules and orders." This was in fact one of the first steps taken in Anne Arundel County (of which Howard was then a part) to pass laws and by-laws governing the actions of the people, to define right from wrong, and to designate that which was legal from that which was illegal. Anyone found guilty of defying these principles was subject to punishment.

For many years culprits or offenders were publicly disciplined. The whipping post was the most common form of castigation. A number of these posts can still be found throughout the country, primarily in small towns where the past has been preserved or restored for today's tourist. Although pillories are also generally included in the reconstruction of pioneer villages as an example of one of the earliest forms of punishment, most historians agree they were seldom used.

In certain areas rooms beneath the surface of the ground, i.e. dungoons, were in constant use; while in others it was an accepted practice for the man appointed sheriff or constable to have erected, outside his home, a crude building with barred windows and doors.

These served as the harshest of all jails. A few still stand and may yet be seen throughout the state, but unless identified by public markers or pointed out by local historians, they are seldom recognized by the casual tourist. Today they are used as tool sheds, storage houses, or even less dignified chicken coops. To the onlooker it seems inconceivable that a man could survive in a place such as this, but survive he did.

*   *   *

Despite the steps taken in 1696 by the Assembly at Annapolis to provide actual police protection as it is known today, it was not until after many other buildings were erected, including the State House, a market house, a school, and a church, that the government finally issued the order to build a jail. Upon its completion, Annapolis became "the chief seat of justice, where all writs were made returnable."

Thus it was that, other than the small jails described above, few public prisons were erected outside the capital. These conditions prevailed throughout the 18th and early 19th centuries.

During the harsh days of the Civil War, for lack of better facilities, acres of ground were frequently fenced and policed by military guards, but no overhead shelter was provided. The prisoner soon learned to improvise for himself. Only in the larger cities such as Washington and Baltimore could one find a prison of any size. As these overflowed with captives, the authorities resorted to using above-ground dungeons such as those to be found at Fort McHenry in Baltimore, and Fortress Monroe at Old Point Comfort, Virginia.

With the cessation of hostilities, Union forces policed the Southern states and jails grew in size and importance. Before the turn of the 20th century, the police force, as such, had become an integral part of the governing body in every town, village and city. Military police became a thing of the past and United States Marshalls demanded, and got, the respect of the people for their courage and fearlessness in maintaining peace and order.

Like all other small towns in the United States, Ellicott City also felt the pangs of growth and progress in the field of law enforcement.

However, until the actual establishment of a modern-day police force, the most important law enforcement officer in town was the sheriff. As far back as 1838 he was considered the chief peace officer in Upper Arundel. As time went by he was charged with many duties including "the supervision of executions, the delivery of prisoners to the state penitentiary, the collection of all fines, penalties and forfeitures imposed by the courts," as well as the custody of county prisoners. The first sheriff was also the tax collector until the appointment of a treasurer in 1850. In addition to a small salary, he received "a fixed sum for the keep of each prisoner," plus a percentage of the money collected. His income was further subsidized by an allowance for traveling expenses.

At the turn of the 20th century the sheriff was authorized to appoint a warden of the county jail, who had living quarters in the building, as well as temporary deputies when necessary.

Today the sheriff "is elected for a term of four years and receives an annual salary... He serves as an agent of the court, maintains and supervises the county jail and is responsible for appointing jail wardens." He may still commission deputies when necessary, but he has no jurisdiction over county police appointed by the local authorities. His records of those committed to jail are kept in the warden's office in the jail house.

*   *   *

According to Dr. J.R. Bromwell Branch, before the turn of the century law enforcement was in the hands of Ellicott City's venerable sheriff, James E. Van Sant, better known as "Mr. Jimmy." To quote Dr. Branch:

> He was a tall, spare, middle-aged man, with a flowing white beard—of this he was inordinately proud, and as he said "kept well laundered." In addition to his police duties, Mr. Jimmy was the town lamplighter. As regularly as the sun set, Mr. Jimmy could be seen walking up Church Street with a ladder over his shoulder to light the lamp in front of the Lutheran Church. This was as far as he went in that direction.

The jailer was Mr. Ray.

*   *   *

In 1904 Julius Wosch, then thirty-one years of age, was sworn in as constable. Later he was appointed chief of police. On occasion he was assisted by E. Russell Moxley, but according to one source, for the most part "he was the town's entire police force for thirty-five years." With his wife, the former Ethel Betts, he maintained a home on Main Street.

Well known throughout the county, Constable Wosch was highly respected by the police force of Baltimore City as well as the
members of the B. & O. Railroad Company, whose property in the
small mill town was carefully guarded by him. Although the people
of the community accorded him great respect, many looked upon
Mr. Wosch in awe, for it is said that his ability to enforce the law
was such that on many occasions he merely sent for the offenders,
rather than go personally, and they would report promptly, no matter what the charge!

It has been written of him:

In 1904 he became Ellicott City's police chief, detective, patrolman and desk sergeant. He set up a police station and magistrate's court in his own home town
at no rental cost to the city.

He personally equipped a complete bureau of identification, with facilities for fingerprinting and other re-
cordings. He exchanged identification records with
other large cities of the country and thereby picked up
many notorious characters wanted by metropolitan police forces. His crime detection methods and their results made him famous throughout the East.

... During his service on the police force Mr. Wosch
had many adventures and several narrow escapes from
death. One winter night a Negro was burned to death on
a nearby farm. Detective Wosch examined the room,
found kerosene stains outlining the spot where the man
had lain on the floor, and promptly arrested a "friend"
of the dead man for murder. He had no difficulty making his case.

On another night, Mr. Wosch climbed into the dark-
ened Baltimore & Ohio Railroad office after an intruder. The man grabbed him and slammed him against
the wall, injuring him seriously. The thief escaped
through the window but was caught shortly afterwards.

Once, singlehandedly, he arrested three holdup ban-
dits.

Mr. Wosch retired in June, 1939.

*   *   *

With the crime rate remaining astonishingly low, Ellicott

City and the surrounding area did not feel the need of a large police force for some time. Then in 1952 the county commissioners passed an act to form a county-wide Police Department and levied taxes on the entire area to cover the cost of maintenance. E. Russell Moxley, the same man who had assisted Julius Wosch in 1904, was appointed chief of police. His assistants were officers Harrison, Linthicum and Zeltman.

As of this writing, the Department is headed by Police Chief G. Russell Walters. The force is staffed by forty-five officers, 8 detectives, 3 crossing guards and a number of civilian employees including dispatchers and clerks. There are also two K-9 dogs in service.

The Department owns one K-9 wagon, 12 marked cruisers and 9 plain cars. The new home of the Department, although not in keeping architecturally with the rest of Ellicott City, is fully e-quipped for any and all emergencies. Meanwhile, the possibility of a sub-station somewhere in Columbia is under consideration.

A booklet, KNOW YOUR COUNTY GOVERNMENT, prepared and released by The League of Women Voters of Howard County, briefly outlines the duties of this department as follows:

> The Howard County Police Department is responsible for preserving the public peace, preventing crime, protecting the rights of persons and property and to arrest all offenders against the laws of the state and the county.

Hence, the law enforcement officer of today is still bound to perform the same duties described by Carl Bridenbaugh as having been exacted of him in 1646, as well as those set forth in 1696 in Annapolis, when each man was charged with "keeping good rules and orders."

Therefore, whether willfully or through persuasion, if any man within the county shall break the laws as set forth by the lawmakers of Howard County or the state, he may well expect to spend some time in the small jail now facing Emory Street. More serious offenders will find themselves transferred to Baltimore.

*   *   *

When first erected Willow Grove actually stood in a grove of trees, from which it derived its name. Under the front gable, cut into the stone, are the names of the county commissioners of that period—Samuel Brown, Jerome C. Berry and William Rowles, as well as the names of the builders—James Rowles, Robert Wilson and John Lang, C.E. The building then consisted of four cells on the ground floor and four above. There were also "dark cells," so called because of their gruesome service. It was here that condemned men doomed to hang were confined until the morning of their execution.

As was the custom, the scaffold was erected in the yard between the jail and the courthouse, where the wooden walk connecting the two buildings now runs. It was not unusual for prominent men of the town to be called as witnesses to these dreaded executions. One such witness spoke to the writer of the last execution to take place in the small town in 1916.

Benjamin Mellor, one of the town's leading citizens, remembers well the horrid details of the hanging. In this case, as in many others, history is not based merely on legal documents and historic sites. Mr. Mellor's vivid memory provides the interested scholar with much of the color and morbidity of the town's experience with capital punishment.

When hangings were discontinued within the confines of the town, the men of Ellicott City felt no regret at being relieved of so harrowing a duty. Today the jail is used only as a place of confinement for those serving limited sentences, or for those awaiting trial.

Although the present jail is considered by some to meet all state and government requirements, the Grand Jury for the March, 1966 term labeled the general conditions as only fair, and its facilities for handling men guilty of serious crimes, "completely inadequate." They further recommended a new jail at a new location after study by a qualified commission. The report stated this to be "mandatory."

With the gradual development of Columbia and the prospect of the county's population more than doubling within the next few decades, there are many who agree with the Grand Jury's recommendation. Others feel that a sizable addition to the present structure is the answer, while a third group favors a tri-county regional jail to serve Howard, Carroll and Frederick Counties. Time is needed for evaluation of the situation.

Until then, the small 90-year-old building facing Emory Street stands firm and solid...a constant reminder of the price of "good rules and orders."

*   *   *

2003 UPDATE

"Willow Grove" seems like an odd name for the former jail that now houses Howard County's Sheriff's Department. Rather than the imagined bucolic setting, the asphalt and cement surrounded, no-nonsense building is connected to the Court House by a "Bridge of Sighs" walkway of sorts. The quaint exterior leads to a state of the art facility inside.

In 1975 Howard County established its first separate Corrections Department. The jail remained in use as such for over 100 years, until a new facility was built at Jessup and opened in April, 1983. For a time the old building continued to be used as a lockup for overflow from Jessup. Concurrently, the Emory Street facility was home to the County's Civil Defense and Emergency 911 services, which relocated in 1976.

Since then the old facility has been remodeled and is now home of the Sheriff's Department, making a convenient base for the officers who maintain order at the Court House next door. Closed circuit televisions monitor events in the Court House, providing immediate information on situations requiring assistance from the Sheriff's Department, while computers and cell phones keep the officers on alert as well.

In 2002 the Police Department celebrated fifty years of service to the Howard County community. The current County Executive, James Robey, is a former Chief of Police, holding that office from 1991 to 1998. He joined the police force in 1966, when police were equipped with barely functioning radios and often had to find pay phones to make calls. In contrast, today's police cars are equipped with computer terminals, and the Department has a $28 million dollar radio system. The current Chief of Police is G. Wayne Livesay, who moved to Howard County in 1952 when he was one year old – a few months after the Police Department was formed.

*   *   *

THE HAYDEN HOUSE
Former Home of the Board of Education

Standing atop Capitoline Hill on Park Avenue, and now adjoining the courthouse, there is a building of beautiful proportions, formerly the home of the Howard County Board of Education. Built in 1840-41 by Edwin Parsons Hayden, it was originally known as Oak Lawn.

The builder, a man of accomplishment, was born in Baltimore August 7, 1811. He was educated at Baltimore College and took his law degree at Yale University, where he was a classmate of Thomas Watkins Ligon, later Governor of Maryland. During his brief life he practiced law at Ellicott's Mills and served in the House of Delegates from October, 1846 to March, 1847 when he was appointed the first Clerk of the Howard County Court by Governor Thomas George Pratt.

Described by his contemporaries as a personable man of good appearance and excellent taste, Mr. Hayden was also recognized as "a lawyer of more than ordinary ability..." Furthermore, he enjoyed a widespread reputation as an interesting and "graceful speaker." His home was considered one of the most handsome in the area, where an atmosphere of gentility and refinement prevailed. This was inevitable, considering the background of this ingenious man.

His father, Dr. Horace H. Hayden, was a noted geologist and one of the founders of the Baltimore Dental College where he served for a time as president. Dr. Hayden was also among those who took an active part in the War of 1812, at the battle of North Point (1814), and later as Assistant Surgeon in the Military Hospital.

Edwin Hayden's grandfather, Adjutant Thomas Hayden, Continental Line, served during the Revolutionary War.

William Hayden of Connecticut, the original settler, was also a soldier, and the first to be decorated for gallantry in the French and Indian War. He was granted land in 1642 for his accomplishments on the field of battle, which land remained in the family for well over two hundred and fifty years.

*   *   *

Edwin Parsons Hayden died May 10, 1850 shortly before his 39th birthday. He left his widow and six children. His lovely home, Oak Lawn, was sold in the 1870s to Henry A. Wooten, whose widow still owned it at the turn of the century. In September, 1937 Howard County acquired the property from John Pue, its most recent owner, and it became the headquarters of the Board of Education. In November, 1962 the present hyphenated passage from the courthouse to the building was erected.

*   *   *

From the beginning education was of primary importance in the small town of Ellicott's Mills, as well as throughout the county. The founding fathers, including Charles Carroll of Carrollton and the Ellicott brothers, contributed greatly of their time, land and money to establish schools within the immediate areas.

As has been noted, the Ellicotts founded the first school shortly after their arrival. Located east of the Patapsco River, it was a simple stone building, possibly consisting of a single room. The Patapsco Female Institute, one of the first seminaries for young ladies in the country, came into being in 1837. It, too, stood on land donated by the Ellicotts. Later, the old Quaker Meeting House also served temporarily as a school.

Meanwhile Charles Carroll, the Signer, contributed a sizable tract of land opposite Doughoregan Manor upon which St. Charles College, a Catholic Seminary, rose. It was destroyed by fire in 1911 but was rebuilt later at Catonsville.

Another Catholic Institution, Rock Hill College, was also obliterated by fire. It stood at the end of College Avenue, towering over St. Paul's Church and Rectory. Founded in 1830 and conducted by the Christian Brothers, it disappeared on January 23, 1923.

A complete account of the public school system in Maryland can be found on record at Annapolis. The Howard County Board of Education also has on file an accurate history of the local system since the establishment of Upper Arundel as an independent county. Therefore the writer will offer only a brief outline of the program as it functioned from the beginning.

*   *   *

In 1840, when the Howard District of Anne Arundel County was created, a public school system was already in existence. The laws of 1825 pertaining to primary schools were in effect and continued until 1843 when the "district trustees administered the affairs of the district, built the schools, bought supplies, and employed the teachers." As is the case today, funds were raised by taxing property owners. But here the similarity ends, for the school system was entirely a local one and not part of a state organization.

It was not until 1864 that centralized state supervision of the county school systems was realized. Until this time there was no uniformity at all. Most of the counties had county boards of education, although several substituted boards of examiners or inspectors. In still others, the county commissioners served as the Board of Education in conjunction with their other duties, while one county had no Board of Education at all. Variety in governing the primary schools until 1864 was accepted as the norm.

"Free Schools," so-called, generally supplemented their funds by charging the pupil a fee. Some counties levied a specific school tax, some demanded a regular tuition, while three counties insisted that "by law, the schools were free."

It was not until 1916 that the present school system was inaugurated. It provided, among other things, that there be "a State Board of Education whose duties are to execute the school laws and bylaws of the state board."

Meanwhile the County Board was instructed to maintain a uniform and effective school system throughout the county. Their duties included the hiring of teachers, the preparation of an annual budget (along with the county superintendent), and—with the written consent of the state superintendent—the election of a county superintendent who was also to serve as the secretary and treasurer of the County Board.

The county school system was further organized into districts, wherein a board of three appointed trustees had "the responsibility of all school property." They acted as advisers in many capacities. By unanimous vote they could refuse to accept the assignment of a teacher to any school within their jurisdiction. It was also within their power to consent to the dismissal of a pupil, or the closing of a school upon the request of the principal-in-charge or a qualified teacher. It was also within their jurisdiction to request the dismissal of an unsatisfactory teacher, by way of written charges filed with the County Board.

With the growth in population throughout the county and the increase in the number of schools, the duties and privileges of the County Board of Education have greatly increased in scope. According to John Yingling, former Superintendent of Schools, at the time of his retirement the Board itself consisted of five members, while the Staff had been increased to include an Assistant Superintendent of Schools, one Assistant in Finance and Purchasing, 13 Supervisors, 2 Supervisors of Transportation, 1 Supervisor of Pupil Personnel, 1 Art Supervisor, 1 Physical Education Supervisor, 1 Social Studies Supervisor and 5 Visiting Teachers. An Advisory Health Committee made up of five members, as well as an Advisory Curriculum Committee of eighteen, had also been created. Hence it is reasonable to assume that as demands for additional personnel and additional committees arise, the School Board will find a way to fill these necessary posts.

A new and unique experiment is now underway in the county, having started in the Glenwood area with the opening of the first "Middle School" in September, 1967. As the title suggests, a Middle School is designed to provide advanced procedures in the education of sixth, seventh and eighth-grade students. Planned by Mr. Yingling and the Board of Education, they are designated "schools between elementary and high school" and "constitute a transition between these two traditional systems."

There are at this time 19 schools in Howard County: 3 Senior High Schools (Grades 9, 10, 11 and 12); 4 Middle Schools (6, 7 and 8th Grades), and 12 Elementary Schools (Kindergarten through 5th Grade.) With the coming of Columbia and Howard County's own population explosion now underway, these numbers will change rapidly. But with larger quarters and better facilities at their new location (the former Harriet Tubman School), Howard County's Board of Education is proving capable of handling the ever-changing situation.

*   *   *

Meanwhile, in November, 1965, the former headquarters of the Board of Education, once famous as the residence of Edwin Parsons Hayden, was designated the People's Court of Howard County—a truly worthy ending for the home of a worthy man and "...a lawyer of more than ordinary ability."

*   *   *

2003 UPDATE

Serving since 1970 as the People's Court, but still a separate structure adjacent to the Court House, the former Hayden House is now physically incorporated into the structure of the Howard County Court House. This was accomplished as part of the 1986 expansion of the Court House.

Imaginative architectural planning and design resulted in an unusual, but little known feature of the old granite structure on Capitoline Hill. On the less visited east side of the Court House, there is a lovely structure featuring two-story grill work reminiscent of New Orleans, now incorporated into the unadorned wall of the larger building.

Conveniently nearby is a resting place of table and benches, a vantage point for viewing this unusual site and admiring the innovative individuals who found this unique way to preserve another deserving structure from the past. We can also wonder how the builder of the original house, Attorney Edwin Parsons Hayden, would react to his home's creative use and surroundings.

*   *   *

On Capitoline Hill, sometimes known as Mt. Misery, there stands still another of Ellicott City's many impressive landmarks, the massive mid-19th century county courthouse. Like most of its neighbors, it too is built of granite quarried locally.

The actual construction of this sturdy building might never have been realized had it not been for the vision and sheer determination of one man—Charles Timanus, prominent architect and builder, man of great foresight, and one of the first to recognize the future potentialities of the small mill town.

The site was chosen on October 6, 1840, and construction started shortly thereafter. Due to many unforeseen problems and the crude equipment with which the men were forced to labor, the building took more than two years to complete. The location selected, although commanding and ideal, proved the greatest of handicaps. For the hill was steep and the road, hardly more than a levelled path cut through and around the hilly terrain, was at times almost impassable. Delivery of necessary materials, including huge slabs of granite and tremendous beams of white oak, was slow and tedious and caused frequent delays. Much of the heavier equipment was hauled by oxen and mules, although a limited number of horse-drawn carts were also used. In bad weather the approach became a virtual quagmire, and for days on end the hill was abandoned. Neither man nor beast could battle the boggy suction of mud and clay. Nevertheless, despite numerous delays the building was finally completed in 1843 and the people of Ellicott's Mills were justifiably proud of their handsome new seat of government.

But even before the completion of the building itself, legal control of the Howard District of Anne Arundel County had been assigned qualified men of local residence. THE INVENTORY OF THE COUNTY AND TOWN ARCHIVES OF MARYLAND (Howard County— Ellicott City), prepared and published in 1939 by the Historical Records Survey Division of Women's and Professional Projects, Works Progress Administration, sheds much light on the subject. The following statement adequately summarizes conditions as they were at the time:

> A court was established at Ellicott's Mills in 1840 and styled the court of Howard District of Anne Arundel County. The orphan's court was set up at the same time, and a register of wills was appointed. Both the circuit and orphan's courts were furnished laws necessary for their guidance by the state librarian. All cases pending in the Anne Arundel Court at the time of the separation were continued in their place of origin. Cases originating in Howard District were, of course, tried there.

The courts referred to were set up temporarily in a house in the Fels Lane area. The old stone building still stands on the corner of Mercer Street and Fels Lane. Although it seems doomed to annihilation, there are those who still hope it will be preserved.

The Classic Revival structure which now serves as the center of all legal activities stands on land once owned by Deborah Disney, erstwhile operator of the town's oldest and most famous tavern. It overlooks the entire town and can be seen from many vantage points. Its tall cupola, one of the first sights to greet the eye of the visitor, is both impressive and picturesque.

Over the years a number of additions have been made to the original building to accommodate the needs of the ever-growing county. As of this writing, still more plans are under consideration to further enlarge existing facilities. With the development of Columbia expansion is inevitable.

*   *   *

Like most of Ellicott City's landmarks, the old courthouse is a ruggedly handsome building. In 1939, when the WPA survey was made, the building consisted of the Circuit Court Room and Judge's Library; 2 Anterooms, a Judge's room and General Library, a Jury Room and a Clerk's Vault, as well as offices for the County Commissioners, the Treasurer, the Clerk of the Circuit Court, the Register of Wills and the Orphans' Court. There were also a number of lesser vaults. In the interim, offices have been expanded and many alterations made.

It is of interest to note here the accumulation of records to be found at the courthouse, varying in both topic and scope. Files and information on the following legal matters are carefully stored in the vaults: Criminal Cases and Executions; Grand Jury Reports, as well as lists of Jurors; Naturalization Cases 1903-6; Land Records dating back to 1839; Deeds and Mortgages from 1840 through the current year; Plats; Stallion Pedigrees (1909); Records of Marriages from 1865-1920 and from 1921 to the present day; Divorce Decrees dating back to 1909; Affidavits of Consent for Minors to Marry (1888); the Census of 1850-70; a Record of Free Negroes in the county from 1840 to 1863 and finally, Howard County Slave Statistics (1868). Truly, a wealth of material lies buried within the confines of this building, the author's list conveying only a limited suggestion of the total content.

Outdoors, the battered British cannon on the front lawn is said to have been captured at the Battle of Bladensburg during the War of 1812 by "Bachelor" John Dorsey. It is one of this country's very few reminders of that ill-fated encounter. Although impressive to view, it is reminiscent of unhappier times.

Another memorial on the grounds of this venerable building is to the left of the main entrance. It is a Confederate monument erected to the memory of those men of Howard County who gave their lives in behalf of "the Lost Cause." Following the dedication of this marker, held on September 23, 1948, a suitable tribute was paid them as members of the United Daughters of the Confederacy stood by. Among those present on this memorable occasion were the Reverend Daniel Cummings, Rev. F. Alan Parsons, Judge William Forsythe, Mrs. W. Harry Parlett, Mr. Richard Talbott and Mr. Edwin Warfield, III.

*   *   *

Many interesting stories are told of the courthouse itself. Not the least of these is how and why this particular site was chosen.

As the story goes, in those days cattle and swine from surrounding farms were driven on foot to the Baltimore market via the old Frederick Road. The grunts and groans of the cows and pigs were far from conducive to the commanding dignity of the courtroom. So the builders chose to rise above the sounds, selecting Mt. Misery as the best location.

Legend has it that the elevation still was not sufficient to drown out all the noise, and an occasional outburst from the herds down below resulted in another equally explosive outburst from the courts above! But time and tide passed, and today the desired peace and quiet reign supreme in the various courts and chambers.

Although the courthouse is today equipped with every conceivable modern convenience, there was a time when this was not the case. During the early days of its existence running water was an unknown luxury, as was central heat. Four chimneys pierced the roof, and alcoves were to be found throughout the building to house individual stoves which supplied an uneven but fairly adequate temperature. As in most 19th century buildings, the halls were cold, and trips through them were hurried and held to a minimum. Even so, at the time the old building offered "the finest to be had" in terms of 19th century conveniences.

When in Ellicott City, the visitor will find much of interest within this rugged building. Although certain branches of the governing body, such as the Police Department and the Board of Education, do of necessity find shelter in other buildings, beneath the roof of the old courthouse there still gather the lawmakers, and those men who are responsible for the government of this enchanting county.

Changes may come, and changes may go, but at least for the present the courthouse on Capitoline Hill—the home of Howard County's governing body—remains the most important building in the county. There are many who hope it will always remain so.

*   *   *

2003 UPDATE

In 1986 the County completed a major renovation and addition to the Court House, dedicating it in a ceremony presided over by then County Executive, Hugh Nichols. Since then the County administration has moved the offices of the County Executive and County Council to the George Howard Building in the County office complex on nearby Rogers Avenue.

In the current atmosphere of heightened security, all visitors to today's Court House are asked to go through a metal detector, and purses and packages are subject to inspection. This is actually quite comforting to the innocent, and is handled well. The Sheriff's Department provides security for the building, and has its own tale of preservation. On May 7, 1975, the Department received its first car, a 1974 Dodge Coronet, which was a hand-me-down from the Police Department. Over a quarter-century later the car was found and restored, and on May 7, 2002, a new set of keys was presented to the Department.

The future of the old Court House is not so comfortably assured. As the demands for Circuit Court and other County services continue to grow, workers in today's Court House again cope with cramped quarters and overcrowding. A decades-old debate has resurfaced on whether to expand the historic facility or relocate the Circuit Court to another location. In January, 2003, the County's state legislators rejected County Executive James Robey's request for state funding for improvements to the building, some expressing the desire, instead, to put efforts and resources into a new court house at a different location. With or without support for improvements to the existing structure, the County hopes to build a $45 million judicial complex around the year 2010.

*　　　*　　　*

LAWYER'S ROW

Across from the county courthouse and winding around Court House Road, the visitor will find a group of small frame structures known as Lawyer's Row. The first of these buildings, located opposite the First Presbyterian Church (now the Historical Society) was built in 1862 by Henry E. Wooten, State's Attorney, to be used as his office. It later served as the office of the late Judge James T. Clark, and is now occupied by his son, Judge John L. Clark.

Until 1878 the ground immediately facing the courthouse and running downhill to Main Street was still open land, with the exception of three occupants: Sprecher's Coal Yard, which was located at the turn of the road; a nondescript building at the corner of Main Street and Court House Road; and facing on Main Street, the Howard House, Ellicott City's well-known combination hotel and public dining room.

Little by little the open land disappeared and additional small but efficient buildings were erected for the convenience of "the men on the hill." One after another they rose until they skirted the entire road. The last one to be built was the brick building which served as the office of the late State Senator Joseph L. Donovan.

A half-dozen years ago, no less than twenty-three lawyers were to be found atop Capitoline Hill, occupying the unique buildings and serving the people of Howard County.

*   *   *

The interiors of most of these offices are much the same. They consist of a tiny entrance hall with doors to the left and to the right. As a rule, two attorneys shared the limited quarters, working together on some cases, and independently on others.

Each building has a general waiting room, a private office for each of the attorneys, and a conference room which also serves as storage room for the many files of legal documents. When last visited by the writer, the buildings were heated by stoves, since space for central heating systems was not available. Other modern facilities were also obviously missing, the closest running water being across the street at the courthouse. The only concession to the 20th century was electricity.

In one building, bare and colorless wooden floors greeted the client, while straight-backed chairs were scattered at random around the room. The secretary's desk took up one corner, while another corner housed files containing the labor of years. Little or no attention was paid to the lack of luxury or modern equipment. It was as though things remained unchanged by choice.

One redeeming feature in the physical appearance of the building was the size and cleanliness of the huge windows which made the interior a little more cheerful, despite its otherwise frugal atmosphere. Only in the private office of each attorney was there any semblance of modern-day accommodations. Comfortable chairs, electric fans and Venetian blinds helped remind the visitor that this was indeed the 20th century!

The writer's first official visit to one of these offices proved informative to be sure. Accustomed to the luxuries and comfort of legal offices in such cities as Baltimore and Washington, she found delight in the quaint disarrangement of the waiting room. The assortment of furnishings and file cabinets, obvious left-overs from past generations, was fascinating but hardly conducive to peace of mind. What sort of man could tolerate such confusion? Was this a measure of his abilities? The author was soon to find out.

When ushered into the inner office a change took place. Suddenly, it was easy to see why the steady stream of clients kept returning year after year. A firm handshake, an alert look in the eyes of the man who stood behind the huge desk, and walls lined with legal books on every conceivable subject were noted within a fraction of a second. Apprehension vanished and in its place satisfaction and a sure sense of confidence prevailed.

*　　　*　　　*

What these buildings lack today in luxury is obvious. But the purpose they have served is equal to any rendered in the larger and more elaborate offices in nearby cities. Nevertheless, with the passing years the small picturesque buildings have started to deteriorate. There are those who insist that the increase in local population and clientele has brought about a need for larger offices and more storage space, making the small frame buildings all but inadequate. A very small minority disagree. Consequently, most of the buildings are gradually being abandoned by Howard County's professional men, including those who do not literally choose to leave.

To date, only one building has been tastefully restored. Another has been kept in moderately good repair, while a third has been taken over in part by the Social Security Agency, with little or no improvement having been made.

Thus the fate of the rest of Lawyer's Row remains uncertain. The convenience to the courthouse cannot be underestimated. Nor can it be equalled elsewhere. But to the average man of this motorized age such considerations are of little importance.

It is to be hoped that some practical use will always be found for these colorful buildings, for Capitoline Hill without Lawyer's Row would lose much of its rustic appeal. Perhaps a little additional thought and imagination on the part of local agencies and private individuals will eventually lead to some reasonable and worthwhile use for these minute but distinctive buildings which have served the county so well for so long.

*　　　*　　　*

2003 UPDATE

The string of picturesque small buildings known as Lawyer's Row still houses lawyers in a location convenient to the Court House, and in a style unimagined by Celia Holland.

The buildings are now equipped with electricity, air conditioning, and running water. Although they appear unchanged on the outside, the interiors are now disparate. Some retain the floor plan described by Mrs. Holland, with the tiny entrance hall and adjacent offices. Others, like the offices of Silverstein and Ostovitz, LLC, at 8355 Court Avenue, have undergone amazing transformation. This firm purchased the building in 1982 and modernized its interior, creating a light, open, and airy space that must be a pleasure to work in.

LOG CABIN—MERRYMAN STREET

Upon leaving Capitoline Hill via Court House Road, one will find still another interesting but little-known landmark simply by crossing over Main Street, on the south side of which the "Road" becomes Merryman Street.

On this narrow lane, perhaps a good city block below Main Street, the visitor can indulge in a brief glance—and a truly passing one at that—at one of the county's oldest forms of shelter, a crude but distinctive log cabin. Older by far than the joined cabin on New Cut Road, this humble building still stands despite nearly two centuries of wear and tear and the profound poundings of the elements.

Dated by Historic Ellicott's Mills, Inc. as having been built "circa 1780," the small shell of a house differs considerably from the log cabin at the other end of town. Most historians would agree that this building bears little resemblance to the slave quarters of old, but rather that it carries the identifying marks of a once-substantial settler's hut. Its measurements and general appearance suggest that it was a single-room-and-overhead-loft structure, such as was erected by the early settler when laying claim to uninhabited or unclaimed land.

The little hut also speaks well of the man who built it, despite the fact that over the years his identity has been lost. For any man who would choose such a spot to split rails and clear the

231

land to build his home must have indeed been a man who loved the sounds of nature. The tiny cabin all but straddles a narrow stream, and despite the development of the surrounding area, this one small plot remains to this day an untouched and undisturbed bit of woodland.

The estimated age of this excellent little landmark, if correct, would further indicate that this was no slave cabin since Ellicott's Mills had already become a center of commerce by 1780, albeit a center surrounded by wilderness.

Although the cabin is today considered one of the town's oldest and most unique attractions, its history, like that of a number of other very early structures, remains questionable. Here, too, information is limited and based only on known customs of almost two centuries ago.

Ellicott City's Merryman Street log cabin is today the property of Mrs. Harry Sanford who uses it primarily for storage.

How much longer the little cabin will stand is unknown. How soon its weakened walls will crumble, unless fortified, remains to be seen. But as of this writing it still defies the elements, and the observer concludes that it is not altogether inconceivable that the landmark will go on standing indefinitely in that little patch of woodland which has shielded it these many generations.

* * *

2003 UPDATE

The Merryman Street Log Cabin, known today as the Thomas Isaac Log Cabin, is one of the finest landmarks on Main Street in the Historic District. Given to Historic Ellicott City, Inc. by the Stanton family, in the interest of preservation, the cabin was dismantled in 1980 under the direction of restoration consultant Andrew Cascio. Mr. Cascio did extensive measurements of the building, as well as drawings, and numbered each log before the building was dismantled to ensure correct restoration at the new site.

The Vintage Lumber and Construction Company, Incorporated of Frederick, specialists in log structures, took the cabin apart piece by piece. Howard County's Departments of Recreation and Parks and Public Works assisted the effort with equipment and trucks. Each log, board and stone, including the foundation, was stored in climate-controlled conditions by the County until the cabin was reassembled on its new site, at the corner of Main Street and Ellicott Mills Drive.

Roland and Enalee Bounds monitored the condition of the cabin and worked with Andrew Cascio on the plans for restoration from 1980 until the work commenced in January, 1987. Martin Stephan headed the project for Historic Ellicott City, Inc. Preservation Associates, Incorporated of Hagerstown, Maryland, completed the restoration.

The group dedicated the cabin in its new location in a special ceremony on July 16, 1988. At that time, Historic Ellicott City, Inc. officially transferred ownership of the cabin to Howard County. Historic Ellicott City, Inc. leased the property from the County for use in its historic and educational programming, including its "Two Centuries on Main Street" program in conjunction with the Railroad Station Museum until 2003, when the cabin programming was taken over completely by the County.

The cabin is well maintained and attracts visitors who enjoy seeing reenactors portraying 18th century life. The cabin is now the headquarters of the County's Ellicott City Historic Sites Consortium.

*　　*　　*

2003 Photo of Cabin now on Main Street by Charles Kyler.

E.A. TALBOTT LUMBER COMPANY

The year was 1845. Young Edward Alexander Talbott, direct descendant of Richard and Elizabeth Ewen Talbott of West River, looked around in the small village of Ellicott's Mills for a suitable location for his planned enterprise. Edward Alexander, representing the sixth generation of Talbotts to hold title to Talbott's Last Shift, the home place in Upper Arundel originally surveyed in 1732, owned the estate from June 2, 1848 to October 15, 1850. But several years before he was to come into possession of the property, he had made his decision to strike out on his own.

Although comparatively young he was a man of great foresight and competence. Recognizing the possibilities of the mill town and its surrounding area, he decided upon a career as merchant, and subsequently opened a sizable store on the east bank of the Patapsco River. Here he sold such items as lumber, an assortment of building supplies, and a complete line of tools.

Edward's wife, the former Mary Wareham of the Eastern Shore of Maryland, shared her husband's enthusiasm for this new venture. Working as a team, they prospered. The firm, known simply as E.A. Talbott, quickly earned the respect and confidence of the people of the community. Before long customers came from far and near to deal with "the Talbotts of Ellicott's Mills."

With the birth of her son Edward in 1847, Mrs. Talbott withdrew from active participation in the growing enterprise and assumed the full-time role of wife and mother.

234

The business grew and suffered no set-backs until the year 1866, when a flash flood caused a loss of approximately $10,000 in damage to both stock and building. This misfortune was a serious blow which nearly resulted in the loss of the entire investment. People of less stamina might not have survived, but the Talbotts were not of average caliber. With renewed courage and energy they rebuilt and restocked their store, borrowing money as needed, and quickly resumed a "business as usual" policy. Then again within two short years, "the great disaster" hit Ellicott City and the raging flood of 1868 all but wiped them out.

Long after this second flood, a safe owned by Henry James yielded two promissory notes, each in the amount of $10,000, representing the monies advanced Mr. Talbott after his two successive crises. On the backs of the notes were records of repayment in amounts of one hundred dollars or more. Both debts had been fully liquidated. The two cancelled notes, highly prized by the descendants of Mr. Talbott, were kept with the family papers for many years. Today, only a notation of the incident remains.

*　　　*　　　*

Still determined to go on with his venture even after the second flood, Mr. Talbott decided to move across the Patapsco, beyond reach of the treacherous waters. He opened a shop in a small brick building west of the B. & O. Railroad station and built his lumber yard in the rear. Shortly thereafter he initiated his son into the ways of the business world. The boy chose to become known as E. Alexander to the people of the community, but the business continued under the original name, E.A. Talbott.

An interesting tale is told of E. Alexander who was but a boy of fourteen when the War Between the States began. Upon learning of the enlistment of his father's friend and neighbor, Dorsey Thompson, into the Confederate Army, young Alexander ran away from home no less than three times to join Company A of the 1st Maryland Cavalry. Each time friends of the distraught family found the boy and returned him to his parents. After three such unsuccessful attempts, his father resorted to locking him in the attic for a time, "for safe keeping." When he was released, the youngster realized that the Southern Army was too far away to be overtaken, so he abandoned his plan to join them and gave his parents no further cause for alarm.

After the war Company A met each summer for many years at nearby Oakdale, ancestral home of Governor Edwin Warfield. It is said that young Talbott frequently attended these annual reunions and that he always considered himself an honorary member of the Company since he had indeed "fought with them in spirit, if not in the flesh!"

*　　　*　　　*

During his apprenticeship, E. Alexander was called upon to do a variety of jobs. His youthful ambition and love of life were exceeded only by his deep sense of humor. On one occasion when a new wing was being added to the main house at Linwood, the palatial home on the crest of Patapsco Heights, there arose a need for 40-foot ceiling joists. Since the B. & O. Railroad was not e-quipped to haul lumber of this great length, Mr. Talbott sent his son to Baltimore in a horse-drawn wagon to bring back the unwieldy material. The wagon had no body, so the lumber was laid between the wheels on the cross sections of the frame. As young Talbott attempted to cross the railroad tracks, the wagon wheels sank into the ground between the two lengths of steel rail, leaving the young man and his cargo stranded. The vehicle would not budge. An approaching train was flagged to a halt.

The story, as told by E. Alexander—possibly with some embellishments, was that the engineer and fireman both jumped from the train and angrily demanded that the wagon be moved and the track be cleared. Young Talbott, in a quiet but provocative way, reminded them that without help the wagon would have to remain where it was, and the U. S. mail (which he knew to be aboard) would be detained indefinitely! Grudgingly, the trainmen offered to help.

Using a long coupling link as a pulley, the four wheels were lifted from the track. At length, the wagon with its big load was released and once again the young driver was headed toward his destination. He departed with a smile on his lips and an ever so polite, "Thank you, boys."

Suddenly, upon realizing there would be no compensation for their efforts, the two men gave vent to their emotions and hurled vicious remarks at their young tormentor. But E. Alexander only smiled to himself and silently drove on. A little way up the road he glanced over his shoulder once more and cried out mischievously, "Goodbye, boys. And thank you so much!" The two men glared as he slapped his knee in glee. Young Talbott's only regret lay in the fact that he dared not share the incident with his father who would have termed it inexcusably disrespectful and dealt with it accordingly. But years later he laughingly spoke of it to his own sons who fully appreciated the ironic humor of the situation.

*   *   *

Upon the death of his parents, both of whom are buried at Oella Cemetery, E. Alexander Talbott became heir to the Sprecher property on West Main Street which his father had bought during his more prosperous years. The property consisted of a brick house and store adjoining the well-known Disney's Tavern. Deciding to expand his business, he tore down the existing structures and replaced them with the present building of brick and granite. The lumber yard was then located on the south side of the street opposite the store.

E. Alexander and his wife, the former Georgianna Laney, raised their family much as they had been raised themselves, stressing the importance of honesty, courtesy and respect for their elders. But they were not above enjoying a good joke, whether the laugh be at their own expense or of a general nature. For a time they made their home on Fels Lane, across from the old R. W. Merrick property. Later they moved to a large stone house on Main Street which has since been razed. There were six children: William Edward, Mary Alice (called Marie), Richard, Thomas Murray, John Wilson and George Alexander.

E. Alexander Talbott conducted an honorable and profitable business and was as respected by the townspeople as had been his father before him. Like his father, he introduced his sons into the business world following their education, although he knew that all five boys would not stay on permanently.

According to the late Richard Talbott, formerly of Church Road, his experiences with some of his father's friends remained his most prized memories. During one conversation with the writer he recalled vividly the time when James E. Tyson, operator of a 200-acre farm on the site of the present Chestnut Hill development, purchased a second-hand grain binder from the store. Although it was a piece of used equipment and was sold as such, when trouble started, E. Alexander sent his son to operate the machine and "iron out the kinks." To quote Mr. Talbott: "It acted up occasionally, ignoring all efforts to discover the problem, no matter how hard I tried."

Mr. Tyson, a shrewd but honest business man, startled the youngster when for the first time he was discovered by the boy "sitting beneath a tree with binoculars, his eyes pinned on me as I worked the fields!" A day's work was a day's work, and Mr. Tyson had no intention of being short-changed by any man, even though one of them happened to be the young son of his closest friend! Although Richard was there to repair a machine which had been bought on an "as is" basis, Mr. Tyson watched from his vantage point and neither party left the field until the job was completed!

Frequently Mr. Tyson was driven to the railroad station in Ellicott City when journeying to Baltimore. On most occasions, upon his return he was met by a member of his own family. But on other occasions when no one was available, young Richard was again called upon to go to the station to "carry him safely home."

With a gleam in his eye, Mr. Talbott spoke of the day he received his first tip. "...a whole dime!" he laughed. All this, for his time and energy! "But," he pointed out, "that dime was the first money I had ever earned on my own, and although it may make us smile today, it was one of the biggest events of my life up to that moment."

*   *   *

Following the death of E. Alexander the business passed to three of his five sons, the other two choosing careers elsewhere. Richard, Thomas and Edward W. became the new proprietors, although Edward devoted much of his time to the Patapsco National Bank where he served as president for twenty-six years. The Talbott boys were all educated in the public schools of Howard County. They then attended St. Clement's Academy, and finally Rock Hill College.

Richard, who was possibly the most active member of the firm, went into the business following his graduation from Rock Hill. He married Miss May Georgia Childs of Montgomery County. Having lived in Ellicott City all of their married life, they shared a deep and abiding interest in both the past and the future of the town.

*   *   *

In 1945 the Talbott brothers decided to dispose of the business, selling it to N. Holzweig and N. Caplan, the present owners. Although it is known today as The Talbott Lumber Company, as long as it remained the property of the Talbott family it was known simply as E. A. Talbott.

For years members of this well-known family witnessed the development of Ellicott City as well as the growth of the county as a whole. Mr. Richard, who lived to celebrate his 93rd birthday, had many tales to tell and the happy faculty of being able to recall incidents of the past near-century. The late Mrs. Talbott, although not native-born, was also equally interested and well-informed, and took great pleasure in recreating the yesteryears. With their passing, Ellicott City lost two of its most gracious people.

In his book, THE HISTORY OF ST. PAUL'S CHURCH AND PARISH, published in 1910, Brother Fabrician refers to "Talbott's great store and yard on Main Street." It is also noted in G. M. Hopkins Atlas of 1878, while the genealogy of the family itself is included in THE FOUNDERS OF ANNE ARUNDEL AND HOWARD COUNTIES, Professor J. D. Warfield's monumental history of the county.

*   *   *

From that first day in 1845 when Edward A. Talbott threw open the doors of his new-found business until today, E. A. Talbott —or Talbott Lumber Company as it is now known—has been a landmark in the busy little town that is Ellicott City. Although no members of the old and respected family are connected with it in any way, it will always be reminiscent of them and of a specific period during which much that will never be forgotten lashed out at the small mill town...the War of 1861, the floods of 1866 and 1868, and the fires of the early 1900s.

From all available evidence, there is no doubt the old lumber company will stand for many years to come. Meanwhile, the descendants of its founder are already bearing witness to the rebirth of Ellicott City. It seems inevitable that both will share in the town's ultimate and hard-won battle for recognition.

This, too, is as it should be.

*   *   *

2003 UPDATE

Although Celia Holland believed that the lumber company would continue to prosper on Main Street for many years to come, she could not have foreseen the emergence of the chain hardware stores in suburban shopping malls that would mark the end of many independent enterprises. The lumber company closed in the mid-1990's, and the property reopened in 1996 as the Ellicott Mills Brewing Company.

The Historic District Commission recognized this creative new use for an old building with an award for the architectural excellence exhibited. Housing the huge copper vats of an in-house microbrewery, the painted brick walls decorated with local artwork and antique industrial equipment, and the finely finished wooden floors attest to the current owners' desire to preserve the unique character of this building.

Where building supplies once had pride of place, now the building stands out as the home of a fine restaurant that is a welcome addition to the Ellicott City dining scene. Owners Rick Winter, Bill Pastino, John Stefano, and Tim Kendzerski rightly share pride in their establishment, which has been termed "Baltimore's Best Brew Pub" by BALTIMORE MAGAZINE and was listed among the "Top Seven New Restaurants" by THE BALTIMORE SUN.

*   *   *

2003 Photo by Charles Kyler.

DISNEY'S TAVERN

Standing in the heart of Ellicott City at 174-76 West Main Street, there is a large duplex house with front porch, finished in rough cast over stone. Although it has been completely modernized, its 18th century architectural features are still apparent to the discerning eye. Identified by both Historic Ellicott's Mills, Inc. and the Howard County Historical Society as the former Disney's tavern, it is today recognized as one of the town's oldest landmarks, having been built in 1790 or thereabout.

Shared for many years by two families, Mr. and Mrs. Norman S. Betts of 176 and Mr. and Mrs. Harvey Wine of 174, the old tavern was well cared for and is today in an excellent state of preservation. Despite its central location, because of its sturdy construction and eighteen-inch walls, both families found it practically soundproof. Neither claimed to be disturbed by outside noises or the constant confusion of modern-day traffic as it flows steadily past the door.

In the spring of 1966 the writer enjoyed the privilege of meeting and spending considerable time with Mr. and Mrs. Betts in their delightful home. It was an experience worthy of note.

Once inside the house, the author found it hard to realize that at one time 174-76 Main Street had been the center of the community's more boisterous social activities. For it was here that in 1840 Mrs. Deborah Disney opened her tavern which was destined

241

to become well known near and far. Catering as she did almost exclusively to male patrons, Mrs. Disney soon found herself operating one of the liveliest places in town.

In addition to the tavern, Disney's also offered overnight shelter for a limited number of tourists and traveling business men. Many Howard County farmers also found the place convenient when called for jury duty. They had only to walk up a short flight of steps from the back yard and cross over a small bridge to reach their destination when court was in session. Even in bad weather there was no need for tardiness. And, indeed, there is no record of any such complaint.

Although a number of people are of the opinion that 176 Main Street or the western half of the building, was built first and served as the tavern, evidence indicates otherwise. Mr. and Mrs. Betts were convinced, as is the writer, that the two houses were at one time a single structure owned and operated by Mrs. Disney as a combination tavern-inn-residence. The attic at 176 extends a full six feet over the adjoining house, while the dining room cupboard also cuts into the house next door, over the basement steps. Then too, the front and rear walls of both houses are unbroken in line and show no signs of having been joined. It has been suggested that before Mrs. Disney took possession of the property, this was one of Ellicott City's more spacious town houses. This theory seems almost self-evident.

The part formerly occupied by Mr. and Mrs. Betts consists of nine rooms (the adjoining house having eight) and is believed to have been the section, at least in part, used by Mrs. Disney as her personal living quarters since the only fireplaces in the entire building are located here—one in the living room, the other in the dining room. Many of the original doors remain, the pegs still visible despite numerous coats of paint. The basement, which once served as a wine cellar, had an earthen floor but has since been cemented.

Mrs. Betts, the former Mary Elizabeth Treakle Sanner, a native of Ellicott City, was born at Angelo Cottage better than a half century ago. She was the granddaughter of John Thomas Ray, one-time owner of the little castle, from whom she learned much of the history and lore of the town. She is possibly as well-informed on these subjects as any of the local residents.

Although Mr. and Mrs. Wine are not natives of Ellicott City, they have made it their home for a number of years, becoming "citizens by adoption."

*   *   *

Very little is known of the occupancy of the building prior to 1840 when Mrs. Disney made of it an Ellicott City landmark. However, it is a matter of record that as late as 1868 it was still operating as a tavern when E. Alexander Talbott took possession of the adjoining property and transferred his lumber business here from the lower end of town.

About five years later Joseph H. Leishear, Sr., Ellicott City's "patriarch of grocers" whose original store was washed away in the great flood, became the new owner. By agreement with his father, Joseph, Jr. made the tavern his home during the years when he helped manage the new store, then located on the site of the present Post Office. He, in turn, was assisted by an aged colored man, Jake Henson, "who delivered heavy groceries on an old-fashioned drag."

According to Mrs. Betts, Mr. Leishear was succeeded by Miss Rebecca Talbott, sister of E. Alexander, who took possession of the old landmark in the late 1800s, following the closing of the Leishear store. A Mr. William F. Lilly then purchased the property, leaving it to his daughter Mrs. Mary Lilly Sage, from whom Mr. and Mrs. Betts rented their side of the building in 1929. Just when it was converted into a duplex house remains uncertain, although it is thought to have been done by Mr. Lilly.

It was not until 1942 that Mr. and Mrs. Betts finally decided to purchase their half of the tavern, making it their permanent home. Although the house was then beautifully redecorated, other than remodelling the kitchen for greater efficiency and installing some much-needed closet space upstairs, they left the interior of the structure basically unchanged.

At the time of the writer's visit, the Betts' unquestionably good taste was everywhere in evidence. The living room, done in a soothing Williamsburg green, was beautifully furnished, each piece showing to advantage the 18th century features of the old home. The dining room—Mrs. Betts' favorite—was panelled beneath the chair-rail with tongue-and-groove panelling. The gay floral pattern of the wallpaper above did full justice to the room's size and appointments, the most handsome of which was a tall cabinet resembling a giant breakfront, but of quality vintage.

In one corner of the lovely room, next to the window, there was an off-set concealing a hollow shaft which ran from the first floor to the attic. It is thought to have been a dumb-waiter when the building was used as a tavern and inn. Trays of food and liquid refreshments were undoubtedly passed to the different floors by means of this handy device.

A collection of unusual prints and pictures, all of Ellicott City, were to be found in the front hall of the Betts home. They were of great interest to the author, depicting as they do, early and rare scenes of the immediate area. One, an unusual panoramic view of the small town many years ago, showed Disney's Tavern as it was during its most active period. Another depicted an old B. & O. train approaching the historic station, the smoke from its engine puffing stoutly, while the third was a photograph of the covered bridge that once spanned the Patapsco. All were realistically tinted and are undoubtedly collector's items.

Mr. and Mrs. Betts were justifiably proud of their home town and constantly contributed to its well-being whenever an opportunity presented itself. One of Mrs. Betts' most prized possessions was a lovely silver platter given her in 1952 by the members of the Patapsco Bank, for which she worked many years. During the flash flood of 1952 when damage ran high and losses soared, she was of outstanding help in saving that which could be saved. When the horrible experience came to an end and panic subsided, she was feted by her fellow-workers at a dinner and presented the beautiful tray which occupied the place of honor in her dining room. It was inscribed simply: "Miss Mary," but it was signed by each and every director of the bank.

The upstairs rooms at 176 Main Street were of average size and equally well furnished. Outdoors, a small covered patio had been built behind the house, within the shadow of the courthouse. A huge boulder of granite, typical of the town itself, was accented by colorful floral plantings. Although the original steps and small bridge had disappeared, the tiny yard remained delightfully picturesque.

Mr. Betts, a quiet and friendly man, seemed to delight in the success he and his wife had achieved in restoring the old landmark. All of his contributions were labors of love, since his pride in the small mill town was as deeply rooted as was his wife's.

Noted in the 1959 Howard County Tour Guide as lending "an air of peace and serenity in the heart of Ellicott City," and described by one of the town's leading citizens as "one of the loveliest little houses around," 176 Main Street lived up to all the writer's expectations. For Mr. and Mrs. Betts had made of it a place of real charm, while retaining all the original features.

*   *   *

Unhappily, on Monday, January 16, 1967 Mr. Betts, a lifetime resident of Howard County and son of Charles W. and Sarah Holden Betts, died at his historic home on Ellicott City's Main Street. A local banker of long standing, he was also a member and Trustee of Emory Methodist Church and treasurer of both the Howard County Public Health Association and the Animal Welfare Society of Howard County. He was a director of the Home Building Association of Ellicott City, Inc. and a member of the Howard County Historical Society. He was survived by his wife and several nieces and nephews.

In June, 1967, after having remained in the lovely old home several months, Mary Sanner Betts notified the author that she intended leaving Ellicott City to make her home in Baltimore. Thus a part of the famous tavern would once again change hands. But the memory of its former occupants—the gracious lady who contributed so much toward the preservation of this historic building, and her kind and gentle husband who proudly worked by her side in this and many other worthy projects—will not be forgotten.

Because of them and their good neighbors, Mr. and Mrs. Harvey Wine, Disney's Tavern remains today an 18th century landmark in an excellent state of preservation. It is to be hoped that the new owner, Harry H. Tanburo, will find as much satisfaction in preserving this valued edifice as did the former owners.

*   *   *

2003 UPDATE

The Disney Tavern duplex today houses several thriving businesses. The left side features Gramp's Attic bookstore, owned by Walter Jackson. This is the place to seek out a copy of one of the original printings of this book, as treasures abound and offerings change frequently. The second and third floors on that side of the building comprise a private apartment. On the right side of the duplex, the first floor houses the law office of Dennis Hodge, who owns the building.

Zip Publishing, a company that produces several local newspapers, recently occupied the second and third floors on the right side of the building.

Their newspapers fill a void left by the Stromberg/Thompson publishing family, offering in depth local stories not found in any other venue. The publishers, Phyllis Greenbaum and Pete Cook, have worked on newspapers all their lives, including time spent working with Doris Stromberg Thompson. The space has since reverted to a private apartment.

At 16 Columbia Road, within a stone's throw of Main Street, the visitor will note a two and one-half story white brick house, today referred to as The Puhl House. Known to have been built well over a century ago, it was at first a modest home with two small rooms on the first floor, two rooms of equal size above, and a "built on" kitchen. There were two fireplaces, both of which are still in use. Of particular interest are the three tiny windows cut into the front wall of the attic, an innovation seldom found in early 19th century homes.

Although the identity of the original builder remains unknown, according to the present owner there is on record at the courthouse a deed to the house—then known as "the French property"—dated 1848. Since most properties in the area were no less than forty years old before the Howard District of Anne Arundel County initiated its program of recording titles and deeds in 1840, the Puhl house is believed to have been built shortly after the turn of the 19th century. Local historians give its date of construction as "the early 1800s."

The French family, long-time residents of Ellicott City and owners of the property for many years, were highly esteemed by their friends and neighbors. Mr. and Mrs. John French are well remembered by a number of the town's senior citizens. Upon their deaths John and Mary, the last of their children to remain single, continued to live in the old home for a number of years before moving to Baltimore.

*　　*　　*

There were other well-known occupants whose experiences also contribute to our somewhat limited knowledge of the house itself, as well as the surrounding grounds. Not the least of these were Mr. and Mrs. John T. Ray who lived here at a later date.

Much has been written concerning the public burial grounds established by the Ellicott family in 1800, but few people know of the existence of an additional graveyard which was laid out in 1844. It is located directly back of the Puhl House. There are still a number of graves remaining, although the markers have disappeared.

One such burial site was purchased by the Ray family even before they made 16 Columbia Road their home. Having suffered the loss of an infant son, they buried the child in the little-known cemetery. A Certificate of Burial issued to Mr. Ray is today in the possession of a grand-daughter, Mrs. Norman Betts, formerly of 176 Main Street. It reads in part:

> Certificate of Burial #34, in the Village of Ellicott's Mills, part of a tract called 'West Ilchester,' laid off in lots, dedicated to the purposes of a Burial Ground under provisions of an Act of General Assembly of Maryland passed at the December Session 1844, Chpt. 13, and recorded among the Land Records of Howard District, in Liber E.P.H. #8, folio 442.....

The document is dated January 9, 1855, and signed by Beal Heleus and John Day.

*   *   *

Mr. and Mrs. Carl Schwartz, from whom Mr. and Mrs. Puhl purchased the house, were residents but a short time. However they did much to improve the property.

According to Mrs. Betts who knew the place well, a wall dividing the two small and dismal rooms on the first floor was removed, thereby converting them into a large and cheerful living room. Traces of the former partition may still be seen on the floor of the "new" room.

Repairs were made as well as a few additional improvements, but a complete restoration was not achieved until several years after their departure.

*   *   *

In 1957 Mr. and Mrs. Adolph B. Puhl became the new owners. But work on the restoration of the old landmark was hardly
underway when Mr. Puhl died suddenly, exactly one year to the day
of the date they had taken possession.

After a reasonable interlude Mrs. Puhl and her son, Edward
D. Puhl, now co-owners, resumed the program begun by their late
husband and father. In addition to restoring many of the old home's
unique features, including a narrow, closed and winding stairway
(believed to be the original), they made several major improvements. The roof of the rear wing was raised approximately eight
feet, thus allowing for an additional room, and living space was
greatly increased.

A beautiful patio which is now accessible from the second-
floor level was also added, as was an unusual serpentine wall. Both
additions contribute much to the basic charm of the house. Finally,
several coats of white paint, applied to the faded brick walls of
questionable color, helped stress the excellent lines of the lovely
old home. Touches of black accent the simple but dignified entrance, while shutters of the same color frame the original twelve-
paned windows.

In its setting of great trees and tasteful foundation plantings,
the Puhl House is a credit to Ellicott City and to its owners. It has
been included in the brochure published by Historic Ellicott's Mills,
Inc. as a house worthy of note, and merits its listing as one of the
better restoration jobs achieved to date in the small town.

*   *   *

2003 UPDATE

The successful preservation of this tiny jewel of a building continues. In the 1970's and 1980's the house was used as a
teahouse and café. It again reverted to private ownership, and
was owned from 1993 to 1999 by Dodie Stewart (formerly
Gaudry) who sold the property to David and Connie Ennis.

The Ennis's transformed the building from a private home
to an upscale salon called 'envy.', which offers a variety of beauty services. Their daughter Leeza, a stylist, runs the business.
Notable is the fact that they adapted the home to commercial use
while respecting the historic integrity of the property, causing
minimal changes to the building. David Ennis served as general
contractor for the project and worked to preserve the historic
elements of the structure.

For example, they used European-style shampoo bowls that didn't require additional drilling into the plaster walls and placing the new electrical system over the existing one. Leeza Ennis acted as interior designer, and her use of antique furniture and traditional paint colors like Federal yellow helps preserve the historic look of the house. This excellent adaptive use of a property in the Historic District is a fine example of how a building, no longer as desirable as a private residence due to surrounding commercial properties, can still be creatively preserved and enjoyed.

*   *   *

2003 Photo by Charles Kyler.

Tongue Row, as seen by Richard Gucker

TONGUE ROW

Cradled in a curve on the west side of Columbia Pike within sight of Main Street, one approaches a cluster of joined houses, conceivably some of the oldest row houses in the state. Perching precariously over the edge of a deep slope and clinging to the side of a steep ravine, they leave one with the impression of "hanging on for dear life!" And in their unique way, they are. In doing so they offer the visitor to Ellicott City one of the town's most famous attractions.

Built in the early 1800s by a Mr. Tongue for millhands and their families, and consisting of four stone structures—the first and last of which are double houses, the remaining two, individual residences—they are separated only by narrow airways, such as are frequently found in the older sections of Baltimore.

Although the doors and windows vary in size and shape and the pitch of each individual roof is different, as a unit, the dwellings give the impression of being uniform. They are a picturesque addition to a picturesque town.

It is said that Tongue Row has been photographed by more people than any other single attraction within the immediate area. In 1962 A. Aubrey Bodine, esteemed photographer and member of the staff of THE BALTIMORE SUN, was given an assignment to undertake another of his photographic ventures. He covered Ellicott City, including Tongue Row, and produced one of the finest photographs of the well-known landmark to date. It was included in the National Trust Traveling Display of 1962-63 and shown throughout the country, thereby winning national recognition.

Artists, too, find much to romanticize in this simple street scene with its glimpse of the courthouse and the Historical Society building in the background. Richard Gucker of Baltimore County, who drew the accompanying sketch, depicts clearly the unique charm to be found here when sought by the discerning and observant eye. He has captured all the appeal that is Tongue Row's.

Another etching in black and white executed by Ted Koppel, a

251

resident of Howard County, has also caught the attention of many who appreciate fine work. Copies are still available in the town and they have proven among the fastest selling items in the tourist trade. The original, once the possession of the late Milton J. Fitzsimmons of the Patapsco Pharmacy, is still on display at the drug store on Main Street, along with other views of the town sketched by the same artist.

When in 1963 Mr. Fitzsimmons, better known as "Doc" Fitzsimmons, was approached by the writer concerning the name of this group of fascinating houses, he replied with an amusing but provocative story. In effect, he said:

> Back in the days when telephones were unheard of, and fans and air-conditioners were in the distant future, the curiosity of the townspeople of that area, and the heat of the day drove the ladies to the front steps of their homes. The houses being so closely joined, by raising their voices a bit, they could exchange all the local gossip without walking a single step. Their words flew, and their tongues wagged. And so the houses became known as Tongue Row.

Not knowing whether to take him seriously, this author resorted to silence. At the time the name of the builder had not been revealed. Even so, there was reason to suspect that this was but a bit of harmless good humor! The twinkle in his eye only confirmed the suspicion! Nevertheless, each time the writer passes Tongue Row on her way to town, she recalls with delight Doc Fitzsimmons and his fanciful narration. But for him, the oft-repeated legend might well have died. As it is, whether named for the man who actually built it, or for the women who found relaxation in "wagging their tongues," Tongue Row remains today one of the mill town's principal attractions. So when in Ellicott City, one should be sure to include this unique sight in his travels.

In the mind's eye blot out the surrounding buildings of little character and see this famous landmark as seen through the eyes of such artists as Mr. Bodine, Mr. Gucker, Mr. Koppel and others. Then, and only then, can the attractive row of houses be visualized as it was in the beginning—back in the early 1800s—when Ellicott's Mills was a place of rugged beauty and imaginative architecture, compared by many to an Alpine village.

Today Tongue Row seems assured of a secure future. Through the Patapsco Land Development Company of Washington, D.C.,

Mrs. Esther Skeel Rettger, a one-time resident of Georgetown, has purchased four of the old properties facing on Columbia Road and undertaken the renovation of the historic site. Although she has faced many difficulties, Mrs. Rettger is not easily discouraged. Her theory regarding the small mill town is best expressed in her own words:

> You can build Columbia and all the new apartments
> you want, but you can never duplicate Ellicott City.

To date, the homes already house a fabric shop, an art and import shop, and a small but appealing antique shop. So it is not without cause that the writer sees every indication that this once insignificant group of millers' homes may well become known as one of the state's most unique and minute shopping centers.

As such, appropriately enough, the old landmark will again live up to the legendary origin of its name: Tongue Row—a place where words fly and tongues really wag!

*   *   *

2003 UPDATE

Tongue Row remains one of the most charming and picturesque parts of the Historic District of Ellicott City. The old stone buildings still house a variety of shops, opening onto Columbia Pike or the parking lot in the rear. During work on the parking lot a few years ago, a ramp was built next to Tongue Row, which allows for easier and more convenient foot traffic to the Columbia Pike-side shops. The ramp is named Roussey Lane, in honor of a fallen police officer who once worked at Tersiguel's Restaurant.

In June, 2000, a production crew from The Learning Channel's 'Great Books' television series used the buildings as a location for a filming of "Les Miserables," finding the gray stone edifices a reasonable approximation of buildings in nineteenth century France. A portable "stone" wall was used to block out passing cars. In the early 21st century the site remains a magnet for photographers and artists.

*   *   *

KEEWAYDIN

When Judge James Clark sat on the bench at Ellicott City, he was known to be a stern man, and one who was feared by those who had reason to know they had violated the law. Completely fearless himself and fully aware of his widespread reputation, Judge Clark could not be persuaded by either threat or cajolery to alter his course once he had fully evaluated the evidence and reached a decision.

But this man was something more than an impersonal custodian of justice. He was also known to be—above all else—just and honest. The accused, appearing in his court, knew well that although he might earn full contempt if found guilty, until proven so "beyond a reasonable doubt" he would also have the unprejudiced eyes and ears of the Judge. For James Clark believed deeply in the tenet, "innocent until proven guilty."

*   *   *

James Clark, the oldest son of John L. and Corinne Talbott Clark, was born and raised at Fairfield on the Clarksville Pike. He received his early education in the one-room school at Oakland Mills which still stands. He also attended Rock Hill College before moving on to St. John's at Annapolis, where he graduated in 1903. He earned his law degree at the University of Maryland well before

254

his 21st birthday. With the laws of Maryland reading that no man was eligible to practice law until he had reached maturity (21), young James worked for two years for the Baltimore & Ohio Railroad Company before opening his office. On October 30, 1912 he married Alda Hopkins of White Hall.

Alda Tyson Hopkins, daughter of Samuel and Martha Tyson Smith Hopkins, was born at White Hall, twelve miles from Ellicott City. (The old home is known today as Hickory Ridge and is the residence of Henry Owings.) One of five children, Alda received but one year of formal education when she attended the Arlington Institute of Virginia, an exclusive private school for girls. The balance of her training was received from her mother and from a series of governesses. Although modest concerning her own abilities, Mrs. Clark's many accomplishments speak clearly of her varied talents and multiple interests.

The first year of their marriage James Clark purchased ten acres of land from his father. There being no "great house" on the farm, he built Keewaydin for his bride, leaving the tenant house free for his farmhand. The Clarks lived in a small house near the site of Keewaydin until it was completed. The name chosen, meaning West Wind, was taken from the beautiful poem "Hiawatha," a favorite of both Mr. and Mrs. Clark.

The cedar-shingled house stands today in the middle of a lovely tract of land, additional acreage having been acquired over the years. There are twelve rooms, including the baths, and a large central hallway with spiraling stairway. The entire house is furnished with pieces from both sides of the family. Says Mrs. Clark: "Everything, from the beds to the dining room table and chairs, to the living room pieces, and even including the silver and china are family pieces. The Judge and I didn't buy a thing!"

Included among the Clarks' most prized possessions are an old Ellicott mug brought from Pennsylvania by one of the original settlers; some very old linens bearing the monogram of Martha Ellicott; beautiful Sheraton chairs from the Tyson family; the first piece of glass made in Maryland; a piece of signed Stiegel glass; a number of very old bedspreads, and handsome china and silver from the Ellicott, Tyson, Clark and Hopkins families.

Of equal interest are the pieces of artwork scattered throughout the house. The colorful drawings in the bright kitchen, executed by Mrs. Clark and depicting Ellicott City many years ago, are particularly appealing.

*   *   *

It was in this house that all four sons were born: John L., Samuel Hopkins, James, Jr. and Joseph Hopkins Clark. And it was from this house that young Samuel, three months shy of six years, was carried to Johns Hopkins Hospital where he died, leaving a void in the lives of this close-knit family.

Mr. Clark practiced law in Howard County from 1911 to 1942. To the people who knew him as their personal attorney, he was more than a professional adviser. He was, instead, an understanding friend who used the tools of his profession in their behalf, never overlooking their anxieties or fears, and never leaving a stone unturned until each case was resolved. At the same time he was their personal friend and confidant. His genuine interest in their families, their successes and failures, was both sincere and wholehearted.

Mr. Clark's career was interrupted temporarily during World War I, when at great sacrifice to himself, he gave up his practice to volunteer for Army Service. He was honorably discharged December 1, 1918, because of "termination of emergency."

He also served twice as State's Attorney, the first time in 1919 when he was appointed by the court to fill out an unexpired term, and then again from 1930 to 1934 when he was elected to office. In 1942 he was appointed Judge by the late Governor Herbert R. O'Conor.

Judge Clark's chief hobby was farming. In 1927 he bought Elioak Farm, also located on the Clarksville Pike. Here he introduced Aberdeen Angus cattle into the area in the early '30s. He imported some of the best blood lines in America for this venture which was highly successful. At one sale he sold nine calves which brought a record price for cattle sold from Howard County. Averaging approximately 1,000 pounds per head, they brought the heretofore unheard-of price of $16.80 per hundred. As a sideline and more for pleasure than profit, the Judge also enjoyed raising beagles and rabbit dogs. His was indeed a full life!

His sudden death of a heart attack on Maryland Day, March 25, 1955, came as a blow to both family and community. His passing proved a great loss to the county, and he was deeply mourned by all who knew him, as well as by those who had more intimate knowledge of his good works and brilliant career.

An oil painting of the Judge which hangs in the living room at Keewaydin is truly representative. The expression in his eyes, as caught by the artist, as well as the set of the jaw, indicate the strength of character that was his. Although a person of strong convictions, he was not a narrowly opinionated man. To the contrary, he kept an open mind at all times and nurtured a persistent urge to pursue knowledge and understanding wherever it was to be found.

The Clarks were members of St. John's Episcopal Church, Ellicott City, where Mrs. Clark was particularly active in the drive to build the new parish house. Following the Judge's untimely death, Mrs. Clark resumed attendance at St. Mark's Parish near White Hall, the scene of her childhood. Understandably, this parish still holds many fond memories for her.

*   *   *

Although Keewaydin can not be classified as one of Howard County's older homes, it is definitely one of rare distinction. For within its walls are housed the treasures and heritages of one of the county's best-known and most accomplished families.

There were many "firsts" that took place at Keewaydin. To name but a few: the annual suppers for the benefit of St. John's Church were initiated by the Clarks and held here for a number of years; the first meeting of the Ellicott City Parent-Teacher Association was also held in this house; and the Howard County Health Department held its first official meeting within these walls. Meanwhile Judge Clark was one of the promoters of the Rotary Club and served as its first president, even as Mrs. Clark was instrumental in promoting the annual County Fairs. Realizing that money was due the county for such a program, she had her husband speak to Warren G. (Buddy) Myers, county agent for many years. Mr. Myers wrote to the Maryland State Fair Association and obtained the allotted money, making possible the first official Fair.

Keewaydin has been, and still is, the center of many of the county's activities. Despite her advanced age, Mrs. Clark has never lost interest in civic affairs. She is the first to defend the preservation of old and historic landmarks, and the last to seek credit for all she has accomplished.

Her love of horses, as well as her joy and delight in riding, is legendary throughout the county. At the remarkable age of 76 she still rides, breeding and breaking her own colts! It was primarily through Mrs. Clark's efforts that the Doughoregan Horse Shows were initiated in 1921, the first one having been held at Keewaydin. After two years they were transferred to the Manor. The first meeting of the Hunt Club also took place at Keewaydin.

Regardless of her comments to the contrary, Mrs. Clark is also an author in her own right. She was deeply devoted to her

258

mother and wrote an account of her life for the benefit of the members of her immediate family, an account she considers of a personal nature. For public consumption she penned a delightful volume entitled HOLD HARD. Dictated to Betsy Fleet and illustrated by the author, the work gives a clear but entertaining insight into the lively and sensitive disposition of the writer. A thoughtful woman of many interests, Mrs. Clark is primarily a lover of life and the good things it has to offer. It is somehow contradictory to visualize her in a depressed frame of mind, even though she has known great pain and suffering as well as happiness and fulfillment.

In 1960 the beautiful and historic First Presbyterian Church was purchased by Mrs. Clark and presented to the Howard County Historical Society (of which she was the founder and first president) as a befitting memorial to the memory of her late husband. It will also serve as a constant reminder of the generous benevolence of its gracious donor. In appreciation, the Society unanimously bestowed upon her a life membership.

On March 12th, 1967 no less than three hundred friends and admirers met in the Society building to honor this delightful and invigorating woman who has contributed so much to the betterment of the county. A portrait, executed by Mrs. Frank Hazel, then of Angelo Cottage, was unveiled. It will hang in the main room of the Society's headquarters.

The roots of the Clark Family are buried deep in the soil of Howard County, and loyalties are as strong now as they were almost two hundred years ago when their ancestors—the Ellicotts, the Tysons, the Hopkins and the Clarks—first founded and settled in and around the famous little town.

*   *   *

2003 UPDATE

Keewaydin was the childhood home of Senator James Clark, who now lives further west in the Ellicott City area on Route 108 at his farm Elioak. Senator Clark, who was president of the Maryland Senate and always interested in conservation, writes lovingly of the property in his memoirs, JIM CLARK: SOLDIER, FARMER, AND LEGISLATOR, published in 1999, saying that he was born in the southwest bedroom of the house. A mile from Main Street, at the corner of Old Columbia Pike and Toll House Road, the house and ten-acre property are part of the area's scenic gateway to the Historic District. According to

Senator Clark, the name "Keewaydin" comes from Longfellow's "The Song of Hiawatha" and means "The Northwest Wind."

In recent years owners attempted to sell the property to various business interests, including one with plans for an 87-room nursing home. The nursing home would have occupied the field in front of the house and thus would have blocked its view, threatening the historic integrity of the site. A more recent proposal involved building as many as 19 houses around the historic house – another obvious threat to the integrity of Keewaydin.

Happily, the property has been saved and will continue life much as it appears today. According to Mary Catherine Cochran, President of Preservation Howard County, this was accomplished through the vision of a buyer for the property, the availability of rewarding tax and easement rules, and the stewardship of Ann Jones, a savvy and determined land use planner who serves on the board of the Howard County Conservancy. A new owner, Edward J. Brush, donated an easement to the Howard County Conservancy that prevents further development on the land, which assures the property's uncluttered setting.

In late 2001, Mr. Brush sold the house and property to his attorney, Lex Ruygrok, who today lives in the house with his wife, Terry, and their triplet sons, Bryan, Dylan, and Kyle. A delightful combination of openness and warmth greets today's visitor to Keewaydin. The original front door opens to a traditional central hallway and stairs; on either side are large front rooms with original flooring and woodwork. The living room features a fireplace with the home's original carved mantle. Former open porches on each side of the house are now enclosed, one side converted to an open eating area, but still featuring the warmth of rustic wooden cabinets; the other side is a play area. The house contains five bedrooms and three living floors, in addition to a basement partially finished as a recreation room.

The Ruygroks have made their own improvements to the 10-acre property, replacing some of the old fencing and installing two stone pillars at the entrance. Three outbuildings remain on the property, providing storage and garage space, and even a habitat for wildlife in the form of a groundhog. The Ruygroks plan additional interior improvements to their charming home.

*   *   *

SEARCH ENCLOSED

Opposite Keewaydin on Columbia Road the connoisseur will find still another stone and frame house of considerable size and age known as Search Enclosed. Having served at one time as a weighing station on the old toll road—then known as the Ellicott City-Clarksville Turnpike—it is today the home of Mr. and Mrs. Melvin W. Chambers.

Many years ago John L. Clark, father of the late Judge James Clark, bought ten acres of land, believed to have been originally a part of Talbott's Last Shift, and the existing house and converted it into a privately owned weighing station. The two scales were located on the road directly in front of Keewaydin before the newer house was built, when all was open land. For a time they were operated alternately by Benjamin Coons, keeper of the toll gate which lay east of the scales, and Grafton Gray, a local smithy.

Before many years passed the station was functioning on a full-time basis and the station master lived in the old house. Here farmers gathered to check the weight of their grain before going on to the mills. It was a busy center and a place where views were exchanged and neighborly conversations took place, a custom not unlike that practiced in crossroad country stores. Scattered families met who might not otherwise see each other for months on end.

Today the once-picturesque weighing station has been converted into an attractive residence by Mr. and Mrs. Chambers, who have not only faithfully restored the landmark but who have, in doing so, preserved still another of Ellicott City's older structures. By adding a few unique features they have also succeeded in stressing the old home's strength and architectural charm. The lacy iron railing and lovely Belgian block terrace enhance the massive painted stone building, while the black shutters and trim set off the gleaming white of the entire house. Indoors, wormy chestnut paneling displays to advantage many pieces of fine antique furniture as well as a colorful collection of early-American glass.

Search Enclosed is, in itself, an excellent example of what can be achieved by exercising a little imagination and good judgment when restoring old but well-designed houses. Such an undertaking, although frequently costly and time-consuming, offers the owner a feeling of accomplishment and individuality. For unlike modern homes, such as are to be found in present-day residential developments, rarely can there be found two identical old homes.

Hence, despite the cost and inconvenience to which the owners are subjected, a restoration such as this is worthy of all the effort required. The ultimate result, as in the case of Search Enclosed, is an ever-stimulating reward—a distinctive residence which gives joy to the owner, and enchantment to the entire community.

*   *   *

2003 UPDATE

Some things are made better with time, and the property known as Search Enclosed is an example of such good fortune. In the past thirty years Bette Chambers has made her home a very personal labor of love. Bette and her husband, Melvin, raised their five children on the property, with time out for stints in Germany from 1973 to 1980, and in New Jersey briefly after that. After leaving the house in the hands of renters for a few years, and seeing the damage that was done, they made the decision to return and further enhance the property.

The Chambers made many changes, while retaining the integrity of the old dwelling. They closed over the front door and replaced it with a window, added a greenhouse, an entrance hall with a skylight, a porch and a family room. A laundry room, powder room and bar enhance the kitchen area. The care, integrity and taste used in these changes illustrate the fact that there is a designer in the family––Bette.

Many of the materials used were recycled from other

sites. When houses on Fels Lane were torn down for the new parking lot, Mel brought home the stone foundations to make the patio. He rescued other large stones used on the property when Tropical Storm Agnes destroyed the trolley bridge in Ellicott City. The Chambers brought them home in a Volkswagen that would never be the same after.

Melvin died in 1989, but Bette continued to enhance the property. She acquired more land from neighbors, allowing her to enlarge her garden, creating an oasis of repose that belies the fact that it is only yards from the bustle of Route 103. Everywhere is evidence of Bette's talents as a gardener and member of the Cross Country Garden Club. The garden was one of the delights of the Maryland House and Garden Tour of 1998, and also shows Bette's sense of fun – the tool shed is a former outhouse once used in Oella.

There can be no doubt that Bette has put her distinctive stamp on this beautiful home.

*   *   *

274 COLUMBIA ROAD

At 274 Columbia Road, almost within touch of the pike itself, there is a small home of particular charm which has become known to visitors as "the house by the side of the road." Considered one of Ellicott City's more picturesque homes, it is an unusually fine example of the rugged type of architecture which prevails in and around the 18th century mill town.

Constructed of native granite and frame siding—three sides of stone, the fourth of clapboard—the house is both striking in appearance and pleasing to the eye. The rear wing, which houses a modern kitchen and additional bedroom above, was added at a later date and is also of frame construction.

The original structure is said to have been built by William (Curly) Davis, a successful farmer, as a home for his three maiden sisters. Standing on land once a part of Talbott's Last Shift, one of the area's oldest estates, it is thought to be approximately one hundred and twenty-five years old.

Upon Mr. Davis' death there followed a series of owners including Josephine Ray, Mr. and Mrs. Harry J. Bloom, Clara C. Klashus, Caleb and Elizabeth Rogers, Joseph and Ella Mae Howes, H. Deets Warfield and Mr. and Mrs. P. Stanley Gault. Credit for restoration of the old landmark is given Mr. and Mrs. Gault.

The one major change made by the Gaults was the removal of a goodly portion of an old porch which originally encircled three

263

sides of the house. This single alteration revealed to advantage the excellent lines of the structure heretofore concealed. The single section of porch that was retained runs parallel to the dining room on the south side of the house. Shielded from the sun by a tremendous spruce tree—considered one of the largest and oldest in the area—this small retreat offers complete relaxation combining, as it does, natural beauty and total privacy.

During their ownership the Gaults installed many closets, there being none in the original house. By using plank doors and wrought-iron lift latches, they achieved the desired effect without sacrificing the look of authenticity.

Today 274 Columbia Road is the home of Mr. and Mrs. Omar J. Jones who take great pleasure in pointing out the ancient features of the house. The 24-inch walls, remaining random-width plank floors, huge natural beams in the basement (with bark intact), and the pegged attic floors are all relics of another era. An unusual feature, seldom found in houses of this age and size, is the full basement under the original portion of the house. (In most instances only small areas were excavated, to serve as root cellars or storage bins.)

Entering the house by way of a surprisingly large and cheerful hallway, the visitor is immediately aware of the good taste exercised by Mrs. Jones who is solely responsible for the interior decoration. Using Williamsburg blue and antique white as her basic color scheme, she has succeeded in highlighting many attractive features. The front door of unusual design, the Tiffany chandelier, the all-white staircase including bannister, balusters and posts, have all been accented by a distinctive patterned wallpaper of colonial design.

The living room, finished in solid blue, boasts the original fireplace and two-tiered mantel. Twin columns support the upper and lower shelves which, in turn, frame a mirror of considerable size. Two long windows, running from the floorboard to within inches of the ceiling, make of this a bright and inviting room.

A large bay window in the dining room admits the sun and sheds light on much of the fine old English china, once the proud possession of Mr. Jones' great-grandmother.

The kitchen, completely remodeled by the present owners, is finished in natural wood. Touches of red and white make it a lively but warm and livable room where members of the family, as well as guests, are inclined to gather. A back stairway from the kitchen to the second floor is reminiscent of the day when there were always "at least two stairways in a home."

The second floor bedrooms and hallway also retain their 19th century charm. The master bedroom is highlighted by three deep-seated windows and is of excellent proportions. The center room, Mrs. Jones' favorite, is over the dining room and has a matching bay window, an extension of the one in the room below. The color scheme here is orchid and off-white and the furnishings, early Victorian. The predominating color in the back room is Williamsburg green and the decor, strictly masculine, this being the son's room.

Lovely old quilts are to be found in each of the three rooms, while other bits of antiquity are scattered tastefully throughout the house.

*   *   *

Mr. Jones, Howard County's newly elected first Chief Executive, was for years an outstanding figure in the field of education. He came to this area from his native Somerset County in 1946, when he accepted the position of principal of Lisbon School. Lisbon then consisted of high school as well as grade school. In 1949 he became principal of Howard High, which assignment increased his responsibilities considerably, there being sixty-five teachers and 1400 students in attendance.

Mrs. Jones claims Charles County as her birthplace. Both she and her husband taught at Glasva School near La Plata before transferring to Howard County. When Mr. Jones became principal of Howard High School, she, too, became a member of the faculty, teaching 10th and 12th grade English.

In 1960 Mr. Jones observed his 25th year of teaching. An "Omar Jones Day" was proclaimed and fitting tributes were paid this man whose entire adult life had been devoted to the instruction and guidance of the young people of this state. Parents, teachers, and students alike joined in the celebration, providing an appropriate and memorable program still cherished by the guest of honor.

On March 26, 1965 Mr. Jones was again honored by the faculty and student body of Howard High School and by many friends for his thirty years of outstanding service in the field of education. This program, depicting highlights of his life as an educator, was presented by the students, followed by the presentation of a portrait of himself which now hangs in the main foyer of the school. Other gifts, including a wood carved scroll signed by every student and faculty member, were presented to him in appreciation for his dedicated work.

Surprised but elated by the unexpected honor bestowed upon him, Mr. Jones thanked all those who in any way contributed to this memorable day. He was given a standing ovation by the more than 1500 persons present. The celebration ended with a bruncheon in the library where he was again feted by members of the faculty and the committee who had developed the program.

Mr. Jones' background in the field of education is noteworthy. In 1966 his name was placed on the State Board of Education's approved list of candidates for the position of county superintendent in the State of Maryland. His talents have also been recognized by the Middle States Association of Secondary Schools and Colleges, for which he has served on twelve evaluation committees in four different states, chairing the last six.

*   *   *

In addition to manifesting his interest in the realm of education, Mr. Jones has also been active in civic affairs. Here, again, the people of Howard County have been appreciative. In November, 1966, after having received the greatest number of votes to serve on the newly-formed Charter Board, he was selected by the Board as their chairman.

In 1968 when a charter form of government was adopted by the county, based on his performance as Chairman of the Board, he was strongly urged to accept the nomination for county executive. After careful consideration he accepted the challenge. Then on January 23, 1969 Mr. Jones won the election and became Howard County's first Chief Executive, assuming office on the 28th of that month.

*   *   *

Thus it is that the little house by the side of the road which for so many years had been known simply as "the old Curly Davis place," has now become known as the home of one of Howard County's most highly respected citizens. Although a native by choice, Omar J. Jones has proven himself a man worthy of recognition and a loyal resident of Howard County.

*   *   *

2003 UPDATE

Owner Content World Hagen, who sold the property in late 2002, extensively renovated this charming home with a new address—4075 Old Columbia Pike. Ms. Hagen and her former husband purchased the home in 1983 from the estate of Omar Jones and his wife. Their caring and thoughtful restoration has greatly benefited the property.

Ms. Hagen made a number of improvements, all blending with the period of the house, which dates to the early 1800's. She replaced the former Victorian windows in the front with specially made windows featuring antique glass, of the period contemporary to the structure. She added new shingles, and trim specially milled in Smith, Virginia. Ms. Hagen had installed a new furnace, insulation, and relined the chimney. Interior improvements are also striking. Period molding enhances the first floor, while the second floor features original plaster.

A special addition to the living room is a mantel dating to approximately 1800 found at a collapsing log cabin, which was probably a slave cabin, in the Mayfield area. Ms. Hagen described with pride the difficult work of removing the existing mantle, only to discover that the Mayfield mantle's height better fit the contours of the original wall, indicating that the home's original mantle had been the same height. Another lucky discovery during restoration was an 1828-penny found on the grounds near the front of the home, an apparent testimony to the building's age.

Throughout the house, Ms. Hagen painted the walls a warm white while the trim varies from room to room, featuring rich greens, burgundies, and colonial blue. Jewel toned Oriental carpets enhance the old wide-planked wood flooring. Ms. Hagen's former husband, an appraiser, found that the attractive light fixture in the entrance area once thought to be a Tiffany was a reproduction. The functional kitchen is warm with yellow cabinets and cheerful accents. Upstairs the master bedroom features a headboard made of an old mantel. The second bedroom has become an attractive office, while the inviting back bedroom includes a wall of books and remarkably small closet. Interesting contemporary art enlivens the décor throughout the house.

Ms. Hagen wished to return to her Virginia roots and although the home held much appeal for her the house has been recently sold.

*   *   *

Main Wing of Talbott's Last Shift from Columbia Road

Rear wing, showing granite construction

TALBOTT'S LAST SHIFT

In 1649 Richard Talbott of England and his wife Elizabeth, oldest daughter of Major Richard Ewen, settled on the West River in Anne Arundel County. As members of the Quaker religion, they were peace-loving and gentle people, although progressive by nature. There were four children of this marriage: Richard, Edward, John and Elizabeth.

According to his will of 1663 Richard Talbott, the emigrant, died a landed gentleman, leaving his heirs a goodly number of acres including Poplar Knawle and Talbott's Range. All properties were located in the West River area.

Edward, son of Richard and Elizabeth Ewen Talbott, married Elizabeth Thomas Coale, a widow, in 1679 and in turn had four children. They were Richard, Edward, Elizabeth and John. John, the last of the four children, married Elizabeth Galloway and upon her death, Mary Waters. Their children were Cassandra, Lucy, Elizabeth, John and Edward.

In 1732 John, son of Edward and Elizabeth Coale Talbott, surveyed Talbott's Last Shift, thereby becoming the first of this noted family to settle in what is now Howard County. The property was described as "being on the Patapsco, adjoining Moore's Morning Choice, Chews Vineyard and Edward Dorsey's estate near Columbia." It consisted of 1120 acres.

This acreage was later sold by John, part going to his two brothers, Edward and Richard, part to Richard Galloway, and the final share to George Ellicott. Edward resurveyed his share and purchased adjoining land until his holdings mounted, finally totalling 1031 acres which he named Talbott's Vineyard.

The present house standing at 214 Columbia Road, exactly one mile from Main Street, Ellicott City, stands on land once a part of the original tract of Talbott's Last Shift, and is believed to be located on that part purchased by Edward from his brother John.

This portion remained in the Talbott family until 1850 at which time it was known as Pleasant Fields.

Over the years the land was sold, a few acres at a time, until there were less than a dozen remaining. Small and large houses soon dotted the once-sprawling fields and Ellicott City spread out to encompass the present home.

The late Edward A. Talbott of E.A. Talbott (lumber company), a descendant of John the first settler in Howard County, was the last of this noted family to own Talbott's Last Shift. Edwin P. Hayden, one-time State Delegate and first Clerk of the Howard County Court (1847-1850), acted as attorney for Mr. Talbott until the year 1848 when he turned the property over to him as had been prearranged. It has been rumored that Mr. Hayden "stayed on in the house until his untimely death May 10, 1850, at the age of 39." However, Mr. Hayden did not live at Talbott's Last Shift, having built and lived at Oak Lawn, his own lovely home back of the courthouse, where his wife and six children remained for many years following his death.

On October 15, 1850 the Talbott property was sold for $3,000 to James W. Rowland by Edward Talbott. Edward Hammond, another of Howard County's more prominent attorneys, succeeded Edwin P. Hayden as legal representative for Mr. Talbott, carrying out the transaction in his place.

The next owner was Abraham Buchwalter who paid $5,000 "current money" in 1865. The Buchwalter family held the property for forty-six years, adding approximately fifteen acres to the estate and changing the name to Sunny Side. Mrs. Buchwalter outlived her husband and upon her death the entire property was sold to Margaret R. Pue Jones on November 21, 1911. Rebecca O. Dorsey is believed to have been a part owner of the estate from 1938 to 1946 when a single lot on the westernmost edge was sold to John S. Ditch and wife.

When Margaret Pue Jones originally bought the land it consisted of "26 acres and 32 perches." After having sold off the lot mentioned above, the balance of the estate was sold to Andrew Lee Nicholson, Jr. and wife in December, 1957. Then on June 30, 1959 Mr. and Mrs. Charles M. Cook, the present owners purchased the house and two acres from Mr. and Mrs. Nicholson.

Although it has been known by a succession of names, Talbott's Last Shift remains an appealing home with many fine and unusual features. It boasts fourteen rooms, random-width floors of

Georgia pine and two black marble fireplaces in the main house or west wing. Beautiful silver-plated keyhole covers are to be found on all the old doors, while the key to the front entrance is also heavily plated and folds in the center.

The rear wing is said to have been the service area and servants' quarters. A large stone fireplace in the main room indicates that this was the original kitchen.

From the road the main wing appears strong of line though harsh in color. Upon closer inspection, however, one sees that it offers great promise. After much careful prodding, Mr. Cook discovered that the yellow tinted stucco covers a solid granite house. The stone was undoubtedly quarried locally. Slowly and painstakingly, he is removing the offensive covering and revealing the handsome ruggedness of the hand-hewn and hand-laid granite structure.

On the south side of the house the outline and rough framework of a window (or door) was uncovered. There is no apparent reason for its having been closed up, but it was never finished before it was discarded, perhaps to allow for additional wall space in the room into which it would have opened. The windows throughout the house are of an unusually large size, in most instances matching the openings for the doors. The old shutters can be used on either windows or doorways, since the measurements are, with few exceptions, nearly identical.

A truly remarkable trim at the roof-line, resembling a massive carved and scalloped cornice, is of cast iron rather than wood. It encircles the entire house, adding a note of rare adornment.

Inside Mr. Cook is doing all the work himself. His knowledge of antiquity and awareness of possible hidden features are truly amazing. He and Mrs. Cook are working on a long-term schedule and are in no hurry, which fact should assure them of a thorough and authentic restoration.

Original materials are being reused wherever possible. Approximately seventy per cent of the old sand glass remains intact in the windows. It is being carefully removed while the framework is scraped and sanded to the bare wood, and replaced only as the refinishing is completed. The house is being restored one room at a time, the only modern innovation being the installation of closets where needed, since none existed in the original structure. All other modern conveniences had been installed some time ago.

The Cooks anticipate at least another half-dozen years of hard work before their antique home will reveal its full charm. In the meantime they are enjoying the luxury of spacious grounds for their children, a new swimming pool, and the knowledge that when finished, they will be the proud owners of one of Ellicott City's finest old homes, once owned and occupied by one of the town's most prominent and respected families. This knowledge in itself should be ample incentive for the years of hard work just ahead.

Mr. and Mrs. Cook impressed the writer as being an ambitious and optimistic young couple who thoroughly enjoy each little act of restoration, as well as each new discovery. They do not look on the work as a chore, but rather as a family project which combines their favorite hobby of collecting the old with that of providing a suitable home in which they can thoroughly enjoy their lives, even as they fulfill their ambitions.

They are cheerfully determined to restore once again the dignity and obvious beauty for which Talbott's Last Shift was once so well known. With such determination, there is little doubt that they will succeed. And because of their success, Ellicott City will just as cheerfully reclaim one of its oldest, but erstwhile unrecognized, landmarks.

*   *   *

2003 UPDATE

Thirty years later Charles and Jo Ann Cook still own Talbott's Last Shift and the restoration continues. As with any old home, keeping up with repairs is a constant, unending challenge. Water damage remains in one of the first floor rooms, an aftermath of a fire several years ago. The fire destroyed original glass in some of the windows, which they replaced with reproduction sand glass from England. Four original shutters were also destroyed; reproduction shutters were made in Pennsylvania. The couple had to restore two sections of driveway, and lost a giant cedar tree.

A true do-it-yourselfer, Mr. Cook has worked magic in every area of the house, but Mrs. Cook is not far behind. When their two children were small, she saw the front porch as a safety hazard and tore it down herself.

The Cooks converted the original coal heat to gas years ago, and they added baseboard radiation in 2001. In the family room, they uncovered an outside door and added a skylight, increasing the natural light in the room. They carefully restored the honey colored random-width floors. The kitchen features the original beamed ceiling. The Cooks have decorated the house with style and flair, and used a judicious amount of color to accent the fine moldings.

Decorative elements brighten every room. The headboard

for the bed in the master bedroom is a window frame recycled from Emory Methodist Church. The only original remaining walls are in the hallway, as Mr. Cook had to build all new walls elsewhere in the house. The couple lived in three rooms when they first moved in and laughingly describe having to light the water heater each time they needed hot water.

Work on the exterior was no less daunting. Mr. Cook has installed frieze board on the structure, a 30-year labor of love not quite completed. On the grounds a large walk-in playhouse charms visitors. Built by Mr. Cook in the mid-1960's, soon after the birth of their daughter Dina, the little house contains a working fireplace and enough room for children's sleepovers. Mrs. Cook even served Thanksgiving dinner there one year. The swimming pool, added by Mr. Cook, can no longer be used, its stability challenged by nearby new development.

Mrs. Cook was born and raised in Howard County, living all but two years of her life on Columbia Road. Mr. Cook, born in Illinois, grew up in nearby Ilchester. Together they have created a rare and lovely home. Luckily they have no plans to move and hope to enjoy their beautiful residence for many years to come.

*   *   *

Quaker Meeting House as it appeared when in use

— *Courtesy of Mrs. Norman S. Betts*

QUAKER HILL

When the Ellicott brothers migrated to Maryland in 1772 and founded their mills in Upper Arundel, they brought with them men, tools, and equipment of their own invention, plus a dream. But more important still they brought a proud heritage, handed down by their elders during the formative years when they were still members of a small Pennsylvania congregation of Quakers.

While establishing themselves in the crevice known as "the Hollow," they overcame many obstacles of cynicism and prejudice, both religious and material. But the practice of their faith, which included attendance twice weekly at public services, proved a more difficult handicap than most other activities. For the closest Meeting House was located near Elkridge Landing about one mile below Thistle (now Ilchester), a great and sometimes impossible distance to travel at that time. Nevertheless, when feasible they did attend, along with the Pierponts, the Haywards, the Reads and others.

Because of the inconvenience of distance as well as the hazard of crossing the Patapsco at Thistle—the only way in which the house of worship could be reached, there being no road connecting the two settlements on the east bank of the river—the Ellicotts planned a Meeting House of their own. It became a reality in 1798, although the deed conveying the entire property including land for two cemeteries, one private and one public, was drawn in 1800 and presented "to the monthly meeting of the Friends of Baltimore, to be held in trust as a place of worship by the Society..." The land, totaling four acres, was located west of the Patpasco, making it more accessible for a greater number of people.

William Hayward of the Elkridge Meeting House, the only minister available, left the old congregation which had been founded in 1699 for the new. Sitting in utter silence, a number of his former members continued to meet in the ancient building, "the remaining members of the faith." Gradually, as roads were cut through the rambling forests, they too became members of the congregation at Ellicott's Mills, which soon became known as "the new Elkridge Meeting house" or Quaker Hill.

The building itself was one-story, measuring fifteen by forty feet, and scarcely twelve feet high. It was built of granite, with a sloping shingled roof. Rectangular in shape, it had two doors—one for the men, the other for the women—separated by two center windows. There was also an additional window on the outer side of each of the doors. Simple panelled shutters adorned the building. They were closed after each service "to keep out the weather." Later two wooden sheds were added, one at each end, to serve as storage space for firewood, implements and other necessary equipment.

The intensity of the Ellicotts' quiet determination to practice their faith despite all obstacles is beyond dispute when we recall that, with the exception of two small voluntary donations amounting to sixty dollars given by Samuel Smith and Samuel Godfrey, the financial burden of erecting the building and establishing the cemeteries was assumed by the family as a matter of course.

The first service to be held in the new Meeting House has been described by one historian as "a meeting of peculiar solemnity." At this meeting Cassandra Ellicott, widow of John Ellicott of the first house of Ellicott & Company, married Joseph Thornburg, senior partner of Thornburg, Miller & Webster of Baltimore, "a mercantile house of great respectability." The ceremony was performed in an impressive manner according to the order of the Society of Friends, as a sizable gathering of members sat in silent attendance.

Across the road from the house of worship a private burial ground for the Ellicott family was laid out. At the same time, east of the Ellicott cemetery a piece of land sloping down to the banks of the Patapsco was designated as a public graveyard for the use of the townspeople including the millhands and their families, as well as the members of the congregation. If markers were used at the time, none remain to identify those interred there, or to tell the story of the first settlers. Nothing is left to indicate that at one time this was the small town's principal cemetery.

*   *   *

Although military service was opposed by the Society of Friends, it is recorded that Andrew Ellicott, the surveyor, accepted a commission as Captain from Governor Johnson of Maryland in 1778. He was later promoted to the rank of Major and served in the Elkridge Battalion of Militia during the Revolutionary War. Further evidence of his convictions concerning religious versus patriotic duty is noted in an account of his service under

General George Washington.

Major Ellicott openly argued that "in regard to defensive war the Friends are all wrong." However, it is to be stressed that this was his belief only in the case of defensive warfare. Although his views were frowned upon by members of the faith, he was never expelled from the Society as was George Ellicott, son of the first George, who was known as "the swearing member" of the family.

*   *   *

In 1800 the number of active members of the Quaker Hill Meeting House was reported to Baltimore as 120, an astonishingly low number, considering the size of the families. Among those mentioned as prominent in the faith at this time were Evan Thomas, Joel Wright, Jonathan Wright, Reese Cadwalader, George Ellicott, John Ellicott, Jonathan Ellicott, Benjamin Ellicott, Gerard Hopkins, Elisha Tyson, Isaac Tyson, John McKim, Philip Thomas,

Graves of the Founding Fathers

Edward Stabler, Samuel Snowden and Philip Dennis. Gerard Hopkins left many written records covering this period.

The first George Ellicott, son of Andrew the founder, was foremost in his loyalty to the little congregation. He and his wife, Elizabeth Brooke Ellicott (cousin of Gerard Hopkins) did all in their power to keep the membership alive. However, with the removal of so many families to other parts of the state and to Pennsylvania, New York and Ohio, the decline in attendance was crippling. When the Hartley family left, only Samuel Smith and Ezra Fell remained, and the Meeting House was forced to close its doors.

From that time until her death in 1853 at the age of ninety-two, the widowed Elizabeth Brooke Ellicott was almost totally responsible for the preservation and upkeep of the abandoned building. At her own expense she had the deteriorating roof covered with tin and painted. The woodwork was also repaired and refinished.

In life the donor had been recognized as "a cultivated woman who had traveled extensively." In death her simple obituary read:

> She was the last Ellicott in Ellicott's
> Mills where she had lived 63 years.

George and Elizabeth Brooke Ellicott and other members of the Ellicott and Tyson families are buried on Quaker Hill. Joseph Ellicott and his descendants and many of the Evans family are buried at Hollofield's, three miles up the Patapsco.

Records show that George and John Ellicott also contributed liberally to the building of the brick meeting house in Sandy Spring in 1813.

*   *   *

In 1864 the Meeting House was put to use again when it served as a hospital. In one account of the part played by Ellicott's Mills during the rugged days of the Civil War, it is recorded that "many wounded in the Battle of the Monocacy were cared for here until they could be sent to Baltimore."

In the 1880s the building was used as a school, thought to have been private. It again served this purpose temporarily from 1915 until 1922-23, when it was used for first and second grade students.

About this time Mrs. A. Marshall Elliott, nee Tyson, owner of Berg Alnwyck (formerly the Patapsco Female Institute), fell heir to or assumed the care of the Meeting House and its grounds. She was the last member of the family to hold herself responsible for its upkeep. It is said that during this period until her death, both the grounds and the building were once again' kept in good repair, although the Meeting House stood idle.

Following a visit to the historic spot at the turn of the century, Emily Emerson Lantz wrote:

> The gray stone Quaker meeting-house, the first
> place of worship to be built in Ellicott City by the Elli-

cott family, more than 110 years ago, still stands in stern isolation, but perfect preservation, upon a rocky summit.

Of the cemetery she commented:

> Nearby is the Ellicott family graveyard, where the founders of the city and their descendants rest in peace. It is surrounded by a granite wall and entered through stone gateways, and the place is kept in the beautiful order that bespeaks Quaker management. It is unique in that such maintainance is secured by a family endowment.

Miss Lantz further observed:

> The still and quiet company of Friends is long since scattered, and in the Ellicott City of today—a place founded and peopled by Quakers whose descendants have been the strength and sinew of Baltimore—not one of the faith remains.

Upon the death of Mrs. Elliott the historic old building, as well as the grounds, was abandoned and fell into disrepair. For a time few, if any, recognized the building for what it was or what it had been. But Quaker Hill was not destined to be forgotten. Instead, before many years passed the Meeting House and the Burial Ground became once again one of the better-known historic landmarks within the borders of the community.

For in 1926 a "friendly suit" was filed against the Safe Deposit and Trust Company of Baltimore, "trustee under the last will of Lily Tyson Elliott, deceased," by Thomas Hunt Mayfield, who wished to purchase the property providing a clear title could be obtained. Based in part upon the assertion that the indefinite trust constituted an "adverse possession," the claim read in part:

> A trust for the purpose of a house of worship and a burying ground "for the society of people called Quakers," was invalid because of the indefiniteness of the cestui que trust, the society referred to not being a corporation.

Later in the claim we find the following statement:

Where, although a trust created for a religious society was invalid by reason of the indefiniteness of the cestui que trust, members of the society took possession of the property and occupied it for seventy-five years, and thereafter persons purporting to act as successors to the original trustees transferred the property to a religious corporation affiliated with the society, and this corporation and its successors in interest took possession of the property and exercised complete control thereover for forty-four years, held that there was a valid title by adverse possession, which a vendee was bound to accept.

A decision was reached March 9, 1926 following which Mr. Mayfield became the new owner. He converted the old building into a suitable residence and took possession upon completion of the necessary alterations.

In 1936, following his death, the property passed from his widow, Mrs. Edna E. Mayfield, to T. Hunt Mayfield, Jr. and his wife Dorothy. In 1943 the old Meeting House again changed hands when Mr. and Mrs. Mayfield sold it to Dorsey M. Williams. Finally, in 1949 it was purchased from Mr. Williams by Mr. and Mrs. Lewis W. Boone, the present occupants.

*   *   *

When the Boones took possession, the property included approximately two acres of ground. They have since purchased additional acreage bringing the total to four acres "more or less."

Overlooking Columbia Pike, Quaker Hill can be reached via a narrow gravel road almost within sight of Main Street. Sitting atop another of the small town's hills, it overlooks the town proper and affords the visitor an excellent view of the many old buildings to be found there, now serving modern day needs.

According to Mrs. Boone who was born within sight of her present home, there was at one time a pleasant custom of holding picnics on the grounds. This idea was initiated by Mrs. Elliott. She permitted the children of the area to play on the grassy slopes west of the building, up which had wound many jubilant wedding parties, as well as equally solemn funeral processions.

Later the Ellicott City Lutheran Church sponsored the picnics, and all the children of the town were invited, regardless of denomination. The evening hours were set aside for the young men and women of the town. Japanese lanterns were strung between the trees, adding a festive note to the affair. Many still remember the fun they had and regret the passing of such a delightful custom.

Mr. and Mrs. Boone enjoy sharing the history of their home with interested persons. Although the house is not open to the public, the writer was fortunate enough to have made several visits and to have had the advantage of her hosts' undivided attention. Having been a lifetime resident of Ellicott City, Mrs. Boone is well-informed and anxious to keep alive the history of her home town. At the same time, although he was born in Baltimore County, Mr. Boone considers himself a bona fide Howard Countian—by choice—and shares his wife's enthusiasm for the town he now calls home. Both are active members of the Howard County Historical Society.

There are many priceless antiques to be seen and enjoyed at Quaker Hill, but one of Mrs. Boone's proudest possessions is a silver medal given her father when he attended school in this same building in the late eighties. It is inscribed: "John Kraft, Quaker Hill, 1884."

The house is furnished with rare and beautiful pieces dating back to the 18th century. Among the choice items in the Boone collection are a Queen Anne commode and lowboy, an unusual 18th century slant-top walnut desk with dovetail drawers, a grandfather clock made by T. H. Perkins of Pittsburgh and numbered 66, and a small half-moon drop-leaf table, believed to have belonged to the Washington family.

Early American glass, fine prints, excellent hurricane lamps, rare books, and bronze eagle candlesticks, said to have been presented to John C. Calhoun by the Continental Congress, are also to be found among the treasures owned and enjoyed by Mr. and Mrs. Boone.

*   *   *

Before leaving Quaker Hill, it is well worth the effort to walk across the gravel road and through the grounds of the old Ellicott cemetery to view the markers now standing within the confines of this small yard. Here you will find the graves of Andrew and John, two of the founders; George and Elizabeth Brooke Ellicott; and other members of this notable family.

Since the cemetery has been preserved exclusively for members and descendants of the Ellicott family, there are to this day at least a few who have expressed their determination to avail themselves of this privilege. One such member is Mrs. Ruth Ellicott Valentine of Washington, D.C. who considers her deed to space within these walls one of her most cherished inheritances.

*   *   *

As has been noted, for a time the burial ground was abandoned and all but forgotten. Then upon the death of Elizabeth King Ellicott of Baltimore—daughter of Francis King, noted attorney and outstanding member of the Society of Friends, and wife of William Ellicott, a direct descendant of the famous Ellicott brothers—it was discovered that a specified sum of money from her estate had been set aside to restore the old and venerable landmark. This endowment spurred other members of the family into action.

On July 24th, 1925, long before the current program to restore and preserve the historic mill town was underway, an organization came into being, incorporated under Maryland law and dedicated to the preservation of the burial ground. Adopting the name "Association for the Care and Improvement of the Ellicott City Graveyard Inc."—which name was later shortened to "Ellicott Graveyard Inc."—it consisted primarily of descendants of the Ellicott family. The original trustees were: Malcolm van V. Tyson, Helen H. Carey, Caroline M. Carey, Charles Ellis Ellicott, Jr., Mrs. Robert Henderson, Andrew Ellicott Maccoun, Caroline Ellicott Boyce and James Carey, III.

In recent years a number of persons genuinely interested in the maintenance of this hallowed spot have been, on occasion, invited to attend special meetings of the association.

At the last regular annual meeting the following persons were elected to office: Valcoulon L. Ellicott, president; Harry Lee Hoffman, first vice-president; Virginia G. Clark, second vice-president; C. Ellis Ellicott, Jr., secretary; Virginia G. Clark, treasurer; and John LeMoyne Ellicott, assistant secretary.

Thus it is that once again a group of dedicated people have assumed responsibility for the burial ground of their ancestors. And once again the place is indeed "kept in the beautiful order that bespeaks Quaker management."

*   *   *

With this visit to the small burial ground by the side of the road, and a walk through its consecrated grounds, our journey through one of Maryland's more unique and historic towns comes to an end. As one reads the brief epitaphs and notes the dates on the few scattered markers, the memory of another era alive with history and romance is awakened.

As we leave, closing the gate gently behind us, an upward glance reveals a simple but eloquent piece of grille-work. For atop the wrought iron gate, in peaks reaching skyward, the name ELLICOTT is spelled out. Letter by letter....peak by peak.

This, indeed, is a fitting and memorable time to say farewell. But even more, it seems an impressive and somehow appropriate way of saying "...lest we forget!"

*   *   *

2003 UPDATE

The former Quaker Meeting House remains a private, well-maintained residence, shielded by trees and topography, and secluded, off Columbia Pike. A visit to the adjacent Ellicott Family Cemetery takes today's visitor back to that peaceful period of the early nineteenth century when the first of the founding family of Ellicotts were laid to rest overlooking the small but vibrant town they had established. The small space is well maintained, the graves neatly tended, and the grass mowed, due to the vigilance of Ellicott Graveyard, Incorporated, a non-profit group that has cared for and maintained the cemetery for over seventy-five years.

Harry Hoffman, President of the Ellicott Graveyard, Inc. wrote in a recent newsletter, "Current events are shaking the foundations of civilization, our nation, and the world. Our faith in God and our neighbor is being severely tested. Yet, we believe that the spiritual and ethical values of our country will be made stronger than ever. If you can, I invite you to make a pilgrimage to the Graveyard. Here you will find tranquility, beauty, peace and a sense of the presence of God. Also you will be touched by the spirit of those who have preceded us in life's often difficult, but also joyful and never ending journey."

In the early 1970's a second Ellicott burial ground was subjected to vandalism and, although re-interment of the bodies was impossible, in 1974 stones marking the graves of other members of the Ellicott family were brought to the Ellicott cemetery at Quaker Hill by Ellicott Graveyard, Inc. There is now a row of tomb stones near one of the walls with the following inscription: " The row of stones near this wall were moved in June, 1974, from the Joseph Ellicott Graveyard near Ellicott's Upper Mills. The original stone of Joseph Ellicott has been lost."

Today, descendants of the Ellicotts continue to be brought to their final resting place at the Ellicott burial ground. A recent marker bears the name of Diane R. Carter, wife of George Carter, who died on January 30, 2000. Three plaques in another part of the cemetery are to be seen: "In Loving Memory" of George Leiper Carey III who died in 1992, Madeleine LeMoyne Ellicott Chesney who died in 1995, and Caroline Ellicott Boyce who died in 1990. And in 2001, Col. Ridgely Ellicott was buried in mid-winter; Col. Ellicott had participated in the June 6, 1944 invasion of Normandy on D-Day in World War II.

The graves of Andrew and John Ellicott remain specially honored. Some of the markers in the cemetery have fading inscriptions, but it is planned that the inscriptions will be transferred to acid-free paper to be deposited in the Howard County and Maryland Historical Societies for preservation. It is commendable that, through Ellicott Graveyard, Inc., Ellicott descendants continue to care for and use this pocket of our local history, continuing a tradition of the family's association and identification with the former mill town.

* * *

2003 Photo by Charles Kyler.

BIBLIOGRAPHY

BOOKS AND PAMPHLETS:

Andrews, Matthew Page. *History of Maryland*.
Garden City, New York: Doubleday, Doran &
Company, Inc., 1929.

- - - *Tercentenary History of Maryland*. 4 vols.
Chicago-Baltimore: The S. J. Clarke Publishing Company, 1925.

Bolzau, Emma Lydia. *Almira Hart Lincoln Phelps:
Her Life and Work*. Pennsylvania: Science
Press Printing Company, 1936.

Bridenbaugh, Carl. *Cities in the Wilderness*. New
York: Capricorn Books Edition, 1964. (O-
riginally published by The Ronald Press,
1938.)

Clark, Alda Hopkins, as told to Betsy Fleet. *Hold
Hard*. Centreville, Maryland: Tidewater
Publishing Corp. 1963.

Cochran, Thomas C., Advisory Editor, and Andrews,
Wayne, Editor. *Concise Dictionary of
American History*. New York: Charles
Scribner's Sons, 1962.

Dulany, Wm. J. C. *Dulany's History of Maryland*.
Baltimore: Wm. J. C. Dulany Company, 1897.

Elderdice, Dorothy. *The Carroll County Caravan*.
Westminster, Maryland: Times Printing
Company, 1937.

Evans, Charles W. *Family History - Fox, Ellicott,
Evans, and Others. 1645-1882*. Buffalo:
Press of Baker, Jones & Co., 1882.

Fabrician, Brother. *St. Paul's Church and Parish,
Ellicott City, Maryland*. Baltimore: Foley
Brothers, 1910.

Freeman, Douglas Southall. *R. E. Lee.* 4 vols. New York: Charles Scribners & Sons, 1934–1935.

Glenelg Country School. *Howard County House Tour.* Howard County, Maryland: 1955 and 1959.

Hopkins, G. M. *Atlas of Fifteen Miles Around Baltimore Including Howard County, Maryland.* Philadelphia: G. M. Hopkins & Company, 1878.

Howard County Historical Society in Cooperation with The Ellicott City Rotary Club. *The Raid of Ellicott's Mills.* Ellicott City, May, 1962.

Howard, George W. *The Monumental City, Its Past History and Present Resources.* Baltimore: J. D. Ehlers & Co., Engravers and Steam Book Printers, 1873.

Kent, Frank R. *The Story of Alexander Brown & Sons.* Baltimore: Norman T. A. Munder & Company, 1925.

League of Women Voters of Howard County. *Know Your County.* Elkridge, Maryland: 1957 and 1964.

Mathews, Catharine Van Cortlandt. *Andrew Ellicott, His Life and Letters.* New York: The Grafton Press, 1908.

Morris, Richard B. and Commanger, Henry Steele, Eds. *Encyclopedia of American History.* Revised Edition. New York: Harper & Row, 1961.

Norris, J. Saurin. *A Sketch of the Life of Benjamin Banneker.* Baltimore: John D. Toy, for the Maryland Historical Society, 1854.

Onderdonk, Henry. *A History of Maryland*. Baltimore: John Murphy & Co., 1868.

Post, A. H. S. *The Early Eighties*. Baltimore: Mercantile Trust & Deposit Co., 1924.

Scott, Joseph. *A Geographical Description of the State of Maryland and Delaware*. Philadelphia: Kimber, Conrad, and Co., 1807.

Shepherd, Henry E. *The Representative Authors of Maryland*. New York: Whitehall Publishing Company, 1911.

Swann, Don. *The Hilltop Theatre, Ellicott City, Md*. Baltimore: 1941.

Torrence, Clayton. *Old Somerset on the Eastern Shore of Maryland*. Richmond: 1935. Reprint Ed. Baltimore: Regional Publishing Company, 1966.

Trustees' Reports. *Annual Reports of the Patapsco Female Institute, Ellicotts Mills, near Baltimore, Maryland*. 1841 through 1845. Baltimore: John D. Toy, 1845.

Trustees' Reports, 12th Annual. *Patapsco Female Institute, 1852-53*. Ellicotts Mills: John Schofield, 1853.

Tyson, Martha E. *Settlement of Ellicott's Mills, With Fragments of History therewith Connected*. Baltimore: John Murphy, 1871. (Md. Historical Society Fund Publication, No. 4.)

Warfield, J. D. *The Founders of Anne Arundel and Howard Counties, Maryland*. Baltimore: Kohn & Pollock, 1905.

Wilson, Edwina H. *Her Name Was Wallis Warfield*. New York: E. P. Dutton & Co., Inc., 1936.

Works Progress Administration. *Inventory of the County and Town Archives of Maryland.* No. 13 Howard County (Ellicott City). Baltimore: The Historical Records Survey, March 1939.

Work Projects Administration. *Maryland - A Guide to the Old Line State.* New York: The Oxford University Press, 1940.

PERIODICALS:

The Baltimore American
The Baltimore Sun
The Central Maryland News
The Congressional Record (House). Vol.112, No. 37. (March 2, 1966)
The Howard County Times
The Star - Washington, D. C.

MANUSCRIPTS:

Branch, Dr. J. R. Bromwell. *The Village.*

- - - - *Memories of the Old Manse.*

Burgess, G. Lee. *History of Emory Methodist Episcopal Church.*

Clark, Mary Dorsey. *History of the First Presbyterian Church of Howard County.*

Hanna, Edwin Jr. *Memories Before the Turn of the Century.*

Howard County Land Records. Court House, Ellicott City.

INDEX

Abercrombie, Dr. Anna S. 168
Adams :
    Edith,166
    Pres. John Quincy, 27, 31, 40
Airlocker (or Erlougher), 47
Allan, Rev. Andrew, 197
Allen, William, 160
AMERICAN PROGRESS, 86
Amos, Rev. Edison, 126
Andrews, Marietta Minnigerode,
    110
Archer:
    George, 193
    Robert H., 160
    Mrs. Robert H. (Mary),
    159, 160
Asbury, Bishop Francis, 126

Bach Family, 52
Baker, Alva S., 10
Balderson:
    H. Sherwood, 73, 75, 76
    Mrs. H. Sherwood, 73, 75
    John, 74, 76
Ball Family, 141
BALTIMORE (magazine), 240
Baltimore-Frederick Tumpike, 23
Baltimore & Ohio Railroad, 4,
    11, 13-21, 40, 70, 84,
    85,113, 134, 135, 166, 214,
    235, 236, 244
BALTIMORE SUN, THE, 42,
    91, 111, 153, 160, 167, 185,
    240, 251, 266
Banneker, Benjamin, 2
Bayard:
    Florence, 166
    Katherine Lee, 166
    Louise, 166
    Mabel, 166
    Thomas Francis, 166

Beaver, Chief, 28, 29
Behavioral Research Center,
Bethesda, 146
Benzinger Family, 54
Berg Alnwick, 167
Berry, Jerome C., 216
Betts:
    Charles W., 245
    Mrs. Mary (Sanner), 131,
      241, 242 ,243, 245, 247
    Norman S., 241, 242, 244
    Sarah (Holden) 245
Bierly's Shoe Shop, 34
Blitz, John E., 97
Bloom:
    Edward, 63
    Harry J., 263
    Mrs. Harry J., 263
Board of Education, 218, 222
Bodine, A. Aubrey, 251, 252
Boone:
    Lewis W., 280, 281
    Mrs. Louise (Kraft), 280, 281
Booth, Dr. Edwin, 126
Bosley, John, 39
Bounds:
    Mrs. Enalee, 105, 106, 107,
    233
    Roland, 107, 233
Boyce, Caroline Ellicott, 282,
    284
Branch:
    Charles, 193, 196
    Desiree, 193, 196
    Eleanor Chinn, 194, 196
    Hardin, 193, 196
    Harrison, 193, 196
    Rev. Henry, 186, 190, 192,
      193, 194, 195, 207
    Mrs. Henry, 193, 194, 195,
    196

Dr. J.R. Bromwell, 84, 103, 190, 194, 195, 196, 213
Breckenridge, Mrs. John P., 160, 166
Brennan:
    Mrs. Manola, 170
    Associate Justice, U.S. Supreme Court, William J. Jr., 145, 146
Brian, John W., 126
Bridcnbaugh, Carl, 211
Bright, Sally, 181, 182
Brown:
    Alexander, 13, 14, 15
    Family, 54
    George, 13, 14, 15
    John, 28
    John Riggs, Sr., 83
    John Riggs, Jr., 83
    Paula, 36, 114
    Rev. Richard, 122
    Robert, 36, 114
    Samuel, 216
    T. G., 38, 39
    Dr. William Hand, 59
    William H. & Co., 86
Brush, Edward J, 259
Buchholz, Heinrich Ewald, 100, 111
Buchwalter, Abraham, 270
Buckler, Dr. Thomas Hepburn, 141
Buetefisch:
    Bertha, 96
    Charles, 96, 115
    Henry Christian, 96
    Tailoring Shop, 34
Burbank, John M., Jr., 44
Burgess:
    G. Lee, 127
    Lionel, Sr., 127
    Samuel F., 127
Burke Family, 52

Burleigh, 183
Buswell, David, 171
Cadwalader, Reese, 277
Calhoun, John C., 110, 281
Cambell, Thomas, 38
Caplan:
    Samuel A., 101, 103, 104, 105, 106, 114, 179
    Mrs. SamuelA., 102
    N., 238
Carey:
    Caroline M., 282
    George Leiper III, 284
    Helen H., 282
    James, III, 2
    Carmel, Meryl, 181
Carmel, Meryl, 181
Carroll:
    Charles of Carrollton, 2, 4, 13, 15, 20, 26, 47, 53, 60, 152, 219
    Mrs. Charles, 169
    John Lee, 59
    Dean William A., 126
Carter:
    Charles Henry of Greenwood, 141
    Diane R., 284
    George, 284
    Rev. J. Pym, 205
    Polly, 161
    Sally Randolph, 161
Cascio, Andrew, 20, 107, 232
Castle Angelo (or Angelo Cottage), 5, 19, 48, 89, 133-138, 234, 242
CATONSVILLE HERALD, THE, 92
CENTRAL MARYLAND NEWS, 150, 170, 172, 173, 174, 178, 179, 180, 192-185, 199-203
Chambers, Bette, 261-262

Chambers, Mr. & Mrs. Melvin
    W., 261-262
Chaney, Richard, 82
Cherry Grove, 183
Chesapeake & Ohio Canal Co.,
    13, 14, 15
Chesney, Madeleine LeMoyne
    Ellicott, 284
CHICAGO TRIBUNE, 91
Chicasaw Indians, 150
Christ Child Convalescent Home
    (Rockville), 142
Christ Child Opportunity Shop
    (Georgetown), 142
Christ Child Playground,
    (Cambridge, Mass.), 142
Christ Child Playground, (The
    Hague), 142
Christ Child Society, 142
Church of the Good Shepherd,
    (Jonestown), 168
Cissel Family, 54
Clapp, Enoch, 152

Clark:
    Mrs. Albina (Watkins), 83
    Mrs. Alda (Hopkins), 35,
        206, 207, 234, 255, 257,
        258
    Mrs. Corinne (Talbott), 254,
        260
    E. T. & Sons, 33, 35, 36
    Edward T., 36, 119
    Family, 3, 54
    Mrs. Garnett, 35
    Judge James, Sr., 206, 228,
        254-257, 260
    Senator James, Jr., 177, 179,
        256, 258, 259
    John L., 254, 260
    Judge John L., 90, 178, 179,
        185, 186, 228, 257
    Joseph Hopkins, 256

J. Thomas, 83,84
Lawrence, 168
Louis Dorsey, 35, 207
Louis T., 35, 186
Mrs. Louis T., 186, 196, 197
Mary Dorsey, 191
Samuel, 256
Dr. Thaddeus, 83
Mrs. Virginia G., 282
William, 83
Clay, Henry, 40, 41, 110
Cleveland, President Grover, 84
CLEVELAND PLAIN DEALER,
    91
CLEVELAND PRESS, 91
Coates & Glennin, 123
Cochran, Edward, 10
Cochran, Mary Catherine, 259
Cole, Mrs. James F., 85
Colt, Margaret Oliver, 166
COLUMBIA TIMIES, THE, 94
COMMON SENSE, THE, 86
COMMUNITY NEWS, THE
    (Reisterstown, Balto. Co.), 92
Confederacy March, 161
Cook
    Mr. & Mrs. Charles M.,
        270-273
    Dina, 273
    Pete, 245
Coons, Benjamin, 260
Cooper, Peter, 4, 13, 16, 17, 20
Cotter:
    Chris, 77
    Janet, 77
    Julia, 77
    Marielle, 77
Corson, Rev. F. P., 126
Coskery, Rev. Henry Benedict,
    47, 48, 54, 58
Courthouse, Howard County,
    217, 222, 223-227
Cowpens, Battle of, 23

Crist, Howard G. Jr., 177
Cromwell Family, 52
Crow, Chief, 28, 29
Cummings, Rev. Daniel F., 61, 225
Curley, Archbishop Michael J., 62
Curran, "Aunt Lizzie", 164

DAILY RECORD, 84
Dale, Col. & Mrs. Frederick A. 169
Danaghy, Rev. Thomas J., 64, 65
Dann, Dr., 146
Davis :
    Family, 54
    Jefferson, 155, 161, 171, 172
    William (Curly), 263, 266
    Winnie, 155, 171, 172
Day, John, 247
Dearborn, Henry, 150
DEMOCRAT, THE, 88
Dennis, Philip, 277
Denny, William, 39
Dickinson, Charles S., 6
Dietz, James H., 10
Diffy, Victor J., 48
Disney, Deborah, 224, 241, 242, 243
Disney Tavern, 4,9, 237, 241-245
Ditch, John S. & wife, 270
Dodson, Linden S., 126
Dohony, Rev. Nicholas W., 61-63, 64
Donaghy, Rev. Thomas J., 64, 65
Dolan, Rev. Thomas S., 60
Donovan, Senator Joseph L., 8, 228
Dorsey:
    Benjamin, 78
    Benjamin H., 84
    Col. Charles, 152
    Edward, 211

Family, 3, 54
John (Bachelor), 225
Rebecca O., 270
Thomas B., 152, 156
Dougherty, Very Rev. John J., 58, 59
Doughoregan Manor, 4, 47, 53, 183, 199, 254
Duffy, Edward Paul, 42, 165, 185
Dunkel:
    Howard, 34
    Jeff, 34
Durke Family, 52

EASTERN BEACON, THE (Essex), 94
Easton:
    Mrs. Annie & Sons, 34
    Milton, 116
Eccleston:
    Archbishop Samuel, 48
    Rev. Doctor, 59
Eckenrode, Msgr. John, 62
Eckert:
    Christian, 34, 110, 111, 112
    Christine (Will), 110, 112
Eisenberg, Dr. Leon, 145
Elkridge Meeting House, 275
Ellicott:
    Andrew (the founder), 2, 22, 26, 184, 281, 284
    Andrew, the surveyor (son of Joseph the founder), 2, 3, 276, 277
    Andrew (son of Elias), 81
    Andrew and wife, Emily, 48
    Barbara Agnes (Peterson),48
    Benjamin, 277
    Cassandra, 276
    Charles Ellis, Jr., 282
    Elias, 28, 48
    Elizabeth (Brooke), 26, 31, 253, 261, 277, 278

Elizabeth (Brown), 22, 26
Elizabeth (King), 283
Family, 54, 171
George (son of Andrew the
    founder), 22, 26-28, 32,
    39, 152, 269, 277, 278,
    281
George (son of the first
    George), 48, 78, 250,
    277, 278
John (the founder), 2, 3, 277,
    278, 281, 284
John (son of John the
    founder) 3
John (son of Elias), 48, 85,
    152
John Le Moyne, 282
Jonathan (son of Andrew the
    founder), 22-25, 26, 31,
    130, 184, 276
Joseph (the founder), 2, 3, 4,
    278
Martha, 28, 29, 30, 255
Nathaniel, 22, 152
Col. Ridgely, 284
Samuel, 121, 124
Sarah (Harvey), 22, 184
Thomas, 13, 15
Valcoulin L., 284
William (Baltimore), 282
William (son of Jonathan and
    Sarah), 184
Ellicott & Company, 34
Ellicott City Bicentennial
    Association, Inc., 11
Ellicott City Business
    Association, 11
Ellicott City Colored School,
    Restored, 11
Ellicott City, History of, 1-12
Ellicott City Lutheran Church,
    280
Ellicott City Restoration

Foundation, 12, 92, 99
ELLICOTT CITY TIMES, 83
Ellicott City's Jail, Constables,
    Sheriffs and Police Force,
    209-217
Ellicott Graveyard, Inc., 282,
    284, 285
Ellicott Mills Brewing Company,
    239-240
Ellicott's Country Store, 100-107,
    119
Ellicott's Second School, 199-203
Elliott, Mrs. A. Marshall, 166,
    168, 252, 278, 279, 280
Ells:
    Joseph A., Sr., 52
    Mrs. Joseph, 52
Ellsler, Mrs. George R., 168
Emmart, David, 122
Emory Methodist Episcopal
    Church, 5, 8, 102, 121-129,
    130, 132, 245, 273
Emporium, The Old, 33-36, 45
Engle, Rev. S. M., 196, 197
Ennis:
    Connie, 248-249
    Dennis, 248-249
    Leeza, 248-249
Erie Canal, 14
Evans :
    Charles W., 23, 28
    Family, 278
Ewen, Major Richard, 269

Fabrician, Brother, 48, 53, 142,
    200, 201, 217, 239
Fahey, John, 47
Falconer, Mahlon, 124
Fell:
    Ezra, 277
    W. E., 123
Fields, Matthew, 81, 82
Fire Department, Howard Co., 8,

115-120
First Presbyterian Church (The
Howard County Historical
Society Building), 8, 151,
186, 190, 191, 193, 199, 203,
204-208, 228, 234, 258
Fishbein
Alan, 99
Brenda, 99
Fisher's Grocery Store, 34
Fitzsimmons, Milton J., 252
Flagg, Rev. Robert S., 62
Fleet, Betsy, 258
Flood of 1868, 7
Foley:
Family, 52
Rt. Rev. John S., D.D., 56
Bishop Thomas, 56
Font Hill, 186
Foote Family, 54
Forrest, John, 121, 122
Forsythe:
Family, 54
Judge William, 225
Judge & Mrs. William H., Jr.,
169
Fort, William, 122, 124
Fountainvale, 2
Franklin, Benjamin, 31
Fraser, Rev. Wallace, 197
Freeman, Douglas Southall, 141
French:
Mr. & Mrs. John, 246
John, Jr., 246
Mary, 246
Friends of the Patapsco Institute,
12, 179, 181, 182 189
Fulton, Robert, 3

Gaither:
Family, 54
James - Livery Stable, 35, 103
Galloway, Richard, 269

Gambrill:
Montgomery, 201
Dr. William B., 35
Flour Mill, 34
Manufacturing Co., 116
Gary Family, 54
Gassaway:
Doctor, 35
W. Greggs, 169
Dr. & Mrs. William F., 73
Gaudry, Dodie, See Stewart,
Dodie
Gault, Mr. & Mrs. P., 263, 264
Gaxton, William, 169
Gerwig:
Arthur L., 94
Charles L., 19, 93, 94, 95
La Rue, R., Mrs., 94
Getz, Louis, 201
Giampaoli, Frank, 175
Gibbons, James Cardinal, 55, 56,
58, 60
Gillum, Rev. Dr. J. M., 126
Godfrey, Samuel, 276
Gorman:
Senator Arthur Pue, 88
Arthur Pue, Jr., 88
Gould, Mitchell, 170
Grable, Michael L., 175
Gramps Attic, 245
Gray:
Edward, 152
Grafton, 260
Greenbaum, Phyllis, 245
Greenberry, Hon. Nicholas, 211
Grey Rock, 166
Grier, Rev. M. B., 192
Grimes, C. W., 125
Gucker, Richard, 251, 252
Guiteau, Rev. S., 191, 205
Guyer, Rev. John, 123

Hagen, Content World, 266-267
Haines Family, 54
Halmead, Rev. William, 123
Hammond:
    Edward, 270
    Family, 3, 54
    Major John, 211
Hanna:
    Edwin F. Jr., 103, 166, 177
    Laura, 166
    William S., 10, 179
Hannon, Mrs. Philip (Jean), 12,
    177, 179, 200
Hardey, John, 85
Harmony Presbyterian Church,
    205
Harper, Rev. James, 205
Harrington, Mrs. Emerson C., 168
Harris, Thomas G., 177, 179
Harrison:
    Eleanor, 160
    Officer, 215
    Rebeckah, 160
    W. S., 123
Hartley Family, 277
Harvey, Sarah, 22
Hawkins :
    E. Holmes, Jr., 179
    Louise, 170, 171, 180
Hayden:
    Edwin Parsons, 218, 222, 270
    Dr. Horace H., 218
    Adj. Thomas, 219
    William, 219
Hayward:
    Family, 275
    William, 275
Hazel, Mrs. Virginia (Watkins),
    134, 135, 136, 258
Hazelhurst:
    Catherine Lilburn, 68, 69
    Elizabeth, 68, 69
    Elizabeth (McKim), 68, 69, 75

George Blagden, 68, 69
Julia, 68, 69
Margaret McKim, 68, 69
Maria Eleanor, 68, 69
Richard Henry, 67, 68, 69,
    71, 72, 73, 77, 79
Heavey Family 52,
Heleus, Beal, 247
Helfenstien, Rev. Edw. T., 168
Henderson, Mrs. Robert, 279
Hendrick Family, 52
Henley, Walter A., 174
Henson, Jake, 34, 243
Herbert:
    Mr. & Mrs. John Henry, 166
    Varina D., 166
    Virginia L., 166
Herrmann:
    Charles A., 102, 115, 126
    H. Lizzie, 126
Herrmann & Carr, 86
Higgins :
    Mr. & Mrs. Charles, 197
    Richard, 175, 179
Higinbothom, Frank C., 102
Hill, Emory, 84
Hilltop Theatre, 169
Hilton, Edward, 115
Historic District Commission, 11-
    12, 80, 99, 107
Historic Ellicot City, Inc., 11, 12,
    20, 21, 77, 79, 80, 99, 107,
    137, 181, 189, 232, 233
Historic Ellicott Mills, Inc.,
    11, 25, 131, 173, 177, 210,
    241
Hodge, Dennis, 245
Hodges :
    Adelaide (Snowden), 185
    George Addison, Sr., 185
    Mrs. William Snowden, Jr.,
        187
Hoffman, Harry Lee, 282, 284

Hogg:
  Ann Thompson, 197-198
  Charles Edward Jr., 197-198
  Charles Edward III, 198
  Julia St. Clair, 198
Holden Family, 52
Holland:
  Celia M., 19, 25, 79, 129,
    174, 179, 189, 203, 230,
    239
  James C., 297
Holley, Rev. Watson, 127
Holmead, Rev. Alfred, 39, 161
Holmes, Jean, 95
Holway, James M., 10
Holzweig, N., 238
Hooper, Rev. W. A., 192
Hopenfield, Morton, 179
Hopkins :
  Gerard T., 28, 277
  G. M., 86, 102, 135, 200
  Johns, 13, 20
Howard County Arts Council, 12
Howard County Historical
  Society, 8, 12, 131, 153, 173,
  199, 203, 205-208, 228, 241,
  245, 258, 281, 284, 285
HOWARD COUNTY RECORD, 83
HOWARD COUNTY TIMES, THE,
  19, 39, 81-99, 165, 179
HOWARD COUNTY TIMES
  100th Anniversary, 91-92
HOWARD DISTRICT PRESS,
  THE, 82
HOWARD FREE PRESS, THE,
  81, 82
HOWARD GAZETTE, THE, 82,
  184
Howard, George W., 14
Howard House, 9, 34, 40, 92,
  109-114, 228
Howes, Joseph & Ella Mae, 263
Hughes, William, 122

Hunt:
  Family, 54
  Thomas H., 116
Hunter Lois, 129
Huntington, Rev. C., 192
Hynes, Joshua H., 122
INDEPENDENT, THE, 82, 86
Indian Affairs, 26-30
INDIANAPOLIS STAR, 91
Ingelow, B.,177
Iron Rail, The, 114
Isaac, Rev. Frank R., 126

Jackson, Andrew, 110
Jackson, Walter, 245
Jefferson, Thomas, 2, 31, 105,
  150, 160, 178
Jenkins:
  Mr. & Mrs. J. Carroll, 131,
    132
  Thomas, 122
Jenkins House, 130-132
Johnson:
  Mrs. Lyndon B., 173, 174
  Gov. Thomas, 276
Johnston:
  Rev. A. A., 197
  Mrs. Robert W., 168
Jones:
  Ann, 259
  Margaret R. Pue, 270
  Omar J., 10, 264, 265, 266,
    267
  Talbot, 15
Joseph Ellicott Graveyard, 284
Joyce, John, 47
Jug Bridge, 23

Kavanaugh Family, 52
Kealey:
  James, 137-138
  Louise, 137-138

Nathan, 137-138
Keeler, Cardinal William, 65
Keenan, Rev. Dennis, 60
Keewaydin, 254-259
Keith, Gene, 90
Kendzerski, Tim, 240
Kent, Frank R., 15
Kerger, William, 112
Kevin, Sr. Mary, S.S.N.D., 62
Keydash, Rev. Casimir F., 61
King:
    Francis, 282
    John, 146
    Thomas O., 93
Kinlein, Julius A., 112
Kinsey:
    T., 102
    Wilbur, 101
Kirby Family, 52
Kirkwood & Getz, 34
Klashus, Clarao C., 263
Klein, John J., 119
Knott, Hon. Lee, 59
Koehl, Prof. Charles, 134
Koppel, Ted, 251, 252
Kraft:
    Dorothy & Sons, 34
    John, 281
    Vernon P., 131
Kraft's Meat Shop, 35
Kroh, J. Edwin, 85, 115
Kronheim, Milton S., Sr., 143,
    144, 145, 146
Kuhn, Joseph, 56
Kunen, James, 146

Landon, Gov. Alfred M., 92-93
Lang, John, 216
Lantz, Emily Emerson, 111, 167,
    168, 199, 200, 278, 279
Larman, William, 15
Larrimore, Jack L., 10

Latrobe:
    Benjamin H., 13, 20
    Benjamin H. Jr., 20
    Thomas, 16
Laumann, Philip A., 115
Laumann's Barber Shop, 34
Lawrence:
    Dawson, 86
    William, 135
Lawyer's Row, 8, 9, 228, 229
Lee Family, 141
Lee, Gen. Robert E., 68, 110,
    141, 147
Leishear:
    Joseph H., Sr., 34, 243
    Joseph, Jr., 34, 243
L'Enfant, Pierre, 2
Lewin, M., 39
Ligon:
    The Misses, 35
    Gov. T. Watkins, 35, 218
Lilburn, 1, 5, 67-77, 78, 79
Lilley, James, 63
Lilly:
    James, 61
    William F., 243
Linthicum, Officer, 215
Linwood, 1, 41, 68, 139-148, 166,
    236
Little Turtle, Chief, 27, 28, 29
Livesay, G. Wayne, 217
Log Cabin - Merryman Street,
    231-233
Log Cabin - New Cut Road, 78-80
Long:
    Henry L., III, 119
    R. C., 38
    Robert Carey, Jr., 152
Longfellow Garden Club, 12
Loughran:
    Family, 52
    John B., 96
    Mrs. John B., 96, 97, 111

MacAlpine, 137
Maccoun, Andrew Ellicott, 282
Maccubbin (Mackubin):
    Mrs. George, 141
    Sisters, 35
Macgill:
    Grace, 131
    Marion P., 130
Mac Gowan, Major, 42
Madison, Pres. James, 31
Maginnis :
    John, Sr., 71, 72
    John, Jr., 68, 70
Mahon Family, 52
Malloy, Reginald, 63
Malone Family, 52
Manse, The Old (Presbyterian),
    130, 163, 190-198
Marburg, Emma, 168
Mark, Dr. Nellie V., 168
Marks, Robert H., 10
Marpau, Chief, 28, 29, 30
Martin:
    David, 57
    Family, 52
    Ike, 34
    Isaac, 34
    James, 122, 123, 124
    Ross, 34, 103
Martin's Drug Store, 34
Maryland Historical Society, 285
MARYLAND LAW RECORD, 84
Massey, George E., 115
Matchett, Annie, 160
Mathias, Senator Charles Mc., Jr.,
    166
Matthew, Woods & Hall, 18
Matthews Store, 1
Matthews, William, 123
Mayfield:
    Blanche, 201
    Dorothy, 280
    Edna E., 280

Maud, 200, 201
Nonie, 200, 201
Pauline, 200, 201
Thomas Hunt, 279, 280
T. Hunt, Jr., 280
William F., 200
McCain, Russell H., 174
McClees Family (Washington),
    161
McComb, Mrs. Ruth, 127
McCreary, Captain, 124
McElfresh, Ariana (Mrs. Charles
    Edward Trail), 166
McKeldon, Mayor Theodore, 145
McKenzie Family, 52
McKim:
    Elizabeth Virginia, 68
    Isaac, 15, 152
    John, 28, 277
McKinley, Rev. Dr. A. H., 126
McKinzie, Jessie, 123
McLaughlin:
    Andrew, 38, 134
    William L., 39
McMullen:
    Family, 52
    John F., Sr., 59
McTavish Family, 53
Meade, Marion, Jr., 134
Mellor, Benjamin, 118, 179, 216
Melvin, James Fisher, 84
Memmel, Albert, 63
Mencken, H. L., 19, 84, 136
Mercer:
    Isaiah, 122, 123
    Pearl (Miss), 18
Merrick:
    Miss Mary, 34, 141, 142,
        143, 147
    Judge Richard, 141
Merrick Camp for Boys, 142
Merrick Camp for Girls, 142
Meyer, Dr. & Mrs. Adolph, 169

Miller:
    Charles E., 10, 178, 179,
        180, 181, 188
    Margaret, 61
    Paul, 189
    Valerie, 189
Millikin, Kent, 169
Minneman, Archie, 137
Mitzel:
    Mrs. Doris (Justice), 127
    Rev. Robert, 127, 128
Monroe, Pres. James, 30
Montague:
    Alice, 163, 164, 185
    Gov. Andrew Jackson, 163
MONTGOMERY COUNTY
    SENTI NEL, 81, 82, 92, 94
Monticello, 160, 166
Moore:
    Victor, 169
    Rev. Katherine L., 129
Morris, John B., 15
Morrow, John B., 84
Morse, Samuel F. B., 13, 20
Moss, Bill, 148
Moxley, E. Russell, 213, 214, 215
Mt. Clare Station, 15
Mt. Ida, 8, 39, 174, 182, 183-189,
    194, 199, 203
Mt. Vernon (Virginia), 141
Mulligan Family, 52
Murphy:
    Harry T., 10
    Rev. R. R., 125
    Victorine, 52
Myers, James F., 97
Myers:
    Warren G., 257
    Rev. G.W., 181
Mylne, Rev. G. W., 197

National Pike, 4, 47
Nelson, Arthur, 169

Nichols, Hugh, 10, 226
Nicholson:
    Andrew Lee, Jr. & wife, 270
    Sir Francis, 111
Norris, Mrs. Mary, 154
Oakdale, 183, 235
Oak Hill, 166
Oak Lawn, 218, 219, 270
O'Brien:
    Family, 52
    John Jr., 52
    Rev. Timothy, 47
O'Conor, Gov. Herbert R., 169,
    256
O'Hara, Mr. (of Michigan), 145
Oldfield Family, 34, 52
Old Manse, The (Presbyterian),
    130, 163, 190-198
Oliver, Robert, 15, 166
OMAHA WORLD-HERALD, 91
Onderdonk, Prof. Henry, 13
O'Neill, Rev. Thomas, 56, 58
Onthank Family, 52
Owens, Mrs. Margaret, 127
Owings :
    Henry, 255
    Minnie L., 166
    Dr. Thomas B., 166

Page, Rev. I. Marshall, 197
Parlett,Mrs. W. Harry, 225
Parsons, Rev. F. Alan, 225
Pastino, Bill, 240
Patapsco Female Institute, 1, 2,
    19, 89, 123, 140, 150-182,
    183, 197, 219, 278
Patapsco Female Institute:
    Graduation, 165
    Life at the, 162-165
    Trustees Report, 155-159
Patapsco Female Institute [as]:
    Maryland Women's War

Relief Hospital (World
War I), 167, 168
Summer Stock Theatre
(Maryland's first), 169
Patapsco Flour Mills, 23
Patapsco Hotel, 5, 38-45, 85, 151
Patapsco National Bank, 48, 84
Patterson, William, 13, 15
Peach, Mr. & Mrs. Frank, 142-143
Pennington, Mr., 43
Peter:
Emily, 141
Family, 54
Gabriella (or Ella), 141
George, 141
Mildred Lee, 141
Park Custis, 141
Major Washington, 140, 141,
144, 166
Mrs. Major Washington, 68,
141
Phelps:
Almira Hart Lincoln, 123,
155, 156, 157, 159, 160,
208
Judge Charles E., 155
John, 39
Hon. John, 155, 208
Pierpont Family, 275
Piot, Rev. Bernard, S.S., 48, 54,
55, 63, 64
Pittinger, Rev. B. F., 192
PITTSBURGH LEADER, 91
PITTSBURGH PRESS, 91
Ponselle, Rosa, 169
Poore, Rev. Allan F., 126
Poorman, Kristine, 77
Poplar Knawle, 269
Potts Family, 52
Powell:
Edward Burr, 87, 88, 90, 91
Col. William Sotheron, 86,
87, 88, 89, 168

Powers Family, 52
Pratt, Gov. Thomas George, 218
Preston, William C., 40, 110
Provenza, Mrs. Barbara, 105,
106, 107
Pue, Johnny, 35, 219

Puhl:
Mr. & Mrs. Adolph B., 247,
248
Edward D., 248

Quaker Hill and Meeting House,
4, 42, 47, 57, 134, 205, 219,
274-285

Radcliffe, S. J. & Son, 33, 34
Radcliffe's Emporium, 35
Raine, John E., 88
Randall, Louis, 90
Randolph, Sarah Nicholas, 160,
166
Raven, Chief, 28, 29, 30
Ray:
John T., 135, 242
Mr. & Mrs. John T., 247
Josephine (Josie), 104, 263
Read Family, 273
Reichenbecker:
Catherine Louise, 112
John, 112
Relay Station, 16
Rettger, Esther Skeel, 253
Reuwer, Donald, 36
Rice, Dr. Francis, 146
Richmond:
Mrs. Mary, 51, 52
Rev. Mr., 47
Ridgely Family, 3
Robey, James, 217, 227
Robinson:
Rev. Linus E., 61
William J., 125

Rock Hill College, 5, 48, 56, 63, 116, 123, 151, 219, 238, 254
Rogers :
    Caleb Dorsey, 102, 131, 132
    Caleb & Elizabeth, 263
    James R., 131
Roosevelt, Franklin D., 92, 93
Rossum, Peter van, 137
Rouse (James), 174
Rowland, James W., 72, 270
Rowles :
    James, 216
    William, 216
Rushville, Chief, 28, 29
Ruth, George Herman (Babe), 65, 203
Ruygrok:
    Bylan, 259
    Dylan, 259
    Kyle, 259
    Lex, 259
    Terry, 259
Ryan, Rev. Michael A., 60, 61, 69

Sachs:
    Bill, 189
    Carole, 189
    Samuel H., 97
Sachse, E. & Co., 82, 161
Sage, Mary (Lilly), 243
Sandlass, Henry L., 179
Sands Family, 54
Sanford, Mrs. Harry, 232
Sanner:
    Mary Elizabeth Treakle, 242
    Wilmer, 177
Schaffner, Dr. Robert, 179
Schofield, John, 40, 82, 85, 184
Schwartz, Mr. & Mrs. Carl, 247
Search Enclosed, 260, 261
Settlement House, 142
Sewell, Rev. Thomas, 123
Sheehan, Lawrence Cardinal, 61

Shipley:
    B. Harrison, 117, 118
    Benjamin H. Jr., 118, 119
Sigler Family, 52
Silverstein and Ostovitz, LLC, 230
Simons, Jeanne, 142-143, 144, 145, 146, 147, 148
Simpson, Lewis W., 173, 177, 179
Sioussant, Mrs. Albert, 168
Smith:
    Otis F., 95
    Samuel, 276, 277
Smith, Rev. Joseph, 191
Snowden:
    Marie Antoinette, 185
    Samuel, 277
Southgate, Rev. Edward, 60, 61
Spalding, Archbishop Martin J., 58
Spence, Karen, 148
Spottswood, Rev. J. B., 191, 205
Sraver, Warren, 148
St. Charles College, 35, 60, 101, 116, 219
St. John's Church (Episcopal), 69, 131, 168, 257
St. Joseph's Church (Sykesville), 61
St. Mary's College, 47, 59, 60, 62
St. Michael's Church, 61
St. Paul's Cemetery, 63
St. Paul's Church (Catholic), 5, 47-65, 67, 69, 78, 79, 99, 121, 135, 219
St. Paul's School, 61, 62
ST. PAUL PIONEER AND DISPATCH, 91
St. Peter's Church, 39, 161, 168
Stabler, Edward, 277
Stackhouse, S. Tracy, 207
Stanley, John, 169
STAR, THE (Glen Burnie, A.A. Co.), 94

Starkweather, N. G., 160
Starr, Rev. William E., 50, 57
Stefano, John, 240
Steuart, William, 15
Stewart, Dodie, 248
Stocken and Stokes, 16
Stockton and Stokes, 20
Stromberg:
    Antony P., 91
    Larue R., 97
    Mary Ellen (Flanagan), 91
    Paul G., 81, 82, 9, 19, 92, 93,
        94, 95, 96
Sullivan, Michael J., 88
Sumner, Rev. S. J., 59
Swain, J. K., 39
Swann, Donn, Jr., 169
Swope, Herbert Bayard, Jr., 169
Sybert, Patricia, 179
Sykes Family, 54

Taggert Family, 141
Talbott:
    Cassandra, 269
    Edward (first), 269
    Edward (second), 78, 269
    Edward (third), 269
    Edward A., 35, 789, 90, 234,
        235, 239, 243, 270
    E. Alexander, 234, 235, 236,
        243
    Edward William, 237, 238
    Elizabeth, 269
    Elizabeth (Ewen), 234, 269
    Elizabeth (Galloway), 269
    Elizabeth (Thomas Coale),
        269
    George Alexander, 236
    Georgianna (Laney), 236
    John (first), 269
    John(second), 78, 269
    John (third), 269
    Lucy, 269

    Mary Alice (Marie), 236
    Mary (Wareham), 234
    Mary (Waters), 269
    May (Childs), 238, 239
    Rebecca, 243
    Richard (first), 234, 269
    Richard (second), 269
    Richard (third), 78, 269
    Richard (of E. Alexander and
        Georgeanna), 115, 225,
        237, 238, 239
    Thomas Murray, 237, 238
Talbott, E.A., Lumber Co., 234-
    240
Talbott's Last Shift, 78, 234, 260,
    263, 269-273
Tanburo, Harry II., 245
Taney, Roger Brooke, 110
Tarro, Rev. Peter, D.D., 51, 59, 63
Taylor:
    Amanda, 160
    Isaac H., 102
Tecumseh, 29
Terhune, Rev. Cornelius A., 197
Tersiguel's Restaurant, 253
Thomas:
    Dr. Allen, 152
    Evan, 28, 277
    Family, 54
    Gov. James, 18
    John Chew, 27
    Philip, 277
    Philip E., 13, 15
Thomas Isaac Log Cabin, 232-233
Thomas Viaduct, 16, 20
Thompson:
    Doris S., 95, 96, 97, 98-99,
        179, 197, 245
    Dorsey, 235
    Miss Mary, 124
    Phillip S., 81, 97, 98-99, 199
Thornburg, Joseph, 276
Tighe, Alfred J., 180

Timanus:
    Charles Jr., 152, 184, 223
    Jake, 123
    William J., 122
Todrig, Rev. Mr., 47
Tom Thumb, The, 16, 20
Tommink Family, 52
Tongue Row, 5, 251-253
Toulmin, Alfred F., 161
Townsend, George Alfred, 155
TOWSON TIMES, THE, 94
Trail, Mrs. Charles Edward, 166
Tribble, Rev. O. Hoyt, 197
Truehart Family, 52
Tucker, Charles, 39
Tudor Place, Georgetown, 140, 141
Tydings, Senator Joseph D., 19
Tyng, Rev. J. H., 154
Tyson:
    Anna M., 184
    Elisha, 277
    Ida, 184, 185, 186, 187, 194
    Isaac, 277,
    James E., 167, 257, 258
    Judge John Snowden, 184, 185
    John, Jr., 184
    Lilly, 167
    Malcolm van V., 282
    Martha E., 150, 199, 200
    Rachel, 184
    Samuel & Martha (Tyson
        Smith), 255

Udall, Hon. Stewart L., 19
Unger, P., 86

Valentine, Mrs. Ruth, 282
Vanderlip, Frank A., Jr., 169
Van Lill Family, 52
Van Royen, Dr. & Mrs. William,
    191, 197
Van Sant, James E., 194, 213

Vaughn:
    James, 179
    Monsieur Samuel, 133, 134,
        135, 136
Verot, Rt. Rev. Augustine, S.S., 56
Vintage Lumber and Construction
    Company, 232

Wagandt, Charles, 32
Waite, Edward, 81
Walker-Chandler House, 100-107
Wallenhorst Family, 52
Walnut Hill, 186
Walters, G. Russell, 215
War Between the States, 5-6, 57-
    58
Warfield:
    Gov. Edwin, 84, 235
    Edwin, III, 225
    Family, 3, 54
    H. Deets, 265
    Prof. Joshua D., 239
    Lee O., 196
    Mrs. Lee O., 196
    T. Wallis, 163
Washington Family, 141
Washington, George, 2, 31, 110,
    277
Watkins :
    Family, 54
    Col. Gassaway, 83
    J. Harwood, 83
    Louis (Lewis) J., 83
    Samuel H., 135
    Dr. William W., 83
Watson, Robert L., 178, 179
Waugh, Bishop, 123
Wayland, Thomas Kirby, 193
Weaver, Mr. & Mrs., 73
Webster, Daniel, 110
Wehland, Charles E., 207
Weiderman, Melvin H., 131
Weir, Mrs. John, 201

Wells:
    Mr. (of Lilburn), 69,70
    William, 27
Werner:
    Charles, 115
    Mrs. Mildred, 104, 105, 106,
        107
Wesley, John, 126
Whisman, Dr. James J., 170, 172
White Family, 54
Whittingham, Bishop William R.,
      154
Whyte, Mrs. T.R., 179
Wilkins & Rogers, Inc., 22, 24
Willard, Emma, 30, 159
Williams:
    Dorsey, 90
    Dorsey M., 280
    E.S., 39
    Col. J. T., 39
Willig, George, 161
Willow Grove, 209-217
Wilson:
    Mrs. Edward C., 168
    Robert, 216
Winans, Ross, 20
Windsor, Wallis, Duchess of, 163,
      171
Wine, Mr. & Mrs. Harvey, 241,
      242, 245
Wingate, James, 39, 81, 82
Winter, Rick, 240
Wollen, James, 198
Woods, Charles, 18
Woodford, Helen, 65, 203
Wooten, Henry A., 219, 228
Wosch:
    Ethel (Betts) 213
    Julius, Jr., 115, 213, 215
Wright:
    Joel, 28, 277
    Jonathan, 277
Wyman Family, 54

Yealdhall, Rev. J. Edward, 62
Yingling, John, 221

Zeltman, Officer, 215